WHY THE
JAPANESE LOST

WHY THE JAPANESE LOST

The Red Sun's Setting

Bryan Perrett

Pen & Sword
MILITARY

First published in Great Britain in 2014 by
Pen & Sword Military
an imprint of
Pen & Sword Books Ltd
47 Church Street
Barnsley
South Yorkshire
S70 2AS

ISBN 978 1 78159 198 7

A CIP catalogue record for this book is available from the
British Library

Typeset in Palatino by
Mac Style Ltd, Bridlington, East Yorkshire
Printed and bound in the UK by CPI Group (UK) Ltd,
Croydon, CRO 4YY

Pen & Sword Books Ltd incorporates the imprints of Pen &
Sword Archaeology, Atlas, Aviation, Battleground, Discovery,
Family History, History, Maritime, Military, Naval, Politics,
Railways, Select, Transport, True Crime, and Fiction, Frontline
Books, Leo Cooper, Praetorian Press, Seaforth Publishing and
Wharncliffe.

For a complete list of Pen & Sword titles please contact
PEN & SWORD BOOKS LIMITED
47 Church Street, Barnsley, South Yorkshire, S70 2AS, England
E-mail: enquiries@pen-and-sword.co.uk
Website: www.pen-and-sword.co.uk

Contents

CHAPTER 1

Turtle Ships, Suits of Armour and Bows and Arrows

The Japanese Empire consists of a series of islands situated on an approximate axis running north-north-east to south-west by south covering an area of some 146,000 square miles and lying off the Pacific coasts of the Russian Federation and the Korean peninsula, from which it is separated by the extensive Sea of Japan. The most important islands in the group are, from north to south, Hokkaido, Honshu, Shikaku and Kyushu. A major part of these islands consists of heavily forested mountains upon which it is not possible to develop towns, farm or establish major industries and because of this most Japanese live on the coastal plains. The empire possesses very few natural resources and consequently the means of manufacture have to be imported from abroad. Until manufacturing was introduced during the modern era, most Japanese earned their living by farming or fishing.

Mother Nature has not been kind to Japan. As emeritus Professor Roy Chester points out in his book *Furnace of Creation, Cradle of Destruction*, the country has the misfortune to be located on the unstable Pacific Rim, making it vulnerable to the effects of constant movement of the Earth's tectonic plates, which creates regular earthquakes and tsunamis. As if this was not bad enough, Japan contains over 100 active volcanoes – some authorities suggest that up to 146 are capable of eruption. Obviously, the effect of these natural disasters upon a crowded population is heavy loss of life which, at the personal level, is tragedy on a scale that is difficult to comprehend. Yet, death on this scale is something that the Japanese have lived with for centuries and is something they have learned to accept.

There is, too, another aspect of Japanese life that must be considered. Crowding begets aggression and, to dilute this, the Japanese have developed an elaborate code of courtesy and good manners in their dealings with each other. However, while controlled, the aggression remains. No other country in the world has developed so many forms of martial art into a leisure activity. And then there is the historical legacy of *bushido*, the code of the samurai, drily described by William Laird Clowes in his history of the Royal Navy as 'hereditary fighters – or, in peace time, hereditary idlers'. At its best *bushido* resembled the Western code of chivalry in which the strong defended the weak. In other respects, its emphasis lay in fighting. Honour existed in fighting an equal or stronger opponent, while glory existed both in his defeat or one's own death in battle. To surrender was to bring the vilest disgrace upon oneself and one's family; there was no place in Japanese society for such an individual, whose only escape lay in self-destruction.

Given the above, it is hardly surprising that violence was an almost constant factor in Japan's history. What is surprising is that so little of it involved the empire's neighbours until the last thirty years of the thirteenth century. In 1274 the Mongols planned to add the islands to their own empire and launched a reconnaissance in force from Korea. This landed in Hakata Bay in northern Kyushu, having already captured the islands of Tsushima and Iki on the way. A hastily assembled Japanese force attacked the invaders but was defeated in spite of possessing the greater numbers. A second Japanese army was formed but, before it could act, a storm damaged part of the invasion fleet and the Mongols embarked for Korea in what remained.

Kublai Khan, the Mongol ruler, decided to acquire the islands by diplomacy rather than war and despatched several envoys to convince the Japanese that they would be better off if they accepted Mongol rule. On learning that his ambassadors had been tortured and killed, Kublai assembled a second expedition in 1281. This sailed from China and Korea in two divisions and has been described as being 50,000 strong, although a more accurate figure is not obtainable. As before, the islands of Tsushima and Iki were captured and established as bases for future operations. On this occasion, however, the Japanese were waiting and a series of ferocious land and sea engagements took place. The Mongols managed to secure a landing area on the north coast of Kyushu but were unable to advance inland beyond this because of the fanatical Japanese defence. Likewise, the Japanese were unable to push the invaders back into the sea. Simultaneously, the outnumbered Japanese launched a series of attacks on the Mongol ships, most of the crews of which were by now ashore. A few days into this prolonged battle of attrition a violent storm wrecked most of the Mongol fleet. The invaders now lacked supplies and were decisively defeated. A mere handful managed to board the few remaining ships and escape. Kublai, furious, promised that he would punish the Japanese with yet another expedition, but seems to have changed his mind.

In Japanese history, the storm is known as the *Kamikaze,* or Wind of Heaven, a name that will appear again later in this story. The episode will almost certainly bring to the reader's mind the fate of the Spanish Armada in 1588. Having been driven up the English Channel, the Armada was forced to abandon its temporary refuge in Calais by fire ships and was left with no alternative other than to make its way home round the north of Scotland and the west coast of Ireland. The voyage was made in the teeth of a gale and resulted in a crippling loss of ships and men. The commemorative medal issued by Queen Elizabeth I is inscribed, in Hebrew and Latin, with the words, 'God blew, and they were scattered'.

Following the wreck of the Mongol fleet the Japanese returned to their internal affairs and for many years remained too preoccupied with clan warfare and a variety of power struggles to be interested in maritime adventures. However, the victor in the Civil War of 1582–84 was General Toyotomi Hideyoshi, a commoner who managed to achieve the unification and pacification of Japan and established himself as the head of a dictatorship. Hideyoshi was a man of enormous ambition who planned nothing less than the invasion of China by way of Korea, and its complete subjugation within two years, at the end of which he, his court and government apparatus would move to Peking.

Unfortunately for Hideyoshi, he had to deal with a Korean admiral named Yi Sung Sin first. At this period most Far-Eastern fleets consisted of war junks that carried a gun or two each and relied upon boarding their opponents and fighting hand-to-hand on their decks. Yi, on the other hand, believed that the gun was the decisive weapon and produced an entirely new type of warship, known as the Turtle Ship, to prove his point. The Turtle Ship consisted of two decks. The lower deck contained ports for six oars, or sweeps, on each side, while the upper deck was equipped with a total of eleven ports for guns of various sizes, with ranges varying from 200 to 600 yards depending upon type. Ammunition for the guns included solid shot and incendiary devices. The deck was roofed, some authorities say with hexagonal iron plates, others with timber baulks, and was covered with numerous iron spikes capable of deterring potential boarders. At the prow was a prominent dragon's head, in the mouth of which was a nozzle capable of discharging sulphurous smoke or noxious gasses; alternatively, the mouth might be fitted with the barrel of a small gun. Protruding from the deck were two masts carrying sails, but when additional speed was required the sweeps would be brought into use. A rudder in the form of a turtle's tail was fixed to the vessel's stern. In action, the Turtle Ship destroyed its opponents with frightening efficiency either by ramming or battering them into wreckage with gunfire. For their part, the latter referred to them as blind ships because not a single crew member was visible on deck. War junks lacked sufficient firepower to inflict critical damage on the Turtle Ships and were prevented from boarding by the latter's defences.

The Korean War lasted from 1592 until 1598. In May 1592 the Japanese captured Pusan and by July had taken Seoul and Pyngyang. At this point Admiral Yi attacked a Japanese reinforcement and supply convoy in the Yellow Sea. In addition to some lesser provincial craft, Yi possessed two Turtle Ships. At the end of the day he claimed to have sunk or set ablaze a minimum of fifty-nine

Japanese ships, while the remnant of the convoy was dispersed and in flight. There is no need to doubt his word as a Chinese army had entered the fray and the Japanese, lacking their promised reinforcements and supplies, were forced all the way back to Pusan, where they entrenched themselves.

When the Chinese withdrew in 1596, Hideyoshi despatched reinforcements to Pusan and the following year the Japanese broke out and began a steady advance across southern Korea, despite further Chinese intervention. Thus far, Admiral Yi's fleet, which now included a much higher proportion of Turtle Ships, had already fought no less than twenty-two engagements during the war. Now, in November 1598, Admiral Yi won his greatest victory at the Battle of Chinhae Bay, destroying almost half the Japanese fleet of 400 ships but losing his own life in the process. The survivors fled to Kyushu, leaving their army without any means of communication with the homeland. However, the following month it became known that Hideyoshi had died in Japan. This almost certainly removed the risk of the army commander being beheaded for failure and, having been granted terms by the Koreans and Chinese, his troops evacuated the peninsula. Sea power had been the decisive influence in the war.

Hideyoshi's death was followed by a power struggle that ended in victory for the Tokugawa Shogunate, which ruled Japan until the second half of the nineteenth century. Fear that the activities of Christian missionaries possessed an ulterior political motive, notably after a violent confrontation between Franciscans and Jesuits, resulted in the expulsion of European priests and the persecution of Christian converts. In June 1609, following a Japanese–Portuguese confrontation in Macao, the Shogun ordered the seizure of a Portuguese merchant vessel, the *Nombre de Dios,* lying in Nagasaki harbour. The ship was surrounded by Japanese war junks carrying some 1,200 soldiers. During the next three days every attempt to board her was repelled but, recognising that escape was impossible, her captain blew her apart. His crew and many of their attackers perished in the explosion and her priceless cargo was scattered across the harbour bed.

Antipathy to foreigners grew steadily. The Japanese were simply not prepared to tolerate the interference of foreigners in their affairs, be they commercial, financial, religious or political. The English merchants left voluntarily in 1623, but their Spanish counterparts had to be forcibly ejected the following year. In the belief that Portuguese traders had encouraged insurgents in a recent rebellion, the Shogun expelled them in 1637. The following year only two foreign trading posts remained in Japan – the Dutch at Hirado and the Chinese at Nagasaki.

Incredibly, the Japanese continued to enjoy a relatively peaceful isolation for the next two centuries, implacably resisting every attempt to involve her in international affairs. Then, in 1853. a squadron of four United States warships under the command of Commodore Mathew Perry dropped anchor in Tokyo Bay. Perry was frank in stating that his intention was the negotiation of a treaty that would end Japan's isolation, pointing out that commerce was a two-way traffic that was of benefit to both parties. Furthermore, the spread of industrialisation could only increase the nation's wealth. Perry's attitude was one of sympathetic understanding and polite argument rather than bullying demands. This was appreciated by the Japanese negotiators who took the pragmatic view that not only was Japan falling far behind her neighbours, she also lacked modern weapons of war and understood little of its methods. She was, in effect, defenceless if attacked by a major power. They therefore agreed to Perry's requests and on 31 March 1854 signed the Treaty of Kanagawa, opening trade with the United States and providing protection for shipwrecked American sailors. Similar treaties were subsequently negotiated with Great Britain, Russia and Holland.

Before proceeding further it is necessary to examine the basic structure of Japanese society at this period. Nominally, the country was ruled by a Mikado. Immediately beneath him was an official known as the Shogun, who assumed the political and military management of the country, eventually leaving the Mikado little more than religious leadership. Below came the Daimios (great nobles) who were the leaders of the country's clans and employed a large class of Samurai as armed retainers. The system was undeniably medieval and was a breeding ground for plotting and the pursuit of sectional interest.

There were, naturally, those who disapproved of the new treaties, wished to retain the old ways and objected to the presence of foreigners in their country. As early as June 1863 members of the Chosu clan, manning coast defence forts around Simonosecki harbour, opened fire first on American and then on French and Dutch vessels, provoking an immediate response from French and American warships.

On 1 August of that year Lieutenant Colonel Edward Neale, the British Charge d'Affaires in Japan, had occasion to write to the Prince of Satsuma regarding an attack on a party of British civilians the previous year.

Your Highness,

It is well known to you that a barbarous murder of an unarmed and unoffending British subject and merchant was perpetrated on the 14th of the month of September last, near Kanagawa, by persons attending the procession, and surrounding the norimon [carriage] of Shamadzu Sabbura, who, I am informed, is the father [actually, uncle] of Your Highness. It is equally known to you that a murderous assault was made at the same time by the same retinue upon a lady and two other gentlemen, British subjects, the two gentlemen having been severely and seriously wounded, and the lady escaping by a miracle. The names of the British subjects here referred to are as follows: Mr Charles Lennox Richardson, murdered; Mrs Borrowdaile; Mr William Clarke, severely wounded; and Mr William Marshal, severely wounded ... I am instructed to demand of Your Highness as follows:- First, the immediate trial and execution, in the presence of one or more of Her Majesty's naval officers, of the chief perpetrators of the murder of Mr Richardson, and of the murderous assault upon the lady and gentlemen who accompanied him. Secondly, the payment of £25,000 sterling, to be distributed to the relations of the murdered man, and to those who escaped with their lives the swords of the assassins on that occasion ... Upon your neglecting or evading to do so, the Admiral commanding the British forces in these seas will adopt such coercive measures, increasing in their severity, as may be expedient to obtain the required satisfaction ...

The prince's reply, received on 13 August, fell so far short of Neale's demands that he immediately requested Vice Admiral Augustus Kuper, Commander-in-Chief of the Royal Navy's East Indies and China Station, to deal with the situation as he thought fit. Kuper's squadron contained as interesting a selection of warships as might be expected at this period of the Royal Navy's development. *Euryalus*, the flagship, was a 35-gun wooden screw frigate; *Pearl* was a 21-gun wooden screw corvette; *Coquette* was a 4-gun wooden screw gunboat; *Argus*, built in 1849, was a 6-gun wooden paddle-wheel sloop and the old lady of the squadron; *Racehorse* was a 4-gun wooden sloop and *Havock* was a 2-gun gunboat of a type built in large numbers during the Crimean War.

Kuper's first punitive action took place on the morning of 15 August. Four of his smaller ships entered a bay to the north of Kagosima and seized three steamers belonging to the Prince of Satsuma, valued at some $305,000. These were secured without opposition and brought down to the squadron's anchorage in Kagosima harbour. It evidently took some time for news of the ships' capture to reach the town for it was not until, following a squall at noon, that the Japanese batteries near the town opened an ineffective fire on *Euryalus*, causing some minor damage to her rigging. Kuper immediately despatched a signal for the prizes to be burned and instructed his ships to form line of battle. Then, despite the worsening weather, the squadron began to engage the batteries at close range.

As the action progressed, *Euryalus* led the squadron along the line of the enemy's defences and became the target of several batteries. Kuper, standing on her bridge, had a narrow escape when a shot killed two officers, including her captain, beside him. The crew of a 7-inch breech-loading 110-pounder Armstrong gun, mounted on the forecastle, had an equally narrow escape. After the shell and charge had been inserted into the chamber, the vent-piece was dropped into place behind them and then screwed against the rim of the chamber. It seems that the connection was insufficiently tight, for when fire was applied to the vent-piece it was blown out as the charge exploded backwards, felling the entire gun crew. Fortunately, the men were only stunned and were hounded by their bellowing, no-nonsense petty officer into fitting the spare vent-piece and getting the gun back into action. Less fortunate were the crew of one of the main deck guns, seven of whom were killed and six others wounded when a 10-inch shell from one of the batteries exploded near the muzzle of their weapon.

As the *Euryalus* reached the last in the line of enemy forts it was possible to see through gaps in the drifting gun smoke and occasional heavy showers that parts of the wood-and-paper town were on fire. The town had not been engaged intentionally, but some of the ships' shells, fired on the upward roll in the deteriorating weather, had passed over the batteries and exploded beyond. At this point, *Racehorse* ran aground, but was got off by the combined efforts of *Coquette, Argus* and *Havock*. The last, under Lieutenant George Poole, was ordered to set fire to five large junks belonging to the prince, and went on to destroy an arsenal, a foundry and adjoining storehouses.

The weather continued to deteriorate steadily until Kuyper decided to break off the engagement and find a more sheltered anchorage across the harbour, under the lee of Sakurasima. The wind almost reached hurricane strength during the night but abated during the following day. Observing men establishing a battery among trees and bushes on the hill overlooking the ships, Kuyper decided that, before it could be brought into action, the squadron would return to its original anchorage and repair the damage sustained the previous day before proceeding to sea. The squadron took advantage of the move to shell batteries on the

Sakura side that had not been previously engaged, and also the prince's palace in Kagoshima for good measure. Having completed its repairs, the squadron sailed for Yokohama on the afternoon of the 17 August. The operation had cost Kuyper fourteen men killed and fifty wounded, half of the casualties being sustained aboard the *Euryalus*. The Prince of Satsuma had paid a heavy price for his failure to deal with his criminal element. Worst of all, his inability to defend his possessions had caused him to lose face. Interestingly, one of those watching the engagement from the Japanese side was a fifteen-year-old boy name Togo Heihachiro who would become one of his country's greatest naval heroes and be publicly acclaimed in the Western press as 'The Nelson of the East'. On this occasion, Togo reached the conclusion that Japan must have, and indeed could not do without, a modern navy of her own.

Only weeks after the successful bombardment of Kagoshima, the Royal Navy was in action again, this time in concert with ships belonging to the navies of France, Holland and the United States. The reason was that the Chosu, like the Satsuma, were one of Japan's powerful south-western clans. They were not only opposed to opening the country to foreigners but were also prepared to defy and if necessary kill the Shogun for approving such a policy. The latter was well aware of what was intended and wrote secretly to Sir Rutherford Alcock, the British Envoy Extraordinary to the Japanese government, sanctioning an attack on the Chusu heartland in reprisal for the clan's interruption of the profitable trade route through Nagasaki.

Once more, Vice Admiral Sir Augustus Kuper was appointed to command. His squadron had been reinforced with the 78-gun battleship *Conqueror*, which had a battalion of Royal Marines aboard, the paddle 18-gun *Leopard*, the gunboat *Bouncer,* and two corvettes, *Barrosa* and *Tartar*. The squadron sailed from Yokohama on 29 August and on 4 September was joined off Himesima Island in the Inland Sea by one ~~American~~ US three French and four Dutch warships, the majority being sloops or gunboats.

On this occasion Kuper's intention was to force the Straits of Shimonoseki, the passage of which was covered by no less than ten coast defence batteries mounting a total of thirty-eight guns of various calibres. At 14.00 on 5 September the Allied warships took up their positions in the Straits and opened fire on the enemy's batteries. The *Conqueror*, drawing more water than the other ships, was forced to stay mid-stream and ordered to remain at the maximum range of her Armstrong guns, yet despite this she grounded twice on a sandbar and was lucky enough to get herself off on each occasion without sustaining damage. During the action a boat carrying a flag of truce approached the flagship from Buzen, on the opposite side of the Straits to Shimonoseki, promising only to fire blank cartridges if the ships refrained from firing live rounds, thereby ensuring their safety and preserving the goodwill of their compatriots.

The Japanese had maintained a steady fire from their Batteries 4 and 5, but this slackened at about 16.30 and died away shortly after. By 17.30 Batteries 6, 7 and 8 had also been silenced. Dusk was now falling but, despite being uncertain of the situation ashore, landing parties from *Perseus* and *Medusa* rowed ashore to Battery No. 5, which they found deserted. Having spiked most of the guns, they then returned to their ships without having incurred casualties.

At dawn the following morning Battery No. 8 opened fire, causing some damage to the *Tartar* and the *Dupleix*, but was silenced again shortly after. Two landing parties were then put ashore, the first consisting of the small battalion of Royal Marines carried by *Conqueror* and the second of the remaining British ships' marines, plus 350 French and 200 Dutch seamen and marines. The batteries were assaulted and taken without the need for serious fighting. All the guns were dismounted and spiked, their carriages and platforms burned and their magazines blown up.

Kuyper was anxious to get the men back on board before nightfall and at 16.00 he gave the order to re-embark. The French and Dutch were already in their boats when those still ashore at Battery No. 5 were counter-attacked by a strong force that came swarming out of the valley behind. The two landing parties quickly re-formed and drove the enemy back up the valley but were halted some 200 yards short of a stockade barracks, where the Japanese made a stand. Here, the seamen came under intense fire from firearms and archery, killing seven of them and wounding twenty-six more. Among those wounded was the column commander, Captain J. H. J. Alexander of the *Euryalus*, Midshipman Duncan Boyes of the same ship, carrying the Queen's Colour, and both of his colour sergeants. That the colour was holed by six musket balls suggests that the Japanese were firing too high; had their aim been lower the landing parties' losses would almost certainly have been higher. As it was, the attackers resumed the assault at a run, swarmed over the stockade and chased the enemy out of the rear entrance of the barracks and into trees beyond. The Japanese left numerous dead behind, including a number wearing the curious samurai armour, consisting of metal plates laced together and helmets with splayed neck protection, which were stripped from their late owners and taken aboard ship as trophies. The barracks was then set ablaze and the landing parties embarked. This was no easy matter as a six-knot tide was running and the wounded had to be handled between vessels attempting to maintain their respective positions in falling darkness.

The engagement resulted in the award of three Victoria Crosses. Midshipman Boyes 'displayed great gallantry in the capture of the enemy's stockade. He carried the Queen's Colour into action with the leading company and kept the flag flying in spite of direct fire which killed one of his colour sergeants. Mr Boyes and the other colour sergeant, who was badly wounded, were only prevented from going further forward by direct orders from their superior officer.' The second award was made to Captain of the After Guard Thomas Pride, who 'was one of two colour sergeants who accompanied the midshipman from HMS *Euryalus* when they carried the Queen's Colour into action in the capture of the enemy's stockade'. They kept the flag flying in spite of the fierce fire which killed the other colour sergeant and severely wounded

Pride. He and the midshipman, however, were only stopped from going further forward by direct orders from their superior officer. The third award was made to Ordinary Seaman William Seeley, a native of Maine, USA, who became the first ~~American~~ ᵘˢ citizen to win the Victoria Cross. His official citation reads, 'During the capture of the enemy's stockade Ordinary Seaman Seeley of HMS *Euryalus* distinguished himself by carrying out a daring reconnaissance to ascertain the enemy's position, and then, although wounded, continuing to take part in the final assault on the battery'.

On 8 September, Admiral Kuper shifted his flag to the *Coquette* and in company with four of the smaller warships, bombarded Batteries 9 and 10, situated on the island of Hikusima, round a bend in the Straits. Fire was not returned and a landing party, having established that the batteries were deserted, destroyed its works. On the same day several envoys from Chosiu, head of the Choshu clan, presented themselves to Admiral Kuper with a request for a truce, claiming that his samurai were tired and hungry, but promising that in forty-eight hours' time they would be happy to renew the battle. In fact, they did nothing of the kind. Instead, a high-ranking Japanese officer arrived with Chosiu's humble submission, his consent to the opening of the Strait and a solemn promise to refrain from constructing new batteries. On 10 September, having completed their work of destruction in the various batteries and embarked sixty-two captured guns, the Allies sailed away.

Thereafter, there were few occasions when foreigners were molested and those involved were not seriously punished. That does mean that foreigners were welcome even if their technology was being adopted slowly. The period 1863–1868 was actually one of internal strife involving intrigue, murder and, at times, actual civil war as the Satsuma and Choshu clans attempted, unsuccessfully, to persuade the Shogun to expel foreigners. The death of Iemochi, the old Shogun, in September 1866 was followed in February 1867 by that of the Mikado. When Keiki, the new Shogun, resigned in November 1867, the country slid into anarchy for several months that was ended only when the Satsuma and Choshu decisively defeated the Tokugawa, who had held an historical hold over the Shogunate, on 4 July 1868 at the Battle of Ueno, near Tokyo. On 3 January 1869 the power of the Mikado was restored when fifteen-year-old Mutshuhito assumed control of the government with Satsuma and Chushu support, initiating what became as the Meiji (Enlightened Rule) Restoration. In this regard the Shoguns had always paid respect to the Mikado as a divine presence on earth, a belief that was to continue until 1945.

Nevertheless, by 1877 the Satsuma were fiercely opposed to the government's policy of raising a conscript army on the Prussian model, as this virtually destroyed the ancient power of the clan. A 40,000-strong army, including a large Samurai presence, advanced on Tokyo but sustained a decisive defeat at the hands of the new, modern, national army at Kumamoto in September. This event is often taken as marking the emergence of Japan into the modern world. That, of course, would include the creation of a modern fleet suited to the Empire's maritime ambitions.

CHAPTER 2

First Victories

It is simply to overstate the obvious that starting a navy from scratch is no easy matter for, apart from the ships and men, there are numerous considerations involved, including recruitment, training of officers and men in seamanship, navigation, gunnery, signalling and marine engineering, the provision of dockyards, and the establishment of procurement and supply administrations and, of course, strategic and tactical aspects as they apply to potential enemies.

The first ships of the Imperial Navy were a hotch-potch, assembled from the domains of the old shogunate or purchased abroad. They included an armoured ram originally built for the Confederate Navy during the American Civil War (rams were popular with many navies during this period, but hardly ever used successfully), a wooden gunboat, a wooden corvette, four paddle steamers and four old sailing ships. Many of these were in need of extensive repairs and the armament of most was unimpressive. Likewise, the quality and experience of their crews was uneven. In effect, in its early years the Imperial Navy was little more than a coast defence force and considerable effort was required before it could be considered a blue water navy.

It was decided that Great Britain's Royal Navy would serve as a model because of its long experience and present dominance of the world's oceans. British assistance was requested and in 1873 a thirty-four strong naval mission, led by Lieutenant Commander Archibald Douglas, RN, arrived in Japan. By the time it left in 1879 the mission had firmly advanced the development of the Japanese Navy which absorbed many British traditions and the outlook of its officers. The year 1879 also saw the arrival in Japan of Lieutenant

Commander L. P. Willan, RN, on a six-year tour of instruction in gunnery and tactics at the Naval Academy. In their turn, several of his pupils became influential instructors at the Naval Staff College. Perhaps the most important of the British instructors was Captain John Ingles, RN, who served at the Naval Staff College from 1887 to 1893 and was responsible for persuading the Navy Minister to embark upon a sustained replacement of sailing ships with steam-powered warships. He also ensured that officers must achieve a thorough grounding in the application of science and modern technology before they would be considered eligible for entry to the Naval Staff College or Naval Engineering School. Particularly important were the series of lectures he gave at the Naval Staff College covering a wide range of subjects involving the practical application of sea power to strategic and tactical situations.

In parallel with the arrival of senior British naval officers in Japan, a group of suitable junior Japanese officers were sent to the United Kingdom to learn all they could about the Royal Navy, its methods and customs. One of them was Togo Heihachiro, who had joined the Prince of Satsuma's small navy shortly after the bombardment of Kagoshima and reached the rank of third class officer. He had served aboard the paddle steamer *Kasugu* in the war against the Tokugawa Shogunate and taken part in the battles of Awa, Miyoko and Hakodate. Having arrived in England, the group was dispersed to different boarding houses so that they would be forced to speak English and learn the customs of the country. Having been used to a diet of fish and rice at home, it took them some time to get used to main meals consisting of meat and potatoes. At this period, their British hosts knew almost nothing about Japan save that as it was located in the Far East; the population were understandably classed as Orientals. The Chinese were by far the best known Orientals, and because the young Japanese officers had a similar appearance to them and used the same style of writing, it seemed likely that they were related. Without intending any form of insult some of Togo's British comrades decided to call him 'Johnny Chinaman', little realising that this would probably not be considered a compliment in Japan. Togo's forceful explanation is said to have ensured that the mistake was not repeated. In 1875, while serving as an ordinary seaman aboard the training ship HMS *Worcester*, he took part in a 30,000-mile circumnavigation of the globe, part of which involved remaining at sea for seventy consecutive days without entering a port.

On his return to the United Kingdom he began suffering from an eye infection that was only cured with great difficulty by Harley Street specialists. In spite of this handicap he studied mathematics at a high level before continuing his training, first, at Portsmouth, and then at the Royal Naval College, Greenwich. During this period the Imperial Japanese Navy ordered three warships from British yards and, using the knowledge he had acquired, he supervised the construction of the frigate *Fuso* at the Samuda Brothers' yard on the Isle of Dogs. He received promotion to lieutenant early in 1878 and returned to Japan aboard the recently completed armoured corvette *Hiei*.

The new navy's seamen were either volunteers or conscripts. A high percentage of them were the sons of fishermen and therefore had a working knowledge of the sea and its ways. Obviously, individuals still required instruction in such appropriate subjects as gunnery, signalling and engineering, depending on their place in a ship's crew, as they would in any navy. The virtues of patriotism, loyalty, courage, discipline and self-sacrifice that were so strongly emphasised in the Japanese Army also existed in the Imperial Navy, and the reason for this was that both armed services possessed something unique. In the eyes of his subjects the Emperor embodied the very spirit of Japan. His will was paramount and the lives of his soldiers and sailors belonged to him. If sacrifice of those lives was demanded it must be given without question. Surrender was an unspeakable act of cowardice that could never be forgiven. However excessive these demands might seem elsewhere, the fact was they gave Japan's armed services a very dangerous edge indeed. For the moment, however, there was little for the Imperial Navy to do except expand its strength, continue training, add mine and torpedo warfare to its skills and send neutral observers to the Franco-Chinese War of 1884–1885.

In this respect the Japanese government could hardly have failed to notice that the Great Powers of the day were regularly using force to bully 'concessions' from the Chinese Empire. The latter was so corrupt that at every stage of any government transaction 'squeeze' was extracted by the responsible officials or mandarins. If, for any reason, 'squeeze' could not be extracted, the performance of contracts might be adjusted for the benefit of those involved. Thus, a proportion of high explosive shells, of which there was a shortage, might be filled with a ceramic paste, sand or even water, while others were thirteen years old and had actually been condemned. Again, that portion of the Imperial Chinese Navy that was based closest to Korea at Port Arthur was known as the Peiyang Fleet. Its commander was a former cavalry officer, Admiral Ting Ju-ch'ang, who depended heavily upon the advice of a number of foreigners. The most important of these advisers was a Prussian army officer, Major Constantin von Henneken, who was in turn advised by a Mr W. F. Tyler, a sub-lieutenant in the Royal Naval Reserve now employed by the Chinese Imperial Customs Service, which was subject to British administration. Finally, there was Mr Philo McGiffen, formerly an ensign in the United States Navy, now serving as an instructor at the Chinese Naval Academy in Wei Hei Wei, who was appointed joint commander of the Chinese pre-dreadnought battleship *Ching Yuen*. At sea, these men were some of the navy's handful of officers capable of communicating with each other as, incredibly, the fleet's signal book was written in English without a parallel Chinese translation.

In 1894 Japan decided to flex her muscles and demonstrate that she, too, was now a power to be reckoned with. She deliberately fomented trouble in the Korean peninsula, which was actually a semi-independent province of the Chinese Empire. Riots were provoked in Seoul, the Korean capital, and these reached such dangerous proportions that the Korean government requested Chinese assistance. In response, Chinese troops were shipped to the port of Asan, some forty miles south-west of Seoul. Simultaneously, at the urgings of a rival Korean faction, the Japanese responded by rushing troops to Seoul through the port of Inchon. By now, the Koreans, having brought the situation under control, requested the withdrawal of foreign troops. Neither China nor Japan was prepared to do so until the other did.

The Chinese troops at Asan were now dangerously isolated and in need of early reinforcement in case the Japanese chose to attack them. As the roads connecting China with Korea were little better than tracks, the rapid movement of armies could only be achieved by sea. However, the Chinese Viceroy, Li Hong Zhang, was forbidden by the Peking administration to risk the Peiyang fleet in an action against the better trained and equipped Japanese Navy. He recommended suspension of the reinforcement convoys and suggested that the Chinese fleet should remain within the defences of its base at Port Arthur. At this point the Chinese Emperor, Guangxu, having been advised that Japanese warships were entering what he believed to be Chinese territorial waters, flew into a rage, accused Li of cowardice, insisted that the sailing of reinforcement convoys should be resumed, and ordered him to remove the Japanese presence.

On 20 July Japan broke the stalemate by seizing control of the Korean government. From this point onwards, matters escalated beyond control. Early on the morning of 25 July the Chinese cruiser *Jiyuen*, under the command of Captain Fang Boqian, left Asan harbour accompanied by the gunboat *Kwang-yi*, intending to rendezvous with the transport *Kowshing* and her escort, the gunboat *Tsao-Kiang*. *Kowshing* was actually a British ship owned by Jardine, Matheson & Company, which traded extensively throughout the Orient. She had been chartered by the Chinese government but remained under the command of her British master, Captain Thomas Galsworthy, and was still flying the British Red Ensign. Aboard were 1,200 Chinese soldiers, twelve guns and a quantity of military stores.

According to the Japanese version of events, *Jiyuan* and *Kwang-Yi*, having reached a point off Pungdo Island, encountered three

Japanese cruisers, *Yoshino, Naniwa* and *Akitsushima,* under the command of Rear Admiral Tsuboi Kozo. The Chinese, the report continues, failed to return the Japanese ships' salute as required by International Maritime Regulations, and then opened fire. For their part, the Chinese claimed that the Japanese opened fire first. Whatever the truth, the fighting took place at close range. The *Jiyuen* sustained heavy damage and lost the use of her steering until one of the German advisors aboard managed to install a jury-rigged tiller. At this point the gunboat *Kwang-yi* made a suicidal intervention that diverted the attention of *Naniwa,* commanded by Captain Togo Haihachiro. This enabled *Jiyuen* to escape, despite being pursued by *Yoshino.* In the meantime, *Kwang-yi* received such serious damage that she ran aground on an outcrop of rocks and was destroyed by the explosion of her magazine shortly after. At about 09.00 Togo ordered the transport *Kowshing* to join the rest of the Japanese squadron. Captain Galsworthy made a formal protest, indicating the Red Ensign, but was forced to bow to the inevitable. The Chinese soldiers aboard promptly threatened to murder his crew unless Galsworthy took them back to China. Four hours of haggling followed, at the end of which the soldiers' attention was diverted, possibly by the shouted report that *Naniwa* had fired a torpedo at the transport. If that was true, it failed to explode, but Galsworthy and his British crew took advantage of the alarm caused to jump overboard and swim to the cruiser. The Chinese fired on them, killing everyone save Galsworthy and two others. Major von Hanneken also jumped overboard, but survived the Chinese fire and was picked up by a Korean fisherman. Togo now ordered his gunners to open fire on the *Kowshing,* sinking her and drowning most of the mutineers, although some managed to swim to nearby islands and a few were picked up by the boats of a French warship, *Le Lion.* The last act of what became known as The Battle of Pungdo took place at 14.00 when the *Tsao-Kiang* was overtaken by the *Akitsushima* and wisely surrendered. The sinking of the *Kowshing* almost led to a diplomatic incident between Great Britain and Japan, aggravated by demands in the former's press for compensation. It was, however, formally adjudged that Togo's action was in conformity with international law relating to the treatment of mutineers.

While small in scale, the action had important consequences on the Korean mainland. Major General Oshima, commanding the Japanese troops in Seoul, marched against the Chinese troops holding Asan. Perhaps, if the reinforcement convoy with its additional infantry and artillery had not been intercepted, the ensuing battle might have been fought on more even terms. As it was, the over-matched Chinese were defeated at Songwhan on 29 July. Hostilities between the two countries had now become a reality rather than a possibility and each declared war on the other on 1 August. A build-up of forces in the Korean peninsula commenced at once, the Chinese crossing the Yalu River and landing through the northern ports while the Japanese were shipped through Pusan and Chemulpo.

No further action took place until the following month. Then, on 15 September, General Michitsura Nozu, commanding a Japanese army in excess of 20,000 strong, some of which had marched north from Seoul while the remainder were recent arrivals from Japan, defeated a smaller Chinese army of some 14,000 men attempting to defend Pyongyang. The remnant of this force withdrew north to the Yalu River, where reinforcements, escorted by the Peiyang Fleet, were in the process of landing.

The greater part of the Imperial Japanese Navy, known as the Combined Fleet, had been involved in the Pyongyang operation under Admiral Ito Yuko, a former principal of the Naval Staff College. Ito was informed that Ting's fleet was in the area and promptly set off north to engage it. Although he was aware that the number of ships present with each fleet was similar, he was by no means confident of the forthcoming battle's outcome, and the thought of losing Japan's only fleet, purchased at great expense abroad, weighed heavily upon him. In simple terms, the balance sheet looked something like this:

The Combined Fleet
6 modern protected cruisers
2 older protected cruisers
4 light fast cruisers
1 auxiliary cruiser
1 gunboat

The Peiyang Fleet
2 ironclad battleships
4 light cruisers
6 gunboats
2 torpedo boats

The two German-built Chinese battleships, *Ting Yuen* and *Chen Yuen*, armed with 12-inch guns and protected by a 14-inch armoured belt, were theoretically the most formidable warships on either side. Together with the fleet's cruisers, they threw a heavier broadside than the Japanese. On the other hand, this was partly offset by the fact that the Japanese employed a large number of quick-firing guns, in addition to which their fleet was the faster of the two. In terms of tactics, the approach of the two sides could not have been more different. Ting preferred to fight in line-abreast with a light squadron on his right flank, instructing his ships to engage ahead and never aft of the beam. Ito fought in line ahead with a light squadron leading. Once in contact the light squadron would break through the enemy's right flank and complete its encirclement in concert with the Japanese main body.

The battle commenced at approximately 12.45 when the Chinese opened fire at approximately 6,000 yards range, twice that at which it might take effect. Moreover, the short, stubby barrels of the battleships' 12-inch guns produced a low muzzle velocity with consequent limitation of range and penetrative power. In addition, gunnery trials held in 1883 revealed that when fired ahead the blast was capable of shattering the flimsy flying bridge above. For the moment, the captain of the *Ting Yuen*, Admiral Ting's flagship, seems to have completely forgotten the fact, for the first round to be fired brought the structure crashing down, killing or injuring those standing on it. Admiral Ting's legs were crushed, disabling him for the rest of the battle, while his entire staff sustained varying degrees of injury. Effective command of the Peiyang Fleet was never resumed for, shortly after, a Japanese shell brought down the ship's foremast, so destroying the flagship's ability to signal.

Despite this, the Chinese fleet opened a steady but largely ineffective fire as the Japanese steered obliquely from port to starboard across their front. With the range now down to 3,000 yards the Japanese concentrated their own fire on the extreme right of the enemy line, scoring repeated hits on the *Chao'yong* and *Yang-wei*. Both of these obsolete vessels had been constructed with wooden hulls sheathed with thin metal, plus wooden upperworks. The impact of so many bursting shells quickly produced raging fires, rendered the fiercer by thick coats of paint and varnish. Finally, *Chao'yong* developed an acute list and sank at 13.25. At about the same time *Yang-wei* ran aground and had to be abandoned. However, the Japanese intention of working round the Chinese right flank was foiled by the arrival of several gun- and torpedo boats, including the *Kuang Ping, Ping Yuan, Fu Lung* and *Choi Ti*.

Despite the fact that superior Japanese gunnery was causing numerous fires among the Chinese ships, on the centre and rear of Ito's line was taking serious punishment, mainly at the hands of the two Chinese battleships, *Chen Yuen* and *Ting Yuen*. Ito's flagship, *Matsushima*, was hit by two 12-inch rounds, the first of which passed straight through while the second exploded in a stack of ready-use ammunition, causing further explosions that killed or wounded over 100 members of her crew, started a raging fire that was only brought under control with difficulty, and caused considerable internal damage. *Hiei*, unable to keep up, survived by a miracle. Her captain, Sakurai Kikunojo, took the bold step of turning out of the battle line *towards* the Chinese. She absorbed the fire of two enemy warships which, believing they were about to be rammed, launched two torpedoes at her, only to see them pass close astern. Still firing at every Chinese warship in sight she passed between her two opponents and into quieter water, but not before a heavy shell had exploded in the wardroom, killing a large number of wounded men receiving treatment there, as well as starting a fire. *Akagi*, under Commander Hachiroto Sasaki also sustained a battering at the hands of several Chinese ships when she went to *Hiei's* assistance. Hachiroto was killed, most of his officers were wounded and casualties among the crew were heavy. In addition, a ruptured steam pipe hindered the supply of ammunition to the forecastle. However, *Akagi* was fighting back hard and at 14.20 one of her shells exploded on the stern deck of her principal opponent, the *Lai-yuen*, starting so serious a conflagration that other Chinese vessels were forced to go to her assistance, enabling *Akagi* to make good her escape. The auxiliary cruiser *Saikyo Maru*, a converted liner, as her name suggests, was actually under the command of a British officer, Captain John Wilson. She had already repaired battle damage to her steering but at 14.50 she was attacked simultaneously from different directions by the *Kwang Ping, Ping Yuen* and a torpedo boat. *Saikyo* concentrated the fire of her few small guns on the torpedo boat, evidently to some effect as her opponent sheared off. A second torpedo boat joined in the attack at 15.10 and fired two torpedoes, both of which were expertly avoided by Wilson. In the meantime, however, *Saikyo* had been hit repeatedly by gunfire that damaged the foremast, started a blaze in the first class cabins below the quarterdeck and wounded a number of her crew. Incredibly, the auxiliary cruiser sustained no fatal casualties and by 15.30 her greater speed had enabled her to shake off her opponents. The experience cannot have been an easy one for Captain Wilson whose ship was carrying a very distinguished passenger in the person of Admiral Kamayama Sukenori, the Imperial Japanese Navy's Chief of Staff, who was visiting the fleet on a tour of inspection. In the manner of senior officers on such occasions, the Admiral got in the way and encouraged Wilson to take on the rest of the Peiyang Fleet despite the fact that *Saikyo* lacked anything heavier than defensive armament.

The heavy fighting that had involved *Hiei, Akagi* and *Saikyo* had caused Admiral Ito such concern that he ordered the light cruisers of his advanced squadron, *Yoshino, Takachiho, Naniwa* and *Akitsushima*, to go to their assistance. This decision marked the beginning of the end of the battle as the Peiyang Fleet was now dangerously placed between Admiral Tsuboi's fast squadron and Admiral Ito with the main body of the Combined Fleet. At 15.30 Ito succeeded in sinking the Chinese cruiser *Chih Yuen* which was attempting to ram his flagship.

Prior to the battle Admiral Ting, aware of the difficulties involved in trying to control movements within the Peiyang Fleet, had ordered his ships to work in pairs and conform to his flagship. By now, however, his fleet was beginning to disintegrate, partly because of its losses, partly because its ammunition supply was either exhausted, inadequate or badly manufactured, and partly because its lower speed rendered it unable to manoeuvre at the same speed as the Japanese fleet. In addition, despite the considerable damage inflicted on several of the latter, there were those who had no inclination to continue the fight, including, on the left of Ting's line, the *Kuang-Chia* and *Chi Yuen*, which simply vanished over the eastern horizon. *King Yuen*, which tried to escape in the opposite direction, was overtaken and sunk by Tsuboi's fast squadron at 16.30, together with a destroyer. Altogether, five Chinese warships had been sunk, while the Peiyang Fleet's personnel casualties amounted to 850 killed and 500 wounded. Nevertheless, the two battleships *Chen Yuen* and *Ting Yuen*, fighting together, their armoured belts impervious to the Japanese fire, formed an effective rearguard for the withdrawal of the rest of their fleet to Port Arthur. The furious reaction of the Chinese emperor to the defeat was seriously unbalanced. Admiral Ting was demoted and stripped of his honours, as were his subordinates and relatives. In contrast, praise was heaped on the fleet's foreign advisers, most notably von Hanneken and Philo McGiffin.

Ito broke contact in the failing light. His casualties included about 300 killed and 400 wounded. Four of his ships had sustained serious damage but he still possessed a fleet in being, although he was forced to transfer his flag from the seriously damaged *Matsushima* to the *Akitsushima*.

The results of the Battle of the Yalu, also known as the Battle of the Yellow Sea and the Battle of Haiyang, provided an object lesson in the use of sea power. On 24 October the Navy convoyed Marshal Iwao Oyama's Second Army to the Liaotung Peninsula, where it effected a successful landing at Pitzuwu, north of Port Arthur. The Japanese advance down the peninsula met negligible opposition, but for some reason Ito permitted Ting and his ships to escape from the base and cross the straits at the entrance to the Gulf of Chihli and enter Wei Hei Wei. Port Arthur was stormed with little difficulty or loss on 19 November.

Oyama formed a fresh Third Army and on 19 January 1895 was convoyed to Jung Cheng, on the eastern coast of the Shantung Peninsula, just twenty miles from Wei Hei Wei. The base capitulated on 31 January after two days of fighting in which the fortifications were bombarded by Ito's warships while the army attacked the landward defences. Within the harbour Ting's fleet now came under fire from the Japanese warships prowling outside the harbour and the guns of the captured coast defence batteries. On the night of 5 February a daring attack by Japanese torpedo boats under Lieutenant Commander Suzuki Kantaro resulted in two hits on the battleship *Ting Yuan*, inflicting such serious damage that she had to be run aground. Two days later Ting ordered his torpedo boats to break out, but only two managed to escape. By 12 February the rest of the fleet had now been so badly damaged that it was beyond use. Accepting the fact, Ting took his own life and his subordinates surrendered. The battleship *Chen Yuen*, the cruisers *Tche Yuen* and *Ping Yuen* and several gunboats were repaired and taken into Japanese service.

The unfortunate Chinese had also had the worst of the land campaign that had been extended to Manchuria the previous October. By the spring of 1895 only bad weather prevented the Japanese marching directly on Peking. The Viceroy, Li Hung-Chang, was sent to Japan to negotiate peace and a treaty was signed at Shimonosecki on 17 April. Under the terms of this China recognised Korean independence, paid Japan an indemnity of 300 million taels and ceded to her the island of Formosa, the Pescadores group of islands and the Liaotung Peninsula. Naturally, there was universal rejoicing in Japan, not just because of her victory, but because it was now apparent that she had joined the ranks of the Great Powers. It was not to last long.

CHAPTER 3

Lessons in Incompetence

Hardly had the ink dried upon the Treaty of Shimonosecki than three of the existing Great Powers – Russia, France and Germany – stepped in to impose their own will on events in the Far East. The fact was that in their eyes Japan, a newcomer to the game of power politics, had upset the local balance of power in no uncertain manner and in their view she must be kept in check for various reasons. Those reasons related to Port Arthur and the Liaotung Peninsula which, under pressure from the Great Powers, had been returned to China. Russia already possessed a fine harbour at Vladivostok in Usuri, the maritime province of Siberia, but this was closed by ice for three months of the year and she desperately needed a warm water port in the Far East. In 1897 anti-foreign riots broke out in China's Shan-tung province. By now Russia was making herself exceptionally agreeable to China, especially in matters such as loans at trivial rates of interest, so that when a squadron of Russian warships entered Port Arthur, ostensibly to guarantee a degree of stability in the area, the Chinese government not only accepted the fact but willingly leased the town and harbour to Russia, together with permission for her to fortify it, plus rights relating to the Chinese Eastern Railway that would permit the construction of a branch line connecting Port Arthur with Russia's own Trans-Siberian Railway. In the matter of international prestige the young German Empire felt that somehow she had been out-witted and promptly obtained a lease of her own on Kiaochow. The United Kingdom's long-term distrust of Russian motives went back many decades and had its roots in the Tsar's apparent interest in India that stopped short of actual war but created a semi-permanent state of irritation by encouraging unrest in India's northern neighbour, Afghanistan. The British response to the leasing of Port Arthur to Russia, namely leasing Wei Hei Wei for an identical period and adding to her Hong Kong holdings, was, in diplomatic terms, not a little pointed.

Japan, embittered by the loss of face resulting from these developments, nevertheless had to accept them as she could not as yet afford to fight another war. The situation, however, was changing rapidly. Inside China, widespread anger at her treatment by the foreign powers led to the formation of a fanatical organisation called the Society of the Righteous Harmony Fists, better known as the Boxers. Their aim was the destruction of all foreign influences and focused mainly on Christian missionaries and their converts, who received little mercy. The Dowager Empress Tzu Hsi and her administration claimed that the Boxers were beyond their control, but the truth was that they made no effort to restore order and actually encouraged the rising. In June 1900 the German Minister, Baron Klemens von Kettler, was murdered by a mob and the Peking Legation Area was besieged, its defence being conducted by small detachments of troops already provided by the powers, including Japan, to defend their legations. An Allied expeditionary force captured Tientsin and fought its way to the capital, relieving the Legation Quarter on 14 August. Subsequently, a series of punitive measures was mounted in the surrounding country. Finally, the Dowager Empress agreed to all the Allies' demands for compensation, including the payment of a crushing indemnity of 450 million taels.

During this emergency, large numbers of Russian troops had marched into Manchuria without the permission of the Chinese government, ostensibly to protect the railway and other private property from the Boxers and groups of local bandits known as Hunhutsus. When the emergency was over it was expected that the Russians would leave Manchuria, but they did nothing of the kind. What they did was to increase their hold on the country and extend it into Korea. There, a Russian entrepreneur named Alexander Mikhailovich Bezabrazoff had secured a concession to cut timber along the Turmen and Yalu rivers. The venture made a great deal of money, so much in fact, that a notable part of the Russian nobility had invested in it and some even said that the Tsar was a shareholder. An investment of such value, to say nothing of the business under the financial control of the Russo Korean Bank, required protection. The Russian government was urged not only to reinforce the Manchurian garrison and the Pacific Ocean Squadron, but also to send troops to the Yalu and later into Korea itself. Since the peace treaty signed by Japan and China, Korea was supposed to be an independent kingdom, but the truth was that it was still being torn apart by factional violence and bloodshed. As to who was actually governing the country, the Queen and her ladies had been murdered and the King had fled to the safety of the Russian Legation, where he agreed wholeheartedly with every suggestion his hosts made.

Naturally, by 1904, Japan found this state of affairs quite intolerable. The Korean peninsula was now firmly in the grip of a potential and very powerful enemy, who also possessed modern squadrons at Vladivostok and Port Arthur. In the summer of 1903 the Russian ambassador to Tokyo was left in no doubt that Japan felt threatened by the huge Russian expansion across Manchuria and into Korea and that if Russia wanted to avoid war she must withdraw her troops from Korea. The ambassador dutifully passed on these views to the Tsar, who summoned Admiral Alexieff, his Viceroy in eastern Asia. Alexieff was not really a sea-going admiral and owed his position to the patronage of Grand Duke Alexei Alexandrovich; it was also whispered that he was the illegitimate son of Tsar Alexander II, and this could have done his career little or no harm. As far as the performance of his duties was concerned, he was a dangerous fool who failed to understand the issues in question and was incapable of appreciating the damage his pronouncements would cause. Thus, when Tsar Nicholas II laid the Japanese warning before him he simply sneered that, if necessary, mighty Russia was capable of crushing little upstart countries like Japan with one hand. Against this, he argued smoothly, one could always discuss the matter.

The talks began at once and continued throughout the year. Six draft treaties were exchanged, each, as the Admiral fully intended, containing elements that neither Russia nor Japan found acceptable. Then, on 6 February 1904. The Japanese ambassador to St Petersburg, a Mr Kurino, requested an interview with Count Lamsdorff, Russia's foreign minister. After the usual opening pleasantries, the Count was politely informed that the discussions regarding Korea were at an end and that he had received his government's instructions to return home and had simply called to take his leave.

In diplomatic circles this fell just short of a formal declaration of war. The foreign minister was dumbfounded as Russia was nothing like ready for war. Half the troops intended to garrison Manchuria had either not left or were delayed somewhere along the inefficient Trans-Siberian Railway, a rickety single-track affair with insufficient passing places far removed from each other, interrupted by Lake Baikal, which had to be crossed by steamer to reach the next part of the line. Those troops that had arrived were short of modern weapons and equipment, while Port Arthur's new forts were far from being completed. It was intended to reinforce the Pacific Ocean Squadron. In the circumstances, most ministers agreed that everything possible should be done to avoid war.

By chance, Admiral Alexieff happened to be visiting Tokyo. He received a rain of frantic telegrams ordering him to stop, or at least delay, this drift into war. He immediately hurried to the Japanese foreign office where unsmiling officials confirmed that, as Japanese patience was now exhausted, further discussions were pointless and for this reason the ambassador to St Petersburg had been withdrawn. War was neither discussed nor even mentioned. Feeling that he had pulled off something of a coup, Alexeieff seemed to find the entire situation rather amusing. He hurried back to his own embassy and telegraphed the Tsar to the effect that the Japanese were simply bluffing, had no desire for war and would be mad to institute hostilities. Unfortunately, while his bland assurances were still travelling along the wires to St Petersburg, Togo Heichachiro, now an admiral, was briefing his captains on the Navy's operations during the opening phase of the war while recently mobilised regiments were boarding the transports that would put them ashore in the war zone.

Thinking was not Admiral Alexeieff's strongest point and one wonders what thoughts might have been passing through his mind concerning the capabilities of the Imperial Japanese Navy. We shall, of course, never know, but we can be certain that they bore no relation to the realities of the situation and probably harked back to the days following the end of the Sino-Japanese War when Japan was forced to return her honestly won territorial gains because she lacked the strength to defend them against major powers. As a result of the subsequent anger and humiliation the Japanese government initiated a huge naval expansion programme. This absorbed the latest technological advances in the manufacture of armour plate and long-range guns, resulting in a continuous process of evolution. For example, to defeat stronger armour it was necessary to employ more powerful guns and to resist these even stronger armour was needed, and so on. Again, there was a tradition among ordnance designers, both military and naval, that if a gun had reached the optimum state of development it was still possible to improve its ammunition. The addition of a ballistic cap to high explosive shells was designed to enable them to penetrate the enemy vessel and explode within rather than against its exterior, thereby inflicting far greater damage. There were, too, other considerations, such as the ability to determine the enemy's range in an era when the usual distance between opposing fleets was opening steadily, including the use of optical range-finders, spotting one's own shell splashes to assist in correcting the fall of shot, and the introduction of central fire control systems. Yet another technical innovation was wireless telegraphy. In connection with the enemy's probable use of torpedoes it was possible to hang heavy defensive netting from booms along a warship's side when she was at anchor, but this could not be done at sea as the netting imposed a heavy drag that seriously reduced the ship's speed and therefore had to be stowed. A more practical solution was a permanent steel 'bulge' extending along much of a ship's length at the waterline and below, providing a space in which the force of a torpedo's explosion could be dissipated between the 'bulge' and the hull.

Because the United Kingdom was still the world's dominant sea power, coupled with the earlier amicable relationship that had existed between her and Japan, it was decided that building the majority of the new warships necessary to complete the naval expansion programme would be carried out in British yards. Following the protracted war against the two Boer republics in South Africa, Great Britain had very few friends among the international community. It was, therefore, simply a matter of mutual interest that the two should conclude an alliance in 1902, the keystone of which was that each would come to the other's assistance if attacked by two or more opponents simultaneously. This meant that Russia's allies would not come to her assistance in the event of her fighting a war against Japan, while, in theory at least, the latter would take care of British interests in the Far East, enabling the Royal Navy to keep more ships in home waters to meet a possible German challenge.

By 1 January 1904 the Japanese naval expansion programme was almost complete. On that date the Imperial Japanese Navy (IJN) possessed the following warships:

6 battleships less than ten years old, plus the ancient ex-Chinese battleship *Chen Yuen,* no longer fit for first line service, and two older battleships serving as coast defence ships;

7 armoured cruisers less than ten years old plus two nearing completion;

13 protected cruisers less than ten years old plus three nearing completion and six older ships;

13 unprotected cruisers, of which three were less than ten years old and three over twenty years;

6 elderly gunboats and 1 nearing completion;

20 destroyers less than six years old plus 3 building;

90 torpedo boats of various types plus 3 building.

Quite possibly, Admiral Alexeieff, who was none too well versed in naval matters, might have considered as impudent any idea that the IJN should even consider engaging the much larger Imperial Russian Navy, which consisted of:

12 battleships ten years old, of which 7 were based at Port Arthur;
5 battleships less than ten years old;
8 coast defence ships, classed as capital ships;
8 barbette/turret ships, classed as capital ships;
10 armoured cruisers, of which 4 were under ten years old (3 based at Vladivostok, 1 at Port Arthur);
12 protected cruisers, of which 8 were under five years old (5 based at Port Arthur, 1 at Vladivostok);
9 obsolete sloops and protected cruisers over twenty years old, including 4 based at Port Arthur.
35 gunboats of various types including minelayers, of which possibly 8 based at Port Arthur;
49 destroyers, all but one less than six years old, of which 25 were based at Port Arthur.

That would have been a very superficial view, but then Alexeieff was a very superficial sort of man. The Russian Navy was dispersed across a huge area, the greater part of it in the Baltic and Black Seas, and some of its ships were even present in the Arctic north of the country. On its own, the Vladivostok squadron was too small to win control of the Sea of Japan, and while at Port Arthur the Pacific Ocean Squadron possessed a small superiority in battleship numbers, the ships themselves were less modern than those in Japanese service, while in other areas it was the IJN that possessed the advantage in numbers. Japanese training and efficiency, too, were markedly better than those of the Imperial Russian Navy. Furthermore, most Russian seamen were conscripted landsmen with neither liking, nor experience, nor understanding of the sea. Worst of all, the relationship between officers and men was based on a corrosive form of mutual dislike, reflecting that of the aristocracy and the bulk of the people in Russia itself. Thus, any attempt by Russia's Pacific Ocean Squadron to dominate the Yellow Sea was far from certain in its outcome.

On 8 February 1904 the squadron was lying at anchor in Port Arthur with the battleships and larger warships in the outer harbour and the smaller craft in the inner. The gun crews were sleeping beside their guns but the torpedo net had not been slung out and at dusk illuminated anchor lights reflected their glow across the water. Overall, a peaceful and relaxed atmosphere prevailed with little to disturb the few men in each crew detailed for harbour watch. Outside the harbour two destroyers patrolled their respective beats without incident, periodically coming alongside the cruiser *Pallada*, the fleet's guardship, anchored in the fairway, to report the fact.

During the day the squadron's commander, Admiral Stark, had become a prey to anxieties. A Japanese steamer had entered the port and then departed as soon as its crew had rounded up all of Port Arthur's Japanese citizens. Stark could do nothing without Alexeieff's permission and went ashore to discuss the matter with the Viceroy, suggesting that the fleet should be brought to a state of readiness. Alexeieff's reaction was positively avuncular. Without actually patting the fleet commander on the head, he remarked that Stark worried far too much and must realise that this was all part of Tokyo's game of bluff. He should return to his flagship and enjoy himself at the family party planned for that evening and in future he should leave worrying to the Viceroy.

Stark did as he was told. For those ashore, in restaurants, cafes, inns and the favourite haunts of the fleet's seamen it was business as usual. Then, at a little before 23.00, things started to happen. The two patrolling destroyers entered the harbour at speed and in a shouted exchange reported to the *Pallada* that ten unidentified ships sailing in line ahead were approaching the port. As the cruiser snapped on her searchlights the destroyers raced on to come alongside the fleet flagship, the battleship *Petropavlovsk*. Scrambling aboard, the captains burst into Admiral Stark's cabin, shouting that the Japanese fleet was approaching. Stark was still trying to make sense of what the incoherent, over-excited young officers were trying to tell him when the shooting started.

By now, most battleships had also switched on their searchlights. The outer harbour was therefore brilliantly illuminated when a flotilla of Japanese torpedo boats, led by the destroyer *Shirakumo*, burst through the entrance. If anything, the searchlights provided too much light and affected the aim of the torpedo men, for some torpedoes ran their course and sank while other beached themselves. Three, however, did find their marks. *Pallada* was hit amidships, the explosion causing a second detonation in a neighbouring coal bunker. Seriously damaged, the cruiser was run aground near the lighthouse on the west side of the harbour entrance. Minutes later the battleship *Retvizan* was shaken by an enormous explosion that blew a 200-foot hole in her port side. Another battleship, the *Tsarevich*, was hit in the stern with the result that bulkheads were blown in and her steering compartment flooded. Then, quite suddenly, the torpedo boats vanished. The Russian warships blazed away into the darkness without the slightest idea what they were firing at.

Gradually, calm was restored. Stark despatched the light cruiser *Novik* to discover the whereabouts of the Japanese fleet, then, having ascertained the extent of the damage to his ships, went ashore to report to the Viceroy. Alexeieff called a conference of his senior officers, although there was no hard intelligence upon which plans could be based. There were, however, wild rumours aplenty, so many, in fact, that the town's Governor, General Anatole Stossel, unkindly nicknamed 'the military manikin', threatened severe punishment on those guilty of spreading alarm and despondency.

The Japanese had simply retired beyond the horizon, but Togo had no intention of letting the Russians off so lightly. As soon as it was light enough for accurate gunnery he headed for Port Arthur once more. Meanwhile, a second Russian cruiser, the *Boyarin*, had been sent out to look for him and at about 10.00 she was spotted returning to the port at speed. Once she was close enough it became possible to read the signal flag she was flying: 'Enemy in sight in force'. By then, the signal was superfluous, for the smoke from numerous Japanese funnels was clearly visible along the horizon.

The news was relayed quickly to Alexeieff's conference. The naval officers present immediately tried to leave and join their ships. Alexeieff sharply ordered them to resume their seats, remarking that he had not finished talking. He continued to talk for the next hour, by which time the fleet's Chief of Staff had taken matters into his own hands, signalling the fleet to weigh anchor and form a single line ahead. The ships had already cleared for action and were actually moving when Admiral Stark, finally released from the conference, chased after them in his steam pinnace and boarded his flagship while she was under weigh.

If the Pacific Ocean Squadron's reaction had been seriously delayed by the Viceroy's verbosity, that of Port Arthur's military garrison simply reflected Stossel's unbelievable incompetence. The troops turned out of their barracks readily enough, but their officers had not been permitted to examine the layout of the defences, nor had they been informed which of the coast defence batteries individual detachments were to man, with the result that several turned up at the wrong place. Even when some detachments reached their designated positions they found that the guns were still smothered in their protective winter coating of thick grease. Elsewhere, other guns lacked ammunition, which was apparently still aboard its wagons in a railway siding some 100 miles distant. Finally, the batteries had not been supplied with provisions and those manning them went hungry throughout the day.

Admiral Togo was leading his fleet past the entrance to the port, ordering his ships maintain as rapid a fire as possible for as long as they were in range, which varied between eight and twelve miles. Their shells landed in the town and also caused serious damage to four Russian cruisers. Stossel's batteries fired in support of the Russian ships, discharging blank rounds when nothing else was available, but shell splashes revealed that all of the Russians' reply was falling short. At the end of forty-five minutes Togo's ships turned away and vanished below the horizon once more.

It is often considered that the attack on Port Arthur marked the beginning of the Russo-Japanese War, but that is not quite true. When Togo led his ships out of Sasebo on the Straits of Tsu Shima he had two tasks to perform. The first was to prevent the Pacific Ocean Squadron interfering with the convoy carrying troops to the Korean mainland, and the second was to eliminate a Russian naval presence that might interfere with the Japanese landing, which was to be made on Korea's west coast near Chemulpo.

These missions were actually executed in the reverse order. On 7 February Togo detached a squadron consisting of several cruiser and torpedo boats under Rear Admiral Uriu to Chemulpo, escorting three transports with 2,500 men, plus an assortment of landing equipment. The squadron's approach was duly noted by the Russian naval presence in the port, consisting of the modern cruiser *Variag*, temporarily detached from the Vladivostok presence, and an ancient unarmoured gunboat, the *Koreets*. Both sailed out gallantly enough to meet their opponents but, outnumbered and outclassed, they scurried back into port where their crews scuttled them and then sought refuge aboard the neutral shipping present. The Japanese landing proceeded without further interruption. Uriu anchored his ships in Asan Bay, where he was joined by Togo and the rest of the fleet late the following afternoon. Togo had now completed the missions he had been set in his preliminary briefings, but he was not satisfied, having hoped to have inflicted far greater damage on the Russians with his torpedoes than had been the case. He therefore began planning a second attack on Port Arthur with the intention of bottling up the Pacific Ocean Squadron for the rest of the war.

Did he but know it, the damage inflicted was far greater than he knew, for the Russian seamen had completely lost confidence in their officers. In the meantime, both countries issued formal declarations of war and the world's press was astounded, and a little amused, that 'little' Japan had had the temerity to kick mighty Russia in the rump. Patriotism ran riot in both Japan and Russia. In the latter case unrest and potential revolution had begun simmering just below the surface, but now the Tsar, assured by his advisers that 'a short, victorious war' was all that was needed to defuse the situation, was welcomed everywhere with demonstrations of loyalty.

Togo now changed tactics. Instead of mounting further attacks on Port Arthur, he decided to blockade the Pacific Ocean Squadron inside the harbour by using blockships to close the entrance. These consisted of old freighters, the holds of which were filled with stone and rubble that would be time-consuming to remove once the ships' bottoms had been blown out by large scuttling charges. There was no shortage of volunteers for this extremely dangerous mission, which would be carried out within range of the fortress's guns. On 23 February the first five blockships, escorted by torpedo boats, commenced their approach to the objective in a heavy sea. They were quickly spotted by the defenders and brilliantly illuminated by their searchlights, so much so that their captains were blinded by the intense light and unable to identify the points at which their vessels were to be sunk. Consequently, three of the blockships were scuttled too far out to sea and two were sent to the bottom by the Russian artillery. Incredibly, the torpedo boats picked up all but one of the seventy-six men who had formed their crews.

The following night the torpedo boats launched an attack of their own, perhaps not knowing that the Russians had moved all their warships into inner harbour with the exception of the grounded *Retvizan* which was now permanently employed as the fleet's guardship at the harbour entrance. None of the Japanese torpedoes found a mark and all sank at the end of their runs. On 25 February Togo's battleships carried out an indirect bombardment of the harbour interior at a range of 9,000 yards with his cruisers reporting on the effects of his fire. The battleships withdrew after an hour, by which time the fortress guns had begun to find their range. The bombardment inflicted damage on the Russian cruisers *Askold*, *Bayan* and *Novik,* killed twenty-two seamen and wounded over forty more. Understandably, it seemed to Togo that the Russians were quite happy to blockade themselves. Nevertheless, Stark's masterly inactivity earned him his relief by Vice Admiral Stepan

Makaroff on 8 March. If anyone in the South Pacific Squadron expected the new arrival to maintain Stark's easygoing, not to say restful, routine, they were in for a dreadful shock. To the horror of many, Makharoff tore through the squadron like a whirlwind, rooted out inefficient officers who considered that their position in society justified their presence and sent them packing. This earned him the respect, and even liking, of his crews, who willingly buckled to and implemented his new regime. An important part of this involved making life difficult for the patrolling Japanese out to sea by mounting a series of sorties.

The results of the change of command were duly noted by Togo, who decided to set a trap for his opponent. During the night of 12 April Makharoff spotted several Japanese destroyers engaged in a minelaying operation outside the harbour. Having taken the necessary bearings, he left orders for the minefield to be swept next day. However, shortly after first light on 13 April a brawl broke out between opposing destroyer flotillas. During this, the Russian destroyer *Strashni* was set on fire and sank. Hurrying to the rescue, the Russian cruiser *Bayan* became involved with a Japanese cruiser squadron. At this point Makharoff believed that it was in his power to inflict some loss on the enemy. At about 08.00, aboard the battleship *Petropavlovsk*, he led out a second battleship, the *Poltava*, and the cruisers *Diana, Novik* and *Askold* and set off in pursuit of the Japanese cruisers, against which he opened a long-range fire. In the excitement, the admiral's instructions regarding minesweeping appear to have been forgotten by everyone, including himself. The pursuit continued until the six dark shapes of Togo's battleships emerged from the mist ahead.

Hopelessly outgunned, Makharoff reversed course and began leading his ships back to port. He was within sight of the anxious spectators ashore when the flagship was blown apart by three huge explosions that were audible many miles away, the first being the detonation of the mine she had struck, the second the explosion of a magazine, and the third the bursting of her boilers. Very quickly, she vanished beneath the waves so that of her 700-strong complement only seven officers, including the Grand Duke Cyril, and seventy-three men were picked up from the scene of the disaster.

This had been witnessed from within the harbour by Makharoff's second-in-command, Rear Admiral Prince Uktomsky, aboard the *Peresiet*. He reacted quickly and, in company with *Pobieda*, covered the return of the rest of the ships. Then, at 10.15 there was another huge explosion as *Pobieda* struck a mine and began to list heavily as water rushed in through an immense hole in her bows. She did not sink but had to be nursed very slowly into harbour. This additional explosion started wild rumours that the battleships had been the target of a Japanese submarine attack, resulting in the pointless expenditure of ammunition as guns blazed away at targets that existed only in fevered imaginations.

The next phase of the war was dictated by the land campaign. General Alexei Kuropatkin, a former minister of war, had been appointed commander of all Russian field forces in the Far East, although he was seriously handicapped by the Tsar's appointment of Admiral Alexeieff, already his Viceroy, as supreme commander. Kuropatkin's strategy was, inevitably, dictated by what the rickety Trans-Siberian Railway could deliver in the way of men, munitions and supplies and he reached the sensible conclusion that he would not be strong enough to take the offensive until the end of summer, and must maintain the defensive until then. Inevitably, Alexeieff insisted that he should attack at once. This was not merely idiotic, it was also dangerous as, in terms of strategy, Russia was already on the back foot. By the beginning of May, General Tamesada Kuroki's First Army had driven the Russians out of Korea, defeated those troops defending the line of the Yalu River, and crossed into Manchuria itself. Between 5 and 19 May General Yasukata Oku's Second Army was put ashore on the Liaotung Peninsula at Pitzuwu, just forty miles from Port Arthur, and began advancing on the fortress. One does not need a high-powered crystal ball to understand that once the hills overlooking the harbour had been taken the Japanese artillery would simply destroy the South Pacific Squadron where it lay at anchor. Alexeieff was quick to spot the danger and decided to make himself scarce. He organised a train for himself in which some of the Russian wounded were placed aboard and a Red Cross flag flown to provide an air of respectability, just in case it was intercepted by the Japanese. It was intercepted and would have been released without incident until, too late, they discovered that the Viceroy was aboard, and travelling in some comfort. Thanks to a quick-witted driver, the train was quickly put in motion and survived the fusillade of rifle fire directed at it.

To return to the naval aspects of the war, the death of Admiral Makharoff was regarded as being a greater disaster than the failure to secure a victory. The Tsar decided that the Baltic Fleet would be sent out to reinforce the South Pacific Squadron, command of which would devolve upon Rear Admiral Vilgelm Vitgeft, who had been Alexeieff's Chief of Staff. For the moment Vitgeft concentrated on repairing his damaged warships and constructing booms across the fairway within the harbour mouth, thereby reducing the potential damage that could be inflicted by the enemy's torpedo boats.

Despite the successes that had been achieved thus far, Togo also had his problems and the author of them was a Captain Ivanoff, commander of the Russian minelayer *Amur*. The Russians had laid a considerable number of mines on the approaches to Port Arthur, but they had done so in an untidy way so that their position was far from being an absolute certainty. The Japanese were therefore almost permanently involved in minesweeping operations. Ivanoff made careful notes on the daily movements of the minesweepers and the larger warships that were escorting them and quickly reached the conclusion that in both cases these followed an invariable pattern. Early on 14 May Ivanoff took *Amur* out in a low-hanging mist above which the masts of the Japanese ships were visible from time to time. Some ten miles from the shoreline he laid mines along the route usually followed by the enemy, and returned to harbour.

The following day began badly for the Japanese. In a dense fog Rear Admiral Dewa's cruiser squadron was patrolling south of the Liaotung Peninsula when the *Kasuga* rammed the *Yoshino* so hard amidships that she sank almost immediately with heavy loss of life.

Simultaneously, off Port Arthur, the minesweepers and their escorts returned to their task as usual. At about 10.00 those ashore heard three heavy explosions out to sea and from their movements it was apparent that all was far from well with the Japanese. First, the battleship *Hatsuse* had struck a mine that had wrecked her steering gear. Shortly after, a second battleship, the *Yashima*, also struck a mine and began to list heavily. The next explosion marked *Hatsuse* striking a third mine, following which she was enveloped in a cloud of steam and smoke before vanishing beneath the surface. Some 200 of her crew, including a number with serious injuries, were picked up. The result of this double loss was to reduce Togo's battleship strength by one-third.

Further Japanese losses occurred on the 16th. For unknown reasons a torpedo boat blew itself apart and sank, the destroyer *Miyoko* struck a mine and went to the bottom in just twenty-five minutes, and two gunboats ran each other down in foggy darkness. This catalogue of misfortune ended the following day when the destroyer *Akatsuki* sank at once after striking a mine. Finally, the small despatch vessel *Tatsuta*, which had rescued Rear Admiral Nashiba from the wreck of the *Hatsuse*, ran aground and stayed there for a month, during which the unfortunate admiral had to be rescued for a second time.

Meanwhile, on land the Japanese, whose strength would rise to 80,000 men with 474 field and siege guns following the arrival of their Third Army under General Marsuke Nogi, were closing in steadily on Port Arthur's defences. Excluding naval personnel, the garrison of the fortress numbered some 40,000 men with 506 guns and sufficient food to withstand a long siege. Unfortunately for them, General Stossel was demonstrating no more ability than he had at the beginning of the siege, although his fine opinion of himself was actually grander. His troops, in the main hardy East Siberian Rifle regiments, deserved far better; indeed, when the Japanese began probing the outer ring of forts in July they met such tough resistance that it was immediately apparent that the fortress would be a very hard nut to crack. On the other hand, the future of the South Pacific Squadron was bound to be much shorter once the Japanese were able to emplace their guns on the high ground. Even the Tsar was so concerned by the problem that he ordered Vitgeft to break out and join the Vladivostok squadron.

At 09.00 on the morning of 10 April, therefore, the squadron followed its minesweepers out of the harbour and set a course south-south-east to a point where it could round the Korean Peninsula and head north-east to Vladivostok. In the lead were its six capital ships, *Tsarevich* (flagship of Rear Admiral Vitgeft), *Retvizan*, patched up but still with several hundred tons of water aboard), *Pobieda*, *Peresviet* (flagship of Rear Admiral Prince Ukhtomsky), *Sebastopol* and *Poltava*. Following these were three armoured cruisers, *Askold* (flagship of Rear Admiral Reinzenstein), *Pallada* and *Diana*. Screening the squadron was the light cruiser *Novik* and eight destroyers, while a hospital ship brought up the rear.

As soon as the Russians were sighted Togo began assembling his fleet. As he now possessed only the four battleships *Mikasa* (flag), *Asaki*, *Fuji* and *Shikishima*, plus the armoured cruisers *Nisshin* and *Kasuga*, he was by no means certain of victory but was determined to intercept the Russians and inflict as much loss and damage as possible. Shortly after midday the two fleets opened fire at a range of approximately 13,000 yards. Togo tried repeatedly to cross Vitgeft's 'T', thereby bringing the fire of some or all of his ships to bear on one of his opponents, but every admiral afloat was aware of the manoeuvre and Vitgeft foiled every attempt by turning away. At one point Togo made the mistake of turning to port instead of to starboard and might well have lost his quarry had he not squeezed every ounce of effort out of his engines. Once the two fleets were in contact again they fought a protracted gunnery duel while running on parallel courses. In this the Japanese sustained as much, if not more, damage than the Russians, some of their guns bursting due to the premature explosion of shells in over-heated barrels. When Togo was reinforced by Rear Admiral Dewa's light cruiser squadron the latter was driven off by the concentrated fire of the Russian battleships, the *Yakumo*, Dewa's flagship, being turned into a virtual wreck.

Then, at 18.40, the explosion of two 12-inch shells aboard the *Tsarevich* changed the entire course of the battle. The first burst near the foot of the mainmast, killing Vitgeft and his senior navigation officer and seriously wounding his chief of staff and flag captain. The second exploded on the conning tower roof, killing or wounding everyone within. The body of the dead helmsman fell across the wheel, jamming it so that the ship began turning wildly in a full circle that nearly brought her into collision with the *Poltava* and the *Sebastopol*. The *Tsarevich* had been followed by the *Retvizan* and the *Peresvyet* until the flagship slowed to a standstill, leaving the battle line in disorder and at the mercy of the Japanese. Suddenly a series of flags rose up the flagship's hoists: 'Admiral transfers command.' The fleet was now under the command of Prince Ukhtomsky. Unfortunately, the *Peresvyet*'s signal halyards and top masts had been shot away so that his intended signal 'Follow me' could only be tied to his bridge rails where it went un-noticed. In addition, he was unable to fly his own admiral's flag and it was therefore unclear which admiral had been killed. The *Tsarevich* had begun to move very slowly but no further signals were forthcoming from her. Whatever was going through the prince's mind at this moment it had nothing to do with breaking through to Vladivostok. Instead, he turned again and headed for the illusory safety in the gathering darkness. Togo followed, observing that the Russians were firing with every gun they retained. As twilight turned to darkness he sent in his torpedo craft to finish off the enemy fleet. Incredibly, though they fired no less than seventy-four torpedoes, not one struck a Russian ship that night, despite fine weather conditions.

Early the following morning the battered South Pacific Squadron returned to Port Arthur. One by one the battleships *Retvizan, Peresvyet, Pobieda, Sebastopol* and *Poltava* entered the harbour to a silent welcome. Then came the cruiser *Pallada* and three destroyers, but after that, nothing. So where were the *Tsarevich, Novik, Askold, Diana* and the remaining destroyers? *Tsarevich* had been unable to keep up with the rest of the battleships, but for a while her senior uninjured officer, Captain Shunoff, had tried to continue the voyage to Vladivostok. Unfortunately, because her funnels were so badly holed, her fuel consumption rose to the point that Shunoff was forced to accept that he would never get there. Accompanied by *Novik* and three destroyers, he therefore headed for the German treaty port of Kiaochow where *Tsarevich* and three destroyers were interned; *Novik* completed coaling within the time permitted by the neutrality laws and set off again for Vladivostok. *Askold* and another destroyer reached Shanghai where they too were interned, as was the *Diana* when she reached Saigon.

Despite this, Togo had little cause for satisfaction. His own fleet had sustained unexpectedly heavy damage and he had failed to destroy the South Pacific Squadron, which in itself was the reason that the Army was heavily engaged in besieging Port Arthur. If the Baltic Fleet succeeded in reaching the Far East the possibility existed that he would find himself between two fires. Within Port Arthur morale had been seriously damaged by the results of what became known as The Battle of the Yellow Sea. There was serious doubt as to whether the South Pacific Squadron would ever go to sea again, and whether it and the fortress would survive to see the arrival of the Baltic Fleet.

CHAPTER 4

Destruction of a Navy

During the early months of the war few within the Russian establishment would have imagined that, as it continued, it would become a matter of urgent necessity for the Tsar's naval presence in the Far East to receive substantial reinforcements on a hitherto unimagined scale. Yet, such were the reports of losses sustained by and the disappointing achievements of Port Arthur's warships that, as early as 20 June 1904, Nicholas convened a meeting of his Higher Naval Board, consisting of those best qualified to advise him. They included the Imperial Navy's most senior officers, General-Admiral the Grand Duke Alexei Alexandrovich, the Minister of Marine, four senior admirals and one comparatively junior admiral, Zenovy Petrovich Rozhestvensty, who had seen active service in the Black Sea against the Turks and in Far Eastern waters. He was considered to be the Navy's top gunnery expert and was noted as a fine administrator who also happened to be a workaholic. Like many Russian senior officers of the day, he possessed pronounced eccentricities. Of these the most notable included flinging his binoculars at the head of any subordinate who happened to annoy him, but as this was anticipated they were able to take evasive action so that the instruments often flew harmlessly overboard. Such furious rages were to earn him the nickname of 'Mad Dog'. There is little doubt that it was at this meeting that he received the order to take Russia's Baltic Fleet, re-named the Second Pacific Squadron, around the world to the Far East and, on arrival there, destroy the Japanese Navy completely.

Naturally, his appointment should have remained the best kept secret in St Petersburg, but in the final decades of Romanov rule it was the custom of those privileged to be members of the establishment to demonstrate their importance by disclosing such secrets to their mistresses and friends, 'in the strictest confidence, of course'. Of course, these confidences would be passed on for similar reasons or sold on to professional intelligence gatherers who would, in turn, sell them to their respective governments or the international press. In this way, Japanese embassies around Europe knew exactly what Russian intentions were and cabled the news to Tokyo. Thus, only days after the meeting of the Higher Naval Board, the St Petersburg correspondent of *Le Petit Parisien* was able to ask Rozhestvensky to confirm that he was bound for the Far East with the Baltic Fleet. Smiling enigmatically, the Admiral replied: 'We shall sail on the 15th July, but of course it is a long voyage taking many weeks. There will be nothing for me to do in the Far East by September. The Japanese will have capitulated long before then.' That such a periodical as *Le Petit Parisien* could obtain such hard confirmation direct from the horse's mouth says everything one needs to know about the level of St Petersburg security.

There were, however, also occasions when Russian operational communications were disastrously slow, notably in the case of Rear Admiral Jessen's squadron, consisting of the three light cruisers *Rossiya, Gromoboi* and *Rurik*, based at Vladivostok. For a short period Jessen's cruisers earned greater credit for the Russian Navy than the rest of the Tsar's Far Eastern warships put together. After leaving Vladivostok they would pass through the largely undefended Tsugaru Strait between Honshu and Hokkaido and cause such chaos among the commercial traffic using the ports along the west coast of the former that insurance rates rocketed to insupportable heights. Great Britain and the United States, neither of whom had any great liking for Russia, protested strongly but these punitive cruises, lasting approximately two weeks, continued.

In addition, the Japanese Navy's loss of face caused Togo to detach a heavy cruiser squadron under Rear Admiral Kamimura to hunt down the raiders. For the moment, however, Jessen enjoyed all the luck. On 25 April two Japanese troopships, the *Kimshu Maru* and the *Goya Maru*, were run down and sunk. Of those aboard, 100 were drowned or killed and 250 were captured. This was bad, but what happened on 31 May was infinitely worse. Jessen's squadron intercepted three transports, *Izami Maru*, *Hitachi Maru* and *Sado Maru*. The first two were sunk together with the twenty-eight 11-inch howitzers they were carrying, without which the siege of Port Arthur could not proceed until replacements were obtained. Also aboard these ships were 1,000 soldiers of the Guard Reserve Brigade, all of whom were shot, drowned or taken prisoner. The *Sado Maru* escaped by the skin of her teeth.

And so it continued. It was this slight encouragement that motivated the Tsar into ordering Admiral Vitgeft to take the Port Arthur warships to sea, defeating Togo and joining Jessen, who would escort him north in triumph into Vladivostok harbour. As we know, none of this happened. Jessen had already left Vladivostok when news reached the city, via the long route through China, that the Port Arthur warships had gone to sea, fought a battle in which Vitgeft had been killed, and were now back in harbour. A fast destroyer was sent after Jessen but failed to intercept him.

On 14 August Jessen was cruising off Ulsan on the east coast of Korea in anticipation that he would be joined by Vitgeft and his ships. To his horror, during the afternoon four Japanese heavy cruisers – *Idyamo*, *Adyuma*, *Tokiawa* and *Iwate*, about half of Kamimura's squadron – appeared on the horizon and turned towards the Russians.

Neither admiral could afford to lose the ensuing encounter. Kamimura's long failure to locate Jessen had resulted in politicians demanding that he should be court martialled for incompetence; stones had been thrown at his home and the type of short sword associated with *hara-kiri* had been delivered to it. The thought must have occurred to him that if he did not defeat Jessen he would have to take his own life. Nevertheless, his estimate of Jessen's whereabouts was an intelligent one. He was aware of Vitgeft's sortie from Port Arthur some twenty-four hours before it was known in Vladivostok and it seemed probable that Jessen would attempt a rendezvous with him in these waters. For Jessen himself there remained just two allthernatives – fight or flight. All the odds were against him – four armoured cruisers against three unarmoured, twelve 8-inch guns against six, and twenty-seven 6-inch guns against twenty-one. Again, he did not know whether any other Japanese warships were present in the area.

Kamimura decided to fight at long range, taking advantage of the fact that he possessed the greater number of heavy guns and was confident in his crews' gunnery skills. Furthermore, the Japanese were fighting with the sun at their backs, enabling them to spot the fall of their own shot better than the Russians. For their part, the Russians sought to make the best of their speed but, after an hour's fighting, the Japanese began to gain the upper hand. They concentrated their fire on the *Rurik*, disabling her steering gear so that she could only be steered by her engines, but further hits, including at least one below the waterline, resulted in the flooding of her engine room. *Rossiya* and *Gromoboi* did their best to draw the enemy's fire away from the stricken cruiser, to no avail. Her fate was sealed when two more of Kamimura's cruisers, *Nanina* and *Tabachiko*, entered the fray at 20.00. Jessen reached the inevitable conclusion that if he did not leave *Rurik* to her fate he would lose his entire squadron.

Rossiya and *Gromoboi*, both of which had a number of their guns disabled, therefore set off at speed for Vladivostok with Kamimura and his four original cruisers in hot pursuit, leaving *Nanina* and *Trabachiko* to finish off the *Rurik*. It was not, in fact, until 21.45 that *Rurik* fired her last shell and even then her senior surviving officer, a Lieutenant Ivanoff, gave orders for the sole remaining torpedo to be launched and for the ship to be scuttled by opening her Kingston valves.

Kamimura continued his pursuit for an hour, at the end of which darkness made accurate shooting impossible. He returned to the scene of the action to find *Nanina* and *Tabichiko* still picking up *Rurik's* survivors, of which there were 625, including 230 wounded. *Rurik* herself had gone down at 22.20, taking a further

170 of her crew with her. As for *Rossiya* and *Gromoboi*, they reached Vladivostok but were in such a damaged condition that it was months before they could put to sea again, and even then *Gromoboi* ran herself hard upon a rock and sustained severe damage. There was now no real Russian naval presence at Vladivostok, while that at Port Arthur was about to be turned into sunken scrap iron by the Japanese artillery.

It will have been noted that Kimamura's victory took place over a month after Admiral Rozhestvensky was supposed to have left for the Far East with the Baltic Fleet. In fact, that fleet was still far from ready. Its crews consisted of a handful of regular officers and petty officers, while the remainder were recalled reservists, conscripts, compulsorily recruited merchant seamen, fishermen and boatmen from Russia's great rivers, and even landsmen. Many were ignorant of discipline and resented its imposition. Others were covert revolutionaries, quite willing to commit acts of sabotage. Still others hated the aristocratic officers who governed their lives and in some cases the feeling was mutual. 'Half of them know nothing', commented one officer on those who lived on the lower deck, 'and the other half have forgotten whatever it was they thought they knew.'

The ships themselves were a very mixed bunch. The best were the four brand new battleships *Suvoroff*, *Borodino*, *Alexander III* and *Oryol*. With their 12-inch guns and speed of 18 knots they seemed impressive, although the truth was that none of them had so much as been through their sea trials. There were also three older battleships, one of which was actually a coast defence vessel. In total, Rozhestvensky's fleet would number forty-two ships including cruisers, destroyers, torpedo boats, hospital ships and a repair ship. Some had a maximum speed of 10 knots which, therefore, became the cruising speed of the entire fleet.

For months Rozhestvensky had bullied and bellowed his way through the tangle of the Tsar's naval bureaucracy until his ships had been properly fitted out, ammunitioned and victualled. During one period he went for three nights without sleep. The one problem he almost despaired of solving was that of establishing an adequate fuel supply. His ships burned enormous quantities of coal, but neutral nations would neither supply it, nor permit the warships of belligerent powers to refill their bunkers within their territorial waters. To overcome this he signed a secret and hugely expensive contract with the Hamburg-Amerika Line whose colliers would supply his ships at sea.

A shakedown cruise at the end of August revealed nothing save glaring inefficiencies in every department. By the end of September most of these had been corrected, if not to the entire satisfaction of the more professional officers. The time to leave was approaching and was marked by farewell banquets and other forms of celebration. For the sake of the fleet's spiritual welfare the pious Tsarina presented expensively crafted chalices and icons to the chapels of the battleships while archbishops in their splendid vestments climbed aboard lesser warships to splash their decks and guns with holy water. Then, on 15 October, the moment to depart finally arrived. Bands played 'God Save the Tsar' and guns fired thunderous salutes. Amid breakdowns, collisions, groundings, lost anchors and shouted recriminations, the ships made an untidy exit from Kronstadt harbour into the Gulf of Finland, so overladen with stores and coal that water slopped onto their decks. Once in the Baltic it became possible to restore some sort of order, but it had been a most unfortunate start to an 18,000-mile voyage.

During its passage of the North Sea the Second Pacific Squadron almost started a war between Great Britain and Russia. Incredible as it may seem, during the night of 21 October the old repair ship *Kamchatka* signalled that she was being chased by Japanese torpedo boats. On the bridge of Rozhestvensky's flagship, the battleship *Suvoroff*, nervous officers saw lights that, in their nervous state, they declared to be the Japanese vessels signalling to each other. Searchlights probing the darkness illuminated a number of small vessels that promptly became the target as numerous warships opened fire on them. At this point more searchlights were spotted dead ahead, accompanied by flashing signal lamps transmitting messages in the Russians' own security code. There were wild suggestions that the Japanese had broken it and were using it against them. These were sensibly countered by the recognition that the new arrivals were simply the fleet's cruiser screen, returning to find out what was happening. The firing was stopped and calmer investigation revealed that the recent targets were fishing boats and that the mysterious lights were nothing more sinister than navigation lights and those usual to fishermen. With a sense of horror, it was also observed that they were flying the British mercantile Red Ensign and that one of them was sinking.

Rozhestvensky was shocked but unrepentant. The British loss was unfortunate, but it was perfectly obvious that the Japanese torpedo boats were hiding among the fishermen – how else could two of his cruisers have sustained damage, to say nothing of a seaman and a priest being killed? He congratulated his crews on their conduct and submitted a glowing report of the 'action' to his superiors. In return, he received the Tsar's commendation and was hailed as a hero by the Russian press. Then the truth came out. His 'opponents' had been the Gamecock Fleet of small 100-ton trawlers based on Hull, which was working at its fishing ground on Dogger Bank. Two innocent fishermen had been killed and their trawler sunk. The fury of the British public brought them out into the streets with demands for war with Russia. The anger spread across Europe and finally Nicholas was forced into an apology and payment of an indemnity valued at approximately £6 million in today's money. The British government's immediate response to the outrage was to send its fastest cruiser squadron to tail the Russian fleet at close quarters. The continued presence of these ships, clean, smart in every detail, slicing through the water at speed, unfriendly and apparently well prepared for trouble with the Russians, must have been intimidating for two reasons. First, however patriotic the Russian officers might have been, the contrast with their own hotch-potch fleet, slopping along at ten knots under a blanket of coal smoke could only have led to the conclusion that they were looking at a real navy; and second, the fact that this was the navy that had trained the Japanese Navy to an equally high standard was no comfort at all.

Having seen the Russians off the doorstep, the British turned for home. Until it reached its appointment with destiny, the story of Rozhenstvensky's fleet holds less interest. The Admiral detached part of it to pass through the Mediterranean and Red Seas to round the Horn of Africa and proceed to Diego Suarez on the coast of Madagascar where it would be joined by the main body, which had sailed down the west coast of Africa and round the Cape of Good Hope. Rozhestvensky made landfall on 29 December, dropping anchor off the hot, steamy little island of Sainte Marie on Madagascar's eastern seaboard. There, to his annoyance, he received word that the detached portion of the fleet, under Admiral Felkerzam, was at Nossi-Be, a bay of many islands some 500 miles distant on the west coast of Madagascar, and had received the Admiralty's approval to overhaul his machinery there. He would not, he added regretfully, be ready for sea for a minimum of two weeks.

Rozhestvensky decided to join him and set off round the island's northernmost point. At about this time he received the devastating news that the original Pacific fleet had been destroyed and that Port Arthur had surrendered on 2 January 1905. The siege had lasted six months, during which five major assaults had been made on the defences. Japanese casualties included 59,000 killed, wounded and missing, plus another 34,000 seriously ill. Some 10,000 able-bodied but starving members of the garrison marched into captivity, a terrible indictment of Stossel's criminal incompetence as the victors discovered that his storehouses contained huge quantities of foodstuffs. Roshestvensky also received a signal from the Tsar informing him that he had formed a Third Pacific Squadron under Rear Admiral Nebogatoff and that this was on the way out to join him. When Rozhestvensky learned that the new squadron consisted of every warship that he had rejected, including shallow-draft monitors dismissively referred to as 'flat-irons', his patience finally snapped and he sent in his resignation. It was rejected on the grounds that he was the only commander capable of carrying out this difficult task.

Intense heat, humidity and ever-present coal dust made the Russians' lives a sort of floating hell in which some men died from tropical diseases and others went mad. Mutinies became commonplace, especially when details of the unrest at home and the savage repression that followed formed the content of those Russian newspapers that reached the fleet. Morale collapsed, many of the seamen believing that they would never see home again. Only the arrival of the wet season provided a little relief as the torrential rain swilled the ever-present coal dust out through the scuppers. In an attempt to shake off the destructive malaise that was gripping the fleet, Rozhestvensky took it to sea for some gunnery practice against a towed target. Only one hit was scored by the entire fleet, and that was on the towing vessel. The only ammunition remaining was considered to be adequate for operational requirements, but none was available for further practice as the store ship meant to be carrying a supply was found to be loaded with winter clothing. Worse still, of a salvo of torpedoes launched, one jammed in the tube, one ran straight but missed the target, and the rest set off in whatever direction they chose. When the Admiral learned that Nebogatoff's unwanted squadron was about to enter the Suez Canal he decided to leave the poisonous environment of Nossi-Be and head for French Indo-China, the next location likely to offer a remotely friendly welcome.

It took three weeks to cross the Indian Ocean. At times the fleet was compelled to halt because of numerous breakdowns, but even when moving its speed was reduced to just eight knots because of the long curtains of tropical weed that had fastened itself to its bottoms. Through the Straits of Malacca it went to round Singapore Island from which observers could view the slow-moving lines of warships under their blanket of funnel smoke. The general opinion of the watchers was the Russians were impressive at a distance, but somewhat scruffy when seen from close at hand. Rozhestvensky had no wish to remain in the area; Singapore was a British naval base and he reminded his captains that another incident similar to that which had taken place in the North Sea could not be contemplated for one minute. The city's Russian consul brought out newspapers and informed the Admiral that a major battle had taken place in Manchuria, where the Japanese troops that had besieged Port Arthur had now joined their comrades. The Russians had deployed 276,000 men and the Japanese 207,000 strong along a front some forty miles long and centred on the important city of Mukden. The Russians' right flank had been turned but General Kuropatkin had disengaged expertly and withdrawn to protect his lines of communication, even though he had to abandon Mukden. Russian losses amounted to some 60,000 casualties and much equipment, while the Japanese had lost about 54,000 men.

At this moment Rozhestvensky did not require reminding that his fleet provided Russia's last hope of a victory. He took a north-easterly course through the South China Sea and if, from time to time, smudges of smoke were seen on the southern horizon, its origin was not Japanese but a shadowing British cruiser squadron, there to remind the Russians to mind their manners. The Russians' destination was, in fact, Kamranh Bay in French Indo-China, in which he dropped anchor on 12 April. He had received a packet of orders from the Singapore consul from which it was apparent that neither the Tsar nor the Admiralty would forgive his disobedience in deliberately failing to wait for Admiral Nebogatoff's Third Pacific Squadron at Nossi-Be. The orders contained three specific points: first, he was to await Nebogatoff's arrival in Kamranh Bay; second, he was to locate the Japanese fleet and destroy it; and third, he was then to proceed to Vladivostok and hand over command of his fleet to Admiral Birilef, who was already travelling east by rail for that very purpose. To his habitual brooding gloom was now added the suppressed fury generated by the insult. There was no disguising the fact that Rozhestvensky and the Admiralty were barely on speaking terms.

'Have arrived Kamranh Bay,' he signalled bluntly.

'Keep us advised of your movements,' the Admiralty responded, providing the Admiral with just the chance he needed to put them in their place.

'I will not telegraph you again before the battle. If I am beaten Togo will tell you. If I beat him, I will let you know.'

When Nebogatoff arrived with his collection of ancient warships he visited the flagship to pay his respects, as naval etiquette demanded. Roshestvensky's greeting was glacial. After acknowledging the presence of the Third Pacific Squadron and a moment or two of formal conversation, he remarked that he would be obliged by Nebogatoff returning to his own ship. He gave him neither orders nor advice, despite the fact that Admiral Felkerzam was seriously ill and expected to die, and that Nebogatoff would almost certainly have to take over as the fleet's second-in-command. Had Nebogatoff been better acquainted with Rozhestvensky, he would have known that he rarely communicated possibilities with his subordinates.

By now the French had begun to attract international criticism concerning the degree of help to which they, as neutrals, were actually providing for the Russians. The latter were politely asked to leave Kamranh Bay, which they did by making an untidy move to the next bay along the coast. Here, they prepared for the last leg of their long voyage, at the end of which they knew they would almost certainly have to fight a battle. Rozhestvensky would have been less than human if he had not been permanently conscious of his mutinous, ill-disciplined, inexperienced crews, his pathetically slow ships with their unreliable machinery and his fleet's dreadfully low standard of gunnery with which to meet his battle-hardened opponents.

Togo, too, knew that he was about to fight a battle. His ships had been kept busy safeguarding the Army's supply line and had seen to it that adequate siege artillery had been delivered to those investing Port Arthur, making good the loss of those sent to the bottom by Jessen's light cruisers. They had, however, been kept in fighting trim and their crews knew exactly what to expect, which their enemies did not. The efficient Japanese intelligence service had provided regular reports on Rozhenstvensky's progress so that now it had become possible to provide a reasonable estimate as to when he would enter Japanese waters. It was, too, possible to predict with reasonable certainty the route he would take to Vladivostok – with his run-down ships and limited fuel supply the Russian commander would almost certainly seek to pass through the Straits of Tsushima with Tsushima Island to port and the Japanese mainland to starboard. Togo planned accordingly. On 24 May he telegraphed the Navy General Staff informing them that he would wait at Chinhae, his base on the south coast of Korea, and if the Russians failed to appear he would move north to Tsugaru Strait.

Rozhestvensky's ships had finally left the Indo-Chinese coast on 14 May, setting a north-easterly course that by-passed the island of Formosa to port. Nothing now lay ahead save the Straits of Tsushima themselves and contact with the enemy could be expected at any time. At about 05.00 on 27 May one of Togo's fast auxiliary cruisers, the *Shinano Maru*, sighted the Russian fleet in the western approaches to the Tsushima Strait, close to the small offshore Goto Islands. Its position was signalled, but then the Russians disappeared into a dense fog and contact was lost for an hour. By 06.30, however, Togo was leading his own fleet out of Chinhae Bay aboard his flagship *Mikasa* and laying off what he hoped would be an interception course.

It is difficult to strike a balance between the two fleets. The Russians had four modern battleships and seven older capital ships and one armoured cruiser, whereas the Japanese also had four modern battleships and eight armoured cruisers. The Russians possessed the greater number of 12- and 10-inch guns, but in terms of secondary armament the Japanese ships mounted 127 guns to the Russians' ninety-two. In the critical area of speed the Japanese enjoyed a marked advantage, being capable of maintaining a fighting speed on 15 knots while the Russians could only produce 10 knots at best.

At 13.39 the Russian fleet emerged from the mist, moving in two parallel columns, some eight miles ahead of the *Mikasa*. Togo promptly broke out his famous Nelsonian signal: 'The fate of the empire rests on this one battle. Let every man do his utmost.' When, at about 14.07, the two fleets were six miles apart, Togo gave the order for his battleships and cruisers to turn fourteen points to port in succession and then steer east-north-east. Turning in succession around a point presented dangers of which the Russians took advantage, opening a concentrated fire on the turning point at a range of approximately 9,000 yards, fortunately without inflicting serious damage.

Both fleets were now running parallel on a north-easterly heading, approximately 7,000 yards apart. The Russians were at something of a disadvantage as they were trying to merge their two columns into one and this was causing confusion as ships were forced to swerve or stop to avoid collisions. By 14.18 a major gunnery duel was in progress. Togo ordered his entire battle line to concentrate their fire on the *Suvoroff*, Rozhestvensky's flagship, and the *Oslyabia*. For their part, the Russian gunners were performing better than had been expected and were scoring hits along the length of the Japanese line. Nevertheless, the majority of the Russian seamen were experiencing the full horror of a naval battle for the first time and it was a nightmare experience. Their comrades were being blown apart or ripped by flying shell splinters that also punctured funnels and tore their way into superstructures. Rozhestvensky also commented in the British Admiralty's official history of naval operations during the war, 'The paint burned with a clear flame on the steel surfaces; boats, ropes, hammocks and woodwork caught fire; cartridges in the ready racks ignited; upper works and light guns were swept away; turrets jammed.'

It was too much. At 14.40 Rozhestvensky tried to open the range by turning four points to starboard, but there was no way of avoiding the terrible punishment his ships were receiving. There was now no question that the Japanese had gained the upper hand. At 14.50 the *Oslyabia* reeled out of the line, mortally wounded, and capsized before sinking by the bows. With her went the body of Admiral Felkerzam, who had died the previous evening. *Suvoroff*, her steering wrecked and belching smoke, turned to port and passed over her own wake before wallowing to a standstill, yet as long as she had a gun to fire she did so. Rozhestvensky had been forced to abandon his wrecked bridge and was now unconscious, having been wounded several times. With difficulty, he was transferred to the destroyer *Buiny*. Now led by *Alexander III*, the fleet sailed past the former flagship, which remained afloat until 19.20, when a Japanese torpedo sent her to the bottom,

Alexander III had caused some confusion by charging the Japanese line, thereby forcing Togo to order a simultaneous turn away at 14.58. For a while, Togo lost control of the battle, partly because of drifting smoke and poor visibility and partly because of the melee being fought out by the opposing cruisers and destroyers. Admiral Kamimura, now commanding the fleet's Second Division, believed quite wrongly that the Russians had escaped to the south and headed off on a wild goose chase, thereby fracturing the cohesion of Togo's line. By the time he returned to the confused scene of the earlier action some doubt existed as to where the Russians had gone, but shortly after 18.00 they were sighted in the distance, running northwards. In addition, to everyone's surprise, they seemed to have reformed their line.

Togo immediately set off in pursuit, his fleet's superior speed enabling him to overhaul the enemy quickly, thereby initiating the battle's second major phase. *Borodino* was leading the Russian line, followed by *Orel*, then Admiral Nebogatov's division, and finally *Alexander III* straggling behind and evidently suffering from heavy damage. Away to the west were the Russian cruisers, destroyers and service vessels in untidy groups, conforming to the direction taken by the main battle fleet.

A sharp exchange of gunfire took place in which the Russians, with the setting sun behind them, seemed to be inflicting the greater number of hits. However, at 18.43 *Alexander III* lurched out of the line to port and shortly after turned over and sank. Daylight was beginning to fade when *Borodino* received a hit that seems to have penetrated a magazine as the ship was engulfed in a huge explosion and sank at 19.20. This evidently destroyed the Russians' will to fight, for they turned away to the west and disappeared into the gathering darkness.

Togo unleashed his destroyers and torpedo boats to launch attacks on any enemy ships that were still trying to break through to Vladivostok. With one important exception, the majority of these failed and there were even serious collisions between Japanese torpedo craft. The exception was the remarkable results achieved by the Fourth Destroyer Flotilla, under the command of Commander Suzuki Kantaro who, it may be remembered, had led a successful torpedo attack against the Chinese at Wei Hai Wei in 1895. It was Suzuki's torpedo that administered the *coup de grace* to the burning *Suvoroff* some hours earlier and now, at about 02.30 on 28 May, he came across the damaged battleship *Navarin*. Without being seen, he managed to drop several lines of linked mines directly across her path. As intended, she steered straight into them and a heavy explosion followed, after which she sank. Next, the destroyers encountered another battleship, the *Sisoi Veliky*, and launched a torpedo attack that damaged her so badly that she was scuttled by her crew the following morning.

The captains of some of the surviving Russian ships, having observed the destruction of so many of their battleships, saw no future in attempting to continue the battle and headed south for neutral ports in which they could be interned. Others, however, were determined, as individuals, to break through to Vladivostok. Others again, but few in number, accepted that their duty lay in remaining with Nebogatov's flagship which, on the morning of 28 May, provided the nucleus of the remaining fleet – two battleships, two armoured coast defence ships and a cruiser. These were quickly surrounded by Togo's battle fleet and, further fighting being quite pointless, Nebogatov ran up a white table cloth in token of surrender and was taken across to the *Mikasa* where he concluded the formalities with Togo. Isolated Russian ships still remained in the area. Some were sunk if they refused to surrender while others chose to scuttle themselves. One, the *Bedovy*, to which Rozhestvensky had been transferred from the *Buiny* during the previous evening, was captured by two Japanese destroyers with the result that the young lieutenant who came aboard to take possession of the vessel unexpectedly found himself to be the captor of a fleet commander.

As for those Russian warships still at large, the cruiser *Almaz* and the destroyers *Bravy* and *Grozny* actually reached Vladivostok. A second cruiser, the *Izumrud*, almost got there but ran onto rocks in the nearby Vladimir Bay and became a total wreck. The sights and sounds of the battle had proved too much for Rear Admiral Enkvist, whose light cruiser squadron was meant to be protecting the transports at the rear of the Russian column, but did each other considerable damage instead. Enkvist claimed to have made several attempts to break through the Japanese battle fleet, none of which seems to have attracted the enemy's attention. He ignored Nabogatov's 'Follow me' signal and, with the cruisers *Aurora*, *Zemchug* and *Oleg*, turned south and called at Shanghai before reaching Manila, where the squadron was interned.

Of the thirty-eight warships and support vessels that Rozhestvensky had led into the Tsu Shima Strait, thirty-four had been sunk, scuttled, captured or interned. The battle had cost the Russians 4,830 killed or drowned and 5,917 captured, of whom a large number were wounded. Japanese losses included three capital ships damaged, three torpedo boats sunk, eight destroyers and torpedo boats disabled but repairable, and 110 men killed. The Japanese victory had been so complete that it became known as The Trafalgar of the East. Subsequently asked how this had come about, Roshestvensky replied that it was because the Japanese shells had found their targets while the Russian shells had not. There was, of course, far more to it than that.

After Tsu Shima there was little fighting. It was President Theodore Roosevelt of the United States who pointed out to the combatants the futility of their continuing hostilities. Russia was too vast for the Japanese to even contemplate invading, and it had become obvious to the Russians that they were neither able to push the Japanese armies back into the sea nor mount a fresh maritime campaign. The terms of the Treaty of Portsmouth, New Hampshire, required Russia to give up Port Arthur, leave Manchuria and cede the southern portion of the bleak Sakhalin Peninsula, across the La Perouse Strait from Hokkaido, to Japan, whose interests in Korea were formally recognised.

CHAPTER 5

Great Power Status

Hardly had the euphoria generated by the victory over Russia and the subsequent acquisition of territory faded away than the Japanese Admiralty, and indeed every admiralty throughout the world save one, was horrified by the discovery that its battle fleet was now obsolete. The reason for this was the launch in October 1906 of the Royal Navy's 20,000-ton battleship HMS *Dreadnought*, armed with ten 12-inch and twenty-four 12-pounder guns, plus five 18-inch torpedo tubes. Protection was provided by an 11-inch armoured belt and 8-inch armour on the turrets, while four turbine-driven screws were capable of producing a maximum speed of 22 knots. The plain fact was that *Dreadnought* made every other battleship afloat obsolete and, like other navies, that of Japan was forced to produce similar warships quickly and at great expense. Guns and engines were still bought from Great Britain but armour plate, now applied more scientifically to cover the ship's vital areas, was purchased from Germany's Krupp organisation, which had a long-established reputation for producing top quality high density steel. Japan still bought warships abroad, mainly from British yards, but her own yards were becoming capable of fulfilling many of the Imperial Navy's requirements.

Two years after the introduction of the Dreadnought type of battleship the Royal Navy introduced an altogether new class of warship, the battle cruiser. This combined the hitting power of the battleship with the speed of a fast cruiser, the intention being to eliminate an opponent's cruiser screen and destroy his fast commerce raiders. Unfortunately, this combination of qualities had been obtained at the expense of one other, namely protection, with unfortunate consequences that should have been foreseen. For the moment, however, it had become almost mandatory that first-class navies must have at least one battle-cruiser squadron with which to lead its battle fleet into action, and Japan was no exception.

For many years it was believed that the Japanese genius lay in adopting and improving Western technology. Such a view was both condescending and superficial. For example, a Japanese chemist named Shimose Masachika developed an extremely powerful explosive based on picric acid, similar to the British Lyddite, that was incorporated in the filling of both shells and torpedoes. Named Shimose after its developer, it was employed by the Imperial Japanese Navy from 1893 onwards, producing devastating consequences for its opponents.

Politically, times were changing. Japan's nearest neighbours were no longer a threat to her. China was incapable of fighting a modern war and her ancient empire would soon be a memory. It would be many years before Russia, in which unrest and revolution simmered permanently beneath the surface, recovered from her humiliating defeat. However, a new neighbour and potential enemy had recently appeared on the scene. In 1898 the United States had won an easy victory over Spain, which had not been a world power for almost a century, although she still possessed a number of colonies. Among them were the Philippine Islands, which were handed over to the Americans on receipt of a trivial purchase price. The Filipinos, who had fought alongside the Americans in the belief that they were securing their freedom, found instead that they had new masters and understandably rebelled. Their insurrection lasted three years and required 100,000 American troops to bring it under control. It is hardly surprising that the subject is seldom discussed in present-day America, despite Rudyard Kipling's well known contemporary poetic urgings to 'Take up the white man's burden' with its reference to 'New caught sullen peoples'.

Nevertheless, the United States wished to be seen in a friendly light by its new neighbours and despatched a squadron on a goodwill visit to Japan. As is usual on such occasions, there was a certain amount of horseplay among the officers and during this

Admiral Togo, wishing to be seen as a good sport, permitted himself to be tossed in a blanket. 'If we had known what the future held, we wouldn't have caught him the third time!' recalled one of the junior officers involved, much later in life. His name was William H. Halsey and one day he would command a fleet the size of which Togo could never have dreamed of. Bonhomie apart, it was inevitable that the senior staff officers in both navies had already begun to regard each other as potential enemies. With the Americans now firmly established in the Philippine Islands, the Japanese were aware that the great expanse of Manila Bay would provide an ideal anchorage for the US Navy. American opinion, however, took the view that it would have been only too easy for the Japanese to bottle up the fleet inside the Bay, if they chose to, just as they had with the Russian's First Pacific Squadron in Port Arthur. It was therefore decided that the Pacific Fleet's permanent base would be Pearl Harbor in the recently acquired Hawaiian Islands, far to the west.

In the years immediately prior to the outbreak of the First World War, the Royal Navy and the Imperial German Navy were engaged in a prohibitively expensive naval construction race. Because of this, the Royal Navy was forced to withdraw a number of its heavy units from the Far East to home waters in order to preserve a decisive majority of warships over the rapidly expanding German fleet. Under the terms of the Anglo-Japanese alliance, their place was taken by Japanese warships in areas of British interest in the Far East. This so enraged Kaiser Wilhelm II that he wrote personally to the US President, promising him that if Anglo-Japanese threats caused him to deploy the entire US Navy into the Pacific, he would make his own High Seas Fleet available for the defence of America's east coast! Wilhelm's blundering forays into international relations were the despair of his diplomatic service and the matter was allowed to die a natural death.

On the outbreak of the First World War the Japanese punctiliously observed the provisions of their treaty with Great Britain. Germany had been one of the powers that had deprived Japan of the fruits of her victory in the war with China, so she had no reservations about depriving Germany of the colonies she had established around the Pacific and in particular the city of Tsingtao and part of the Shantung Peninsula, leased from China in 1898 for a period of ninety-nine years. Immense quantities of money, approximating to £20 million in the sterling of the day, had been poured into Tsingtao, not only as an example of the finest Germany had to offer but also as a major Far Eastern trading centre with rail links with China, and as a naval base, all of which was protected by a system of modern forts. This was the base of Germany's East Asia Squadron, commanded in 1914 by Vice Admiral Count Maximilian von Spee and consisting of the heavy cruisers *Scharnhorst* and *Gneisenau*, plus a number of light cruisers. While the war clouds were gathering, Spee, familiar with the story of Port Arthur, had reached the correct conclusion that, whatever else it was, as far as his ships were concerned, Tsingtao was a trap. He had taken them to sea before war broke out and made a remarkable voyage across the Pacific to the west coast of South America, where he defeated a small British squadron off Coronel before being defeated and sunk himself at the Battle of the Falkland Islands.

Having issued a suitable ultimatum, Japan despatched an expeditionary force to Shantung. This consisted of a reinforced corps with ample siege artillery under the command of Lieutenant General Kamio. In immediate support was a squadron under Vice Admiral Kato, joined by several British warships from the China station. On 27 August several small islands clustered around the harbour mouth of Tsingtao itself were occupied and work began on sweeping the surrounding waters clear of mines. The first major landings took place on 2 September in Lungkow Bay at the base of the Shantung Peninsula. This was actually in Chinese territory, some eighty miles from Tsingtao itself, and therefore beyond the likelihood of any German interference.

The German garrison of the colony consisted of approximately 5,000 men plus volunteers and was commanded by its Governor, Admiral Meyer Waldeck. In the harbour were a number of smaller warships of which the most important were the Austrian light cruiser

Kaiserin Elizabeth and a handful of river gunboats, some of which had handed over their armament to converted civilian vessels that had left before the arrival of the Japanese and were serving as commerce raiders. To the north-east of the town were three low hills – Bismarck Hill, Moltke Hill and Iltis (Jaguar) Hill – that had been heavily fortified to the extent that they were crowned by ferro-concrete forts, the guns of which were housed in revolving cupolas. A fourth such fort was located on the Hsiao-ni-wa promontory to the south-east of the city. In the open country to the north-east of the city were trench lines stretching from coast to coast, fronted by barbed wire. At the eastern end of these outer defences was a prominent feature named Prince Heinrich Hill. Despite these defensive measures, the situation of the Tsingtao garrison, outnumbered, outgunned and far beyond any sort of assistance, was obviously hopeless. Thus, while the Kaiser might order them to defend the fortress for as long as breath remained in their bodies, only a tiny minority of wild-eyed fanatics could possibly have regarded this as a realistic option.

Fortunately for Waldeck, Shantung was famous for its torrential autumn downpours. Insignificant streams became torrents that roared off the hills, saturating the coastal plain so that floods spread and spread until they became lagoons. For the moment Kamio was unable to make much progress, although his aircraft landed bombs on the German wireless station, the electricity generating station and various ships in the harbour. On 13 September they supported a successful attack on the railway station at the head of Kiao-chau Bay, covering the western shore of German concession. The Japanese were now twenty-two miles from Tsingtao and able to make better progress along the railway's track bed, which was adequately drained.

Meanwhile, a small British force consisting of the 2nd Battalion South Wales Borderers and half of the 1st Battalion 36th Sikhs, a total of some 1,400 men under the command of Brigadier General Bernardiston, was en route from Tientsin, escorted by the pre-Dreadnought HMS *Triumph*. After stopping to pick up 250 mules from the nearby British treaty port of Wei Hei Wei, the force landed in Laoshan Bay, on the eastern or seaward side of the peninsula, on 22 September.

The British contingent took their place in the centre of the Allied line. The floods were now beginning to subside, enabling the Japanese to bring forward their artillery, which ultimately numbered 140 siege guns ranging in size from 11-inch howitzers to 8-inch guns. On 28 September Prince Heinrich Hill was taken without difficulty, providing a view across Tsingtao's hinterland to the enemy's main defence line, some five miles distant. On 30 September German warships in Kiao-chau Bay attempted to bombard the Allied right, but were driven off by the vigorous action of Japanese aircraft, which had already caused damage inside the town with their bombs. Simultaneously, a German counter-attack was easily driven back inside the defences

The fate of the fortress was now sealed. On 30 September, the Emperor's birthday, the Japanese guns began firing a sustained bombardment, supported by the Allied warships lying off shore, that lasted for the remainder of the siege. By day a cloud of black smoke, originating in burning oil storage tanks, hung over the town, while at night the flames from burning buildings illuminated the scene. In the harbour, the remaining German ships scuttled themselves. Curiously, after the first day the guns of the great German forts remained silent save for the occasional shot, apparently saving whatever ammunition remained to meet a major attack. By 6 November the Allies were through the outer defence line and closing up to the inner redoubts. General Kamio had decided that the final assault would be delivered the following day, but it was already clear to Admiral Waldeck that the end had been reached and the following morning white flags were fluttering along his lines. By 19.30 that evening the formalities had been concluded and Tsingtao had become a Japanese possession.

German casualties were surprisingly light in the circumstances, amounting to 200 killed, 500 wounded, approximately 3,000 prisoners who were shipped to Japan, some minor warships scuttled and a quantity of ordnance captured. Japanese losses had been comparatively heavy and included 1,455 killed, 4,200 wounded, an old cruiser, a destroyer, a torpedo boat and three minesweepers. British losses amounted to just fourteen killed and sixty-one wounded.

Tsingtao may have fallen, but Japan had by no means finished with Germany's Far Eastern and Pacific colonies. A Japanese task force secured the Mariana, Caroline and Marshall island groups in the central Pacific without difficulty, for very few of these contained more than a handful of German residents who were heavily outnumbered by Chinese merchants and the indigenous population so that, by the end of October 1914, the German Imperial Flag had ceased to fly east of Suez, the exception being that of the cruiser *Emden* whose spectacular career had a little longer to run.

More Japanese warships took over some of the duties hitherto carried out by the Royal Navy's China Squadron. Elsewhere, Australian and New Zealand troops occupied German holdings in the Bismarck Archipelago, Northern New Guinea, the Solomon and Samoa Islands. For a while the battle cruiser *Ibuki* formed part of the escort of a large convoy carrying Australian and New Zealand troops bound for the Middle East. Belching smoke from her three funnels she ploughed along at 22 knots abeam the transports, earning sincere admiration for her clean lines. Another Japanese warship, the cruiser *Idzumo*, took part in the hunt for Admiral von Spee's fugitive East Asiatic Squadron off the west coast of the Americas.

In 1917, following Germany's declaration of unrestricted U-boat warfare, Japan acceded to a British request for a destroyer squadron to be sent to the Mediterranean, where the activities of some thirty-four German and Austrian submarines was stretching the available escort vessels beyond the limits of safety. Commanded by Rear Admiral Sato Kozo, the squadron arrived at Malta in April and was immediately involved in escorting troopships between Marseilles, Taranto, Alexandria and Port Said. Although no kills were claimed, the unexpected appearance of the squadron led to a sharp reduction in sinkings by U-boats for the remainder of the war. One destroyer, the *Sakaki*, sustained serious torpedo damage and heavy loss of life, but managed to limp back to Malta.

CHAPTER 6

Times They Are a'Changing

With the ending of what came to be known as the Great War the old certainties vanished. The German, Austro-Hungarian, Russian and Ottoman Empires ceased to exist and many of their component regions achieved independence based on ethnicity. Likewise, former colonies changed hands. The process was, however, not a new one. The ancient Chinese Empire, one of Japan's close neighbours, had ceased to exist in 1911 and become a republic under the presidency of Marshal Yuan Shih-k'ai the following year. During the winter of 1915–16 there was considerable unrest when Yuan announced that the empire was to be re-established with himself on the throne, but the issue remained unresolved when he died on 6 June 1916, being succeeded as President by Li Yuan-hung. A revolt the following year actually re-established the rule of the Manchu Dynasty, but only for twelve days, after which Li resigned and Feng Kuo-chang was installed as the new president. On 4 August 1917 China declared war on Germany and Austria-Hungary. She did not play an active part in the fighting but supplied the Allies with labour battalions that were employed on a number of fronts. In recognition of this, she secured the termination of all German and Austro-Hungarian concessions and privileges in China. Japan, meanwhile, had taken advantage of Imperial Russia's internal collapse and occupied Vladivostok in strength. It began to seem as though she intended taking permanent possession of Russia's Maritime Provinces and this, added to the fact that she had let it be known that she was now the dominant influence in Chinese affairs, caused serious alarm in London, Paris and Washington. It began to seem that 'the plucky little Jap', once the victim who had gone on to fight mighty Russia to a standstill, had now turned into something of a bully. As

Japan now possessed the world's third largest fleet, this was not a welcome situation.

Nevertheless, the idea of starting a fresh naval construction race that would drain national exchequers was not acceptable. Indeed, American President Woodrow Wilson had envisaged a huge United States Navy possessing over fifty capital ships. This was neither necessary nor practical and his successor, President Warren Harding, and the United States Congress, quickly abandoned the concept. Indeed, within certain limitations the majority of the world's powers were in favour of arms limitation and in 1921 Harding accepted their view that a conference should be held in Washington to discuss reducing the number of capital ships possessed by any one power to equal its known responsibilities. Delegations attending the conference included those of Great Britain, the United States, Japan, France and Italy. Delegations from the governments of China, Holland, Belgium and Portugal attended only those sessions limited to discussions of matters concerning the Far East. Germany's fleet was now a mere fraction of its former self, already governed by the Treaty of Versailles.

The outcome of what became known as the Washington Naval Treaty was that the Royal Navy, the United States Navy and the Imperial Japanese Navy were respectively restricted to a capital ship tonnage in the proportion of 5 : 5 : 3, while those of the French National Navy and the Royal Italian Navy were both allowed 1.75:1.75. No restrictions applied to the construction of other types of warship. Superficially, the treaty achieved its object of reducing naval expenditure to acceptable levels. The American government, however, had always had an ulterior motive for calling the conference, based on historical Anglophobia and resentment of British primacy at sea. As that primacy was currently reinforced by the Anglo-Japanese alliance, it was determined to break it, not by any direct means, but by substituting a Four Power Treaty signed by the United States, Great Britain, Japan and France, agreeing to consultation in the event of a controversy arising between any two signatories. Understandably, the Japanese felt that they had been let down by their old friends and mentors, the more so as they had reached a mutual agreement with the United States not to fortify their bases in the Western Pacific.

As already mentioned, the Japanese already viewed the United States as a potential enemy, a sentiment duly noted by those with a professional interest in naval matters. One such was Hector Charles Bywater, the second son of a respectable Welsh family that had emigrated to the United States in 1901. Intelligent, well-educated and a fluent speaker of German, by the age of nineteen Bywater obtained part-time employment with the *New York Herald* for which he wrote a series of articles on naval subjects. Recognising his worth, the *Herald* sent him to London as foreign correspondent at the time of the Anglo-German naval construction race. His worth was also recognised by British naval intelligence who recruited him as an agent. He was recalled to New York in 1915 and prevented a German bombing campaign in New York's dockland. Already aware of the possibility of war between Japan and the United States, in 1921 he published his book *Sea-Power in the Pacific: A Study of the American-Japanese Naval Problem* in which he predicted such a conflict. In 1925 he developed the theme in a second book, *The Great Pacific War*. Both books contained elements that were to prove remarkably prophetic. They began with a Japanese air attack on the American Pacific Fleet, which at the time was based in the Philippines rather than in Pearl Harbor. Many actions, both Japanese and American, were accurately predicted, as was the Japanese obsession with winning a great decisive battle in the manner of Tsu Shima and the American ' island-hopping' campaign. With the ending of the Second World War both the Allies and the Japanese admitted that they had used *The Great Pacific War* as a resource when planning strategic operations. Bywater died from 'undetermined causes' a year before the attack on Pearl Harbor; no autopsy was performed and his body was cremated with surprising haste.

In the meantime, a major debate was taking place within the admiralties of all the great powers as to the form that naval warfare would take in future conflicts. The conservative element believed that decisive results could only be obtained by fleets of which big-gun battleships formed the major element. Others put forward the submarine as the future war winner, but the fact that Germany's U-boat campaign in the First World War had finally been defeated by the adoption of escorted convoys and the use of depth charges tended to dilute their argument. A third alternative, however, had become the subject of serious discussion since the war, and that was air power. Of course airships, both inflatable and of rigid construction, had played a part in the war's naval operations, but since then they had largely disappeared. The question was, did aircraft possess the ability to inflict critical damage on enemy warships? Part of the answer was provided by the cross-channel ferry *Ben-my-Chree*, which had been converted to the role of seaplane carrier. In 1915, piloted by Flight Commander C. H. K. Edmonds of the Royal Naval Air Service, one of her Short seaplanes had sunk a Turkish transport with an air-launched torpedo. In addition, a series of trials, some of them with fatal consequences, had proved that it was possible to launch and recover fixed-wing aircraft from ships, leading to the Royal Navy commissioning its first aircraft carrier before the war was over. The next question, therefore, was whether bombs dropped from these aircraft could sink an enemy warship and, more especially, one that was armoured. In 1921 a definitive answer was provided by Brigadier General William Mitchell of the US Army Air Service, albeit that his tests were heavily loaded in favour of the bombers. His principal target was the *Ostfriesland*, a German dreadnought surrendered to the United States at the end of the First World War. It was intended that the bombing attack was to cease with each hit so that its effects could be analysed, but Mitchell chose to ignore his orders and treated his anchored target to a rain of 1,000- and 2,000lb bombs until it sank. Next came three retired US battleships, the *Alabama* , also in 1921, then *Virginia* and *New Jersey* two years later. It has been said that these experiments guaranteed the future of naval aviation, although doubters, mainly those who continued to place their faith in the battleship, continued to argue that attempting to bomb a moving target armed with anti-aircraft weapons was unlikely to guarantee similar results. Mitchell, however, was a fanatic and, worse still, a fanatic with an ungovernable temper. As far as technical discussions within an armed service are concerned, there are limits beyond which insubordination cannot be tolerated, however heated the argument. Mitchell's downfall came about following the loss of the US airship *Shenandoah*, when he described both the Army and the Navy as being 'incompetent, criminally negligent and almost treasonable'. This was too much; he was court-martialled on disciplinary charges and found guilty but permitted to resign from the service.

Interestingly, a calmer and more balanced view of naval aviation's potential was expressed by the then Commander Isoroku Yamamoto, who would in due course rise to command the Imperial Japanese Navy. To those who continued to express the view that the only weapons capable of destroying a battleship were the main armament of another battleship, he was fond of quoting an ancient Japanese proverb: 'A swarm of ants can overcome the largest snake.' In 1920 the Japanese had requested the British government to provide an aviation mission in preparation for the completion of their first carrier, the *Hosho*, two years later. As the Royal Air Force was fully stretched the mission was commanded by Lord Sempill, a former Royal Naval Air Service officer, who recruited a number of ex-RNAS officers and warrant officers to bring it up to strength. Sempill's mission was to re-organise, equip and train the Imperial Japanese Air Service. He was also to advise on the necessary types of aircraft, of which he was to place orders for 200, plus the required operating equipment and spares. On his return home he expressed a sincere admiration for his pupils, whom he described as 'distinctly high in ability ... keen and hard-working'.

Sempill almost certainly met Yamamoto while serving in Japan. On the latter's return to Japan he served as an instructor at the War College and was then appointed to the Air Planning Section of the Naval General Staff. After this, he commanded the Naval Air Development Station, a high security installation beside Lake Kasumigo-Ura. There he put his pilots through an exacting course, involving their landing and taking off on flight decks constructed on barges, plus bombing and torpedo runs demanding a high standard of accuracy. A second tour of duty in the United States as naval attaché at the Washington Embassy not only acquainted him the more important figures in the American establishment, but also made him fully aware of the country's vast natural resources and enormous industrial capacity. His view of the United States Navy, possibly influenced by the social round to which every defence attaché is subject, was that, by Japanese standards, it was relaxed to the point of giving the impression that it was 'a club for golfers and bridge players'. When the time came, he would accept that such a view was mistaken.

The year 1928 saw the US President Herbert Hoover elected to office. Hoover was anxious to put an end to Anglo-American bickering on naval matters that had their roots in misunderstanding. The following year Ramsay Macdonald, who held similar views, became the United Kingdom's Prime Minister. Macdonald acknowledged that as the United States required a two-ocean navy he would accept the American claim to parity in naval strength. As a result of bilateral talks between the two navies, another conference of naval powers was held in London during 1930. The conference ended the long era of British naval supremacy. War debt, the great financial depression and a general public hostile to defence spending ensured so great a comparative reduction in strength that none of the Far Eastern naval bases could be adequately defended, nor could a battle fleet be sent into Far Eastern waters without compromising the safety of the home country. To a lesser extent, the United States was also keen to limit expenditure. This enabled Yamamoto, now a rear admiral, to persuade the conference to accept Japanese tonnage equal to 70 per cent of the US Navy's in cruisers and destroyers, plus parity in submarines. Cleverly, Yamamoto argued that Japan needed a large cruiser fleet to protect her trade routes and a widespread island empire. He also managed to steer the conference away from any discussion of naval aviation and submarine warfare, enabling Japan to continue building an expanding aircraft carrier fleet.

Concurrently, work continued on the design and manufacture of the aircraft which would arm the carriers in the event of war. There was general agreement throughout the international naval aviation community that the ideal combination consisted of torpedo bombers, dive-bombers and fighters whose function was not only to defend them, but also the ship itself, against the enemy's aircraft. First to enter service was the Aichi D3A2 dive-bomber, which first flew in August 1936. Known as Val to the Western Allies, it carried an 816lb bomb load. The Nakajima B5N torpedo bomber, codenamed Kate by the Allies, was the first monoplane carrier aircraft in the world. It entered service in 1937, had a speed of 235mph and was armed with one 1,760lb torpedo. Perhaps the most famous carrier fighter of the Second World War's early years was the Mitsubishi A6M Zero-Sen single-seater carrier fighter. Designed around the average Japanese physique, it was small in size but possessed a high maximum speed of 331mph, was highly manoeuvrable and heavily armed with two 7.7mm machine guns and two 20mm cannon. It came as an unpleasant shock to the Allies to find that their land-based fighters were easily out-performed by the Zero, which continued to be known by that name despite being codenamed Zeke. Despite its many virtues, the Zero's principal defect was its inability to absorb punishment.

Simultaneously, the Japanese had been developing one of the most deadly naval weapons of all time. In 1927 a naval delegation visited the Whitehead Torpedo Works in Weymouth, intent on studying and possibly buying a standard version of the Whitehead torpedo. They came across several oxygen cylinders and became convinced among themselves that the Royal Navy was employing torpedoes powered by oxygen-enriched fuel. In fact, the cylinders were simply part of another manufacturing process. Be that as it may, the delegation returned home and began trying to produce oxygen-powered torpedoes. The result was a series of fatal explosions. Gradually, the cause of each of these was eliminated. By 1932 the production of such a torpedo seemed possible and further development was put in the hands of a team under Captain Kishimoto Kaneharu.

Further detailed work revealed the necessity of avoiding contact between oxygen and the torpedo's moving parts. Finally, in 1933, trials conducted aboard the cruiser *Chokai* proved successful and the torpedo entered production. Its official designation was the Type 93, although it is now generally referred to as the Long Lance, a name conferred by Samuel Eliot Morison, the US Navy's historian. It was a huge torpedo with a length of 29 feet 6 inches and a diameter of 24 inches; in contrast the American Mark 15 torpedo was only 24 feet in length and 21 inches in diameter. The Long Lance carried in excess of 1,000 pounds of high explosive, enough to blow a destroyer apart and inflict critical damage on a cruiser. It could reach a maximum speed of 48 knots and had a range in excess of 45,000 yards, depending on the launcher's settings. Perhaps one of the most frightening things about it was that it barely produced a wake, making its approach all but invisible during the hours of darkness.

The Imperial Navy employed a large number of submarines that were capable of operating in the vast expanses of the Pacific, although living conditions aboard were uncomfortable and reduced crew efficiency. The Japanese never realised the full potential of their submarine fleet, perhaps because of too strict an interpretation of the bushido code. There was for example, honour in sinking an enemy warship, but none in sending a merchant vessel to the bottom. It was apparently not understood that a 'wolf pack' type of attack on an enemy troop convoy would not only inflict heavy loss of life and therefore damage operational capacity, but also damage civilian morale on the home front. Another area of submersible activity was that of midget submarines, an area of development in which Captain Kishimoto Kaneharu was also involved. These two-man submersibles entered production in 1939 and were each armed with two 17.7-inch torpedoes. Operationally, twelve midget submarines could be ferried into the forward area by a seaplane carrier and generally employed in conditions of great secrecy alongside fleet operations.

Despite these interesting developments, there were serious gaps in Japanese war planning. For example, troop and supply convoys often sailed with inadequate or no escort despite the immense areas of operation in which any war with ~~America~~ the USA would have to be fought. Again, the lack of local raw materials and their derivatives meant that they had to be imported in bulk, including large quantities of scrap iron and steel. Most of this was reserved for the Navy and, after the Army's basic requirements had been met, very little was left for tank production. The generals might save face by emphasising that theirs was essentially an infantry army quite capable of dealing with tankless opponents like the Chinese, but the fact was that the Navy's incessant demands meant that such tanks as were being produced were technically a generation behind those in service with balanced armies and, in the long term, the results would be disastrous.

By now, although it was not immediately apparent, the fuse that would eventually lead to the explosion of the Second World War had actually been lit. Following the Chinese Revolution of 1911 the country was in such a troubled state that Japan was permitted to station troops in Manchuria. Twenty years later political power within China remained fragmented, the rivals being Chiang-Kai-Shek's Kuomintang (Nationalist) Party, Mao-Tse-Tung's communists, and a large number of local warlords. In 1932 the Japanese, unable to establish a working relationship with the Manchurian warlords, forcibly ejected them and set up the puppet state of Manchukuo with Pu-Yi, the former Emperor of China, as its head. The reaction of the colonial powers was to orchestrate the expulsion of Japan from the League of Nations.

Within Japan, it was the generals, with the support of Emperor Hirohito and the *kempetai* (political police), who enjoyed unchallenged power, and they pursued a 'salami slicing' type of expansion policy that left them in possession of more and more Chinese territory and natural resources. If approached on the subject, they simply replied that they were simply continuing the policies carried out by the great powers during the nineteenth century. Fighting was sporadic but there was little or no doubt that it could escalate into a full scale war. This began on 7 July 1937 with a carefully staged 'incident' at the Marco Polo Bridge at Lukouchiao near Peking when Japanese troops, allegedly on 'night manoeuvres', clashed with local Chinese forces and then launched a full-scale invasion. This action is frequently taken to mark the beginning of the Second World War.

While Japan possessed the more modern army, an aggressive air force and the third largest navy in the world, China was too large and its population too numerous for her to win an outright victory. She succeeded in occupying the coastal cities and a number of enclaves inland but, even in the latter areas, all she held was the towns while the Chinese conducted a guerrilla campaign from the surrounding countryside. Suddenly the West became aware of the savage cruelty lying concealed within the Japanese character. In efforts to break the Chinese will to continue fighting, prisoners were bayoneted, beheaded, nailed to walls and emasculated, to no avail. The result was counter-productive, for the West initiated a supply line from Burma that remained open for much of the war.

There were, too, times when Japanese arrogance or stupidity or a combination of both seemed to have got the better of them. Despite the dangerous conditions existing throughout the country those Western powers that could did their best to keep their commercial traffic moving on the Yangtse river. However, on the morning of 11 December the British liner *Wantung,* with 600 passengers aboard, was first shelled from the shore near Nanking, then attacked by aircraft. Had the Japanese airmen been wider awake, they would have seen that the liner was escorted by two gunboats, HMS *Scarab* and *Cricket.* These promptly opened up with their 3-inch and Lewis guns, causing the Japanese to veer wildly away and drop their bombs in open water.

The following day the gunboat HMS *Ladybird* was approaching Wuhu, fifty miles upstream from Nanking. Her White Ensign was clearly visible yet a number of Japanese field batteries and several machine guns opened fire on her, killing a sick berth attendant, wounding all her officers and a seaman. Again, the Japanese had been unfortunate in their choice of target for, at that moment, a boat had left the gunboat and was heading straight for one of the batteries. Its passengers included Lieutenant Colonel Fraser Lovat, the British military attaché to the Nanking government, and the British consul at Nanking, who had travelled to Wuhu with the object of preventing just this sort of incident. Incandescent with rage, Lovat grabbed the nearest battery commander, frogmarched him through his guns, pointed out the extensive damage that had been caused and forced him to cease firing. Shortly after a second gunboat, HMS *Bee*, had appeared on the scene, someone fired a single artillery round at her, but missed. Aboard was Rear Admiral R. V. Holt, Senior Naval Officer Yangtse, who was actually on his way to meet his Japanese opposite number. He immediately wiped the floor with the Japanese Area Commander, a Colonel Kingoro Hashimoto, extracting not only an apology for the unprovoked attack, but also a promise to supply a guard of honour for the dead seaman's funeral the following day.

Incredibly, even while this discussion was taking place, one of naval history's most calculated atrocities was taking place. The background to this was the Japanese capture of Nanking, notable for wholesale massacre and rape of its inhabitants. The river gunboat USS *Panay*, under the command of Lieutenant Commander James Hughes, was ordered to evacuate American citizens and others from the city and transport them to Wuhu. Among the passengers were two newsreel cameramen, Norman Alley of Universal News and Eric Mayell of Movietone News. Both had carried out extensive filming of the atrocities and were seen to be doing so by the Japanese. *Panay* was escorting a convoy of three tankers belonging to the Standard Oil Company, the *Mei Ping*, *Mei An* and *Mei Heia*, and had reached a point approximately halfway between Nanking and Wuhu. Hughes had informed the Japanese of the movement and informed them that the convoy would drop anchor some twenty-eight miles upstream from Nanking, which it did at 11.00 on 12 December. On the way it had been fired at, without result, by a Japanese artillery battery lining the bank, despite the fact that Hughes had displayed two large Stars and Stripes flags across the ship's awnings and she was also flying her ensign. At 13.00 the entire convoy came under heavy and sustained air attack from Yokasuka B4 Type 96 biplane bombers and Nakajima A4N Type 97 biplane fighter-bombers. *Panay* replied with her Lewis light machine guns but was hit repeatedly by bombs and began to settle. Hughes, seriously wounded, gave orders for the rest of the wounded to be taken off, only to see their boat deliberately machine gunned by two fighters. The sinking gunboat was then abandoned. Any remaining doubts that she had been attacked in error vanished when a Japanese landing craft appeared and opened fire on two chief petty officers who were returning to the ship to fetch medical supplies. Shortly after, the gunboat turned on her side and went down by the bows. The Japanese then turned their attention to the merchant vessels, sinking two and driving the third aground.

At the headquarters of the US Asiatic Fleet in Shanghai, anxiety was growing concerning the *Panay*'s welfare. She was not replying to radio signals and so sudden had been the Japanese attack that she had not herself transmitted a signal. Admiral Harry Yarnell, commanding, contacted his British counterpart to enquire whether there had been any sightings, but at that moment Holt was attending the funeral of the British rating. However, as soon as he was informed of the attack he headed for the scene at full speed with *Bee* and *Ladybird*. All he found were two burned-out oil tankers, a third aground and abandoned, and *Panay*'s bullet riddled motor sampan. *Bee* began sounding her siren at regular intervals and, after a while, a number of figures appeared on the river bank, some of them wearing naval uniform. Once contact had been made Holt was informed by local people that they had taken the gunboat's survivors to a village away from the river, believing that if they remained where they had landed they would almost certainly have been murdered by the Japanese. While the Americans were being taken aboard the British vessels two Japanese gunboats arrived from Shanghai 'to render assistance'. Understandably, their offer was refused but their presence was interesting. Were they, perhaps, under orders to 'clean up' and destroy the cameramen's evidence of atrocities in Nanking? Or was some deeper scheme involved? The order for the air attack on the *Panay* had been given by Hashimoto, who knew the gunboat's exact location. The recipients were a naval air station which, unused to receiving direct orders from the Army, naturally requested confirmation. This was given and the attack proceeded. The fact was that Hashimoto was an unpleasant and rather dangerous man who lived in a world of intrigue and secret societies. Whatever his wider intentions might have been, the *Panay* incident resulted in the deaths of two American ratings, the master of one of the tankers and an Italian journalist; in addition, five American officers, thirty-five ratings and several civilians were wounded. Japan became epicentre of an international storm of protest and, in their shame, many Japanese citizens contributed to a relief fund for those in need. The Japanese government made a formal apology, paid an indemnity in excess of $2 million and, at Washington's request, dismissed Hashimoto. Inevitably, the disgraced colonel continued to cause trouble in political circles until his career was finally ended by the post-war war crimes tribunal in Tokyo.

One of those offering a formal apology to the American government through its ambassador was Vice Admiral Isoroku Yamamoto, now serving as Deputy Minister of the Navy. Yamamoto had not agreed with the Army's involvement in Manchukuo, and had opposed the war with China from the beginning. He was also against joining the Tripartite Pact with Germany and Italy, negotiations for which began in Tokyo in 1937. While these were taking place the Prime Minister, Prince Konoe, asked him how he thought the Imperial Navy would fare in a war with Great Britain and the United States. With remarkable prescience, Yamamoto replied that it would 'run wild for six months or a year, but after that I have utterly no confidence'.

Such a war was already in view, but in the meantime the Army had rashly chosen to throw its weight about on the border between

Manchukuo and Mongolia. The frontier was only vaguely defined at the point where Manchukuo, Korea and Siberia met. Soviet troops had fortified a feature named Chaungkufeng Hill, situated near the mouth of the Tumen River. The Japanese believed that they had no business to be there and, on 11 July 1938, mounted a month-long series of attacks intended to dislodge them. When these failed, the subsequent truce permitted the Russians to remain in possession of the hill. The Army's leadership, finding it difficult to accept the defeat, decided to mount a major offensive into another disputed area, this time along the Khalkin river in Outer Mongolia. Several divisions were employed in the offensive, which began in May 1939. At first the Japanese were successful, taking a feature named Bain-Tsagan Hill. However, by the middle of summer the Russians had brought up three divisions and no less than five armoured brigades under the command of General Georgi Zhukov, who would prove himself to be a master of mechanised war and win his marshal's baton during the Second World War. Zhukov struck on 20 August, expertly combining artillery fire with air attacks to cover the advance of his troops. The Japanese, who believed that the correct role of tanks was support for their infantry, after which they were withdrawn into reserve, were completely thrown off balance by the Russian armoured brigades' sweeping drives around their flanks to enclose their centre in a double envelopment. Those units that had been by-passed were left for follow-up groups to eliminate. The last remaining Japanese defences, located on Remisova and Namon-Han-Burd–Obo Hills, were overrun and their garrisons annihilated. Those of their army that could fled back across the frontier, the line of which they accepted in a treaty signed on 15 September. The Japanese admitted that the venture had cost them some 18,000 casualties while the Russians admitted to 9,800.

This diversion had done nothing to further the prospect of a Japanese victory in China. By now the generals were in agreement that such a victory was not possible without adequate supplies of steel, copper, tin, rubber and oil. These were becoming increasingly difficult, if not impossible, to obtain from the United States and the colonial powers on the grounds that Japan was fighting a war of aggression. Most of these commodities were obtainable in colonial territories far to the south – Malaya, Burma, the Dutch East Indies, French Indo-China and the Philippine Islands but stocks of them held within the home islands had begun to shrink at an alarming rate – indeed, it was calculated that the stock of fuel oil would be exhausted by the end of 1941. Furthermore, there was hardly a village in the home islands where a family was not mourning the loss of a son, grandson or other male relative, killed in China. Without the intervention of a miracle, the generals faced a bleak future.

They were in luck. The miracle took place between 10 May and 25 June 1940 when the German *Blitzkrieg* overran Belgium and Holland, occupied most of France and forced the British Army to withdraw from the continent of Europe. For the moment, the United Kingdom remained alone, fighting for its life. The Royal Navy was fully committed in the Atlantic and the Mediterranean with comparatively few assets east of Suez. Malaya was held by troops who were either untrained or inexperienced and the same was true of Burma. The Dutch maintained a squadron of warships in the East Indies, plus ground troops, although the latter were widely dispersed. France had some 50,000 troops in Indo-China and these resisted when the Japanese invaded on 22 September 1940. However, under pressure from Hitler, Marshal Pétain, now head of the French state, ordered his forces to cease fighting and treat the Japanese as guests. Indo-China therefore became a springboard for further Japanese expansion. The only remaining threat to this was the American Pacific Fleet, based at Pearl Harbor.

Admiral Yamamoto, now Commander of the Imperial Navy's Combined Fleet (a title approximating to the Royal Navy's Admiral of the Fleet) was ordered to prepare detailed plans for a pre-emptive strike that would ensure the destruction of this. He did so reluctantly, knowing full well America's capacity for mass production, her wealth of raw materials and the fury with which her people would react to such a treacherous act. He expressed his opposition to the idea, just as he had to the invasion of Manchuria and the war on China, which had already made him unpopular with the generals. His assassination was plotted, but when word of this reached him he saw to it that he spent as much time as possible at sea. Nevertheless, his patriotism was beyond question and he began examining the various alternatives available to carry through the projected operation. As a gesture of their new-found goodwill the generals assured him that they envisaged only a short war, at the end of which a treaty would be concluded with their opponents, restoring their territories to them, save for those considered important for Japan's continued well-being.

CHAPTER 7

Climbing Mount Niitaka

On 17 October 1941 General Hideki Tojo replaced Prince Konoye as Prime Minister of the Japanese Empire. Tojo had served as the Kwantung Army's Chief of Staff in Manchuria since 1937 and the following year received the Emperor's permission to hold military and political posts simultaneously. He served as Vice Minister and then Minister of War and in 1940 was prominent in negotiating the Tripartite Pact with Germany and Italy. In addition to holding the office of Prime Minister, Tojo retained the posts of War Minister and Army Chief of Staff. Despite wielding immense power, he was not an absolute dictator in the manner of Hitler, Mussolini and Stalin. Rather, he supported the Army's belief that only by fighting a short victorious war against the Western powers could Japan obtain the resources she needed to win her war in China. He concurred with the Army's view that such a war would present the West with a fait accompli and place Japan in a position of unassailable strength in any subsequent peace negotiations. One of his first acts was to order the occupation of French Indo-China, although he preserved the fiction of negotiating the possibility of relaxing the embargo of the supply of war materials to Japan by despatching delegates to Washington, even while the details for an attack on the US Pacific Fleet in Pearl Harbor were being finalised.

In December 1941 the Imperial Japanese Navy's Combined Fleet possessed eleven battleships, the same number of aircraft carriers, eighteen heavy cruisers, twenty-three light cruisers, 129 destroyers and sixty-seven submarines. At the same time, the United States' Pacific Fleet could muster a total of nine battleships, three aircraft carriers, thirteen heavy cruisers, eleven light cruisers, eighty destroyers and fifty-six submarines. Together, the British Royal Navy, the Royal

Australian and Royal New Zealand Navies had a total strength in the Pacific of two battleships, one heavy cruiser and thirteen destroyers. The only other navy likely to offer opposition to Japanese designs was the Royal Netherlands Navy which, now isolated from its German-occupied homeland, could deploy three light cruisers, seven destroyers and thirteen submarines. These figures, of course, would be changed rapidly by losses and reinforcements once war became a fact.

Planning the attack on Pearl Harbor was, of course, the responsibility of Fleet Admiral Isoroku Yamamoto. This was not a task he wanted, although he accepted reluctantly that it was one that duty required him to perform. There were still admirals of the Imperial Japanese Navy who took the conservative view that the war's decisive naval battle would be fought by battleships. This, as has been mentioned already, was not an opinion shared by Yamamoto. He accepted that battleships still had a place in his own and the US Navy's order of battle, but he now firmly believed that the real battle winners were aircraft carriers, a belief emphasised by an event that had taken place during the night of 11 November 1940, far away in the Mediterranean Sea. There, twenty-one noisy biplane Swordfish bombers, so ancient in this era of fast monoplanes that their own crews called them Stringbags, lumbered into the air from the flight deck of the carrier HMS *Illustrious* and set a course for the Italian naval base of Taranto. While ten of them carried flares that would be used to illuminate the Italian battle fleet, as well as bombs that would be dropped on oil storage tanks, a seaplane base and small warships, the remainder were armed with torpedoes for use against the enemy's battleships. Curiously, the Stringbag's low speed (138mph maximum) served to protect it, for most of the Italian anti-aircraft gunners' fire criss-crossed ahead of the aircraft as they aimed off to allow for speed. One battleship was sunk, another was forced to beach herself and a third was out of action for six months. Only two Swordfish were lost, and only two of their crew lost their lives. Needless to say, the raid caused a sensation throughout the naval world.

The raid that Yamamoto was planning against the US Pacific Fleet in Pearl Harbor bore strong similarities to that on Taranto, but rather than being carried out by a score of aircraft it would be delivered by several hundred, attacking in at least two waves. To further ensure its success, Yamamoto capitalised on his awareness of the American love of golf and by its taking place early on a Sunday morning. That, he knew, was the time that senior officers of both the Army and the Navy would either be on the golf course or travelling to it and therefore beyond immediate recall by their respective headquarters. As far as the troops and the warship crews were concerned, most would still be sleeping off the effects of Saturday night with just a few handfuls of duty men taking their breakfast.

In order to avoid speculation, the attacking fleet would assemble in Tankan Bay, a remote anchorage in the Kurile Islands. Ships would arrive singly or in pairs from different directions without even their captains suspecting the reason for the rendezvous. When fully assembled the fleet was made up as follows:

Attack Force
Vice Admiral Chuichi Nagumo
Carriers *Akagi, Kaga, Soryu, Hiryu, Zuikaku, Shokaku*

Support Force
Vice Admiral Gunichi Mikawa
Battleships *Hiei, Kirishima*
Heavy Cruisers *Tone, Chikuma*

Scouting Force
Rear Admiral Sentaro Omori
Light Cruiser *Abukuma*
Nine Destroyers

Supply Force
Eight Tankers

Midget Submarines
Five

Nagumo's striking force left Tankan Bay on 26 November and began its 3,000-mile voyage across the Pacific. Yamamoto's plan was approved by the Emperor and his Cabinet on 2 December. The following day the coded message 'Climb Mount Niitaka' was flashed to Nagumo, confirming that he was to attack Pearl Harbor and other targets on the island of Oahu. The fleet paused to refuel on 3 December then crossed the international date line and turned south-east to a point 275 miles north of Pearl Harbor where it would launch the first attack wave of aircraft. If Nagumo's force was detected prior to its final approach to the target, the operation was to be aborted.

Did they but know it, the Americans had broken the Japanese codes and were aware that something of major importance was taking place. They had been tracking the whereabouts of major Japanese formations and suddenly the First Air Fleet had disappeared from the air waves. The American intercept operators passed on this information upwards so that General George C. Marshall, the US Army's Chief of Staff, and Admiral Harold H. Stark, the US Navy's Chief of Operations, possessed sufficient information to recognise that an attack on Pearl Harbor was a distinct possibility. Their respective subordinates in Hawaii, Lieutenant General Walter C. Short and Admiral Husband E. Kimmel, were alerted but failed to appreciate the full extent of the danger they were in. It does not seem to have occurred to either of them that the reason for the apparent disappearance of the Japanese First Air Fleet was that it was aboard Nagumos's six carriers and maintaining strict radio silence. However, two of the fleet's aircraft carriers, the USS *Enterprise* and USS *Lexington*, were already at sea and out of harm's way, while the third, the USS *Saratoga*, was at San Diego naval base in California.

On the morning of 7 December the Japanese carriers reached the point at which they would launch their aircraft during the dying hours of a tropical storm. This caused the ships a certain amount of pitching, but not sufficient to cancel the raid and Nagumo ordered the same battle ensign flown by Togo at Tsu Shima to be hoisted. At 06.00 the first wave of aircraft, 183 strong, began taking off and, having formed up, headed for Oahu. In overall command of the attack was Commander Mitsui Fuchida, who would remain over the target until the second wave had completed its attack and then return to his carrier and report the success of the raid to Nagumo.

Shortly after 07.00 an operator at the radar station on the northern point of the island noted growing activity on his hitherto empty screen. In accordance with his standing orders, he immediately telephoned his immediate superior, Lieutenant Kermit Tyler, and reported the development. Tyler was expecting a flight of B-17 Flying Fortresses to reach the island from the American mainland at about this time. 'Don't worry about it,' he replied and rang off. The radar station closed down in accordance with its daily routine.

The raiders closed in at 10,000 feet. Fuchida examined the harbour area and the island's airfields carefully and was astonished by what he saw. There were no patrolling warships on picket duty round the island, no flights of fighter aircraft deployed ready for an emergency take-off, no activity around defence establishments, and no torpedo nets slung alongside the battleships, clearly visible with the majority moored in pairs beside Ford Island in the centre of the harbour. The bad weather he had left behind had been replaced by ideal conditions for the attack. Reaching for his microphone he broadcast the signal for the surprise attack to begin: 'Tora! Tora! Tora!'

The rest of the story has been told many times. At 07.58 the alarm finally blared out: 'Air raid Pearl Harbor! This is no drill!' Amid the uproar of exploding bombs and torpedoes, the incessant rattle of machine guns and the roar of aero engines, men ran from mess decks and barracks to man their weapons through the smoke and flames of burning buildings and aircraft. The Zero fighters, not required to engage their opposite numbers, strafed the ranks of parked aircraft at the Ewa, Kaneohe Bay, Hickham and Wheeler air bases, destroying 188 USAAF and US Navy aircraft, mainly on the ground. The flight of B-17 bombers flew straight into the heart of the fighting and was destroyed as they tried to touch down after their long journey. Kate torpedo bombers tore across the harbour at almost suicidal height to release their weapons, over half of which found their targets. As a result, the Pacific Fleet's battleship element was almost wiped out. The recently refitted *Arizona,* ablaze and belching smoke, had blown up and gone to the bottom on an even keel, taking over 1,000 of her crew down with her. *California* and *West Virginia* were settling, while *Oklahoma* and *Utah* had capsized and the light cruiser *Helena* was severely damaged.

Some fifty minutes after the first Japanese attack wave struck, the 170 aircraft of the second wave arrived over the harbour. By then the captain of the *Nevada* had got her under way and was heading for open water in the belief that she would be less vulnerable at sea. Bombers swarmed round her with the intention of sinking the battleship in the narrow entrance, blocking it. They failed, although they did cause sufficient damage to require her being beached. Also damaged were the battleship *Pennsylvania* and two destroyers, undergoing repair in dry dock.

Nevertheless, the brief pause between the two attacks enabled a number of American fighters to take to the air and these were responsible for shooting down the majority of the twenty-nine Japanese aircraft destroyed, the remainder falling victim to anti-aircraft fire. The Japanese also lost all five of their midget submarines without producing any known results. None of this could hope to conceal the fact that the Pacific Fleet had been badly hurt in material terms, as well as having 3,581 of its personnel killed or wounded.

On the mess decks of the Japanese carriers there was rejoicing at what had been achieved by those who had taken part in the attack, but in the command quarters there was concern that the three American carriers, the greatest prize of all, had escaped destruction. Nagumo was sharply criticised for not mounting a third strike, but he believed that if he did so while the position of the American carriers remained unknown, the risk of their making a strike against his own force while half his aircraft were away was too high and was not one he was prepared to take. Instead, he ordered his fleet to turn west and head for home waters. Having crossed the international date into 8 December, he detached what he considered to be a suitable force under Rear Admiral Sadamichi Kajioka to capture the American base on Wake Atoll, lying to the south. Wake's importance was that it possessed an airstrip and lay between the American islands of Guam and Midway, providing a stepping stone in the wide expanses of the Central Pacific. In overall command of its garrison was Commander Winfield Scott Cunningham, who had at his disposal the US Marine Corps 1st Defence Battalion under Major James Devereux. The battalion's heavy weapons included six 5-inch ex-First World War battleship guns, which were formed into three batteries, and twelve 3-inch guns intended for air defence, and eighteen .50 calibre machine guns. A welcome addition on 4 December was the arrival of the Wildcat fighters of Major Paul Putnam's Marine Fighter Squadron 211 (VMF – 211).

The first Japanese air attack took place on 8 December, delivered by twin-engined bombers flying from Roi-Namur, 700 miles to the south. Thereafter, air attacks came in regularly. They caused extensive damage but received a mauling from VMF-211 and anti-aircraft fire. At 03.00 on 11 December Kajioka's invasion force arrived off the atoll. It consisted of the modern light cruiser *Yubari*, two older cruisers, six destroyers, two destroyer transports, two transports and two submarines. Aboard was a 450-strong naval infantry detachment intended to effect a landing.

Yubari and her consorts began their bombardment runs, at the end of which they reversed course, each turn bringing them a little closer to the shore. Devereux held his fire until the range was down to 5,700 yards, at which A Battery punched two 5-inch shells through *Yubari*'s side, bursting in the boiler room and machinery spaces. Belching smoke and steam, she turned away, but at 7,000 yards another round slammed into her, causing serious internal fires. A destroyer attempted to lay a smoke screen between the battery and the *Yubari* but stopped a round intended for the cruiser and was forced to turn away herself with a wrecked forecastle. B Battery scored a hit on the leading destroyer which retired, trailing smoke. However, the prize for the day's shooting must surely go to L Battery, which put both rounds from its third salvo into the destroyer *Hyate*, causing a huge internal explosion that broke her back and sent her to the bottom. Further hits were scored on a second destroyer and a transport and a large fire was started on the stern of a cruiser.

Kajioka had had more than enough. At 07.00 he ordered his battered command to retire. Unfortunately, the transports had already started disembarking their troops into their invasion barges in a heavy swell. Recovering them was difficult, doubly so under fire, and a number of the troops were undoubtedly drowned when their craft overturned.

The Wake garrison had not quite finished with their visitors yet. VHF-211 took off and made sortie after sortie, harrying the retreating ships with their machine guns, dropping 100lb bombs, then returning to the island to replenish their munitions. Hits were scored on both the older cruisers, and a destroyer transport and a major petrol fire started aboard a second transport. Two bombs struck the full depth-charge racks of the already damaged destroyer *Kiseragi*, tearing her apart in the resulting explosion. All the Wildcats returned to the island, although some of them had sustained serious damage. Kajoika must have broadcast his woes for, at 10.00, some thirty bombers approached the island from the north-east. VMF-211 shot down two and sent another, burning, on its long flight home. The anti-aircraft guns destroyed another and sent three more trailing smoke. Only superficial damage was caused by the remainder. Incredibly, American casualties on 11 December amounted to just four marines slightly wounded.

Kajioka had lost an immense amount of face. Just how he explained his physical losses and the deaths of 700 men to his superior, Vice Admiral Inoui Shigeyoshi, would have made interesting listening, for Inuoi was not unduly popular with the Navy's most senior officers. He had been set the task of capturing Guam and Wake and given adequate ships, aircraft and troops for the job, but now, at a time when the Empire was celebrating one victory after another, Kajioka had returned with a pathetic defeat to report!

This was not something Inuoi was prepared to tolerate. In comparison with the size of its objective, a huge force was assembled to ensure its capture. In command was Rear Admiral Hiroake Abe who had at his disposal the carriers *Soryu* and *Hiryu,* six heavy cruisers and six destroyers. The unfortunate Kajioka was made responsible for the amphibious landing. He was given one modern and two older destroyers, plus a transport and a seaplane to accommodate the enlarged naval infantry contingent, which now numbered 1,000.

On 22 December the last of VMF-221's aircraft was destroyed. The following day's dawn revealed Wake encircled by enemy ships. The atoll was strafed and bombed by the carrier aircraft to cover the landing of the naval infantry, who met the most determined resistance and lost heavily. However, by 13.30 the little garrison had been all but swamped and Cunningham, seeing no point in losing further lives, gave the order to surrender. In the midst of unremitting bad news from around the Pacific, Wake's heroic defence had provided an inspiration for the American people. It could now be clearly seen that the Japanese were not invincible, giving rise to the universal conviction that, given time, they would be beaten.

For the moment, however, there would be a great deal more bad news to be borne. Commanded by Admiral Thomas C. Hart, the American Asiatic Fleet, based in the Philippines, was tiny compared with the Pacific Fleet and consisted of one heavy cruiser (USS *Houston*), two light cruisers (USS *Boise* and *Marblehead*), thirteen destroyers, twenty-eight submarines, a flotilla of fast patrol torpedo (PT) boats and other craft. Thanks to a far-sighted directive from the Navy Department, much of this was already in process of being withdrawn to Java; all that remained were four destroyers, the submarines, a squadron of flying boats and their tender, the PT boats and a regiment of marines. American and Filipino ground troops, under the command of General Douglas MacArthur, included 10,400 American regulars, 12,000 regular Philippine Scouts, 3,000 Philippine Constabulary, and the 107,000 Philippine Army, which was neither fully organised and trained nor equipped. MacArthur's air element, the US Far East Air Force, was commanded by Major General Lewis H. Brereton and contained 125 combat aircraft, including thirty-five recently-arrived B-17 Flying Fortresses.

Details of the attack on Pearl Harbor had reached Manila at 02.30. Brereton had also received a telephone call from Washington warning him that a Japanese strike on the Philippines was likely. MacArthur's intention was to employ his B-17s in an attack against the enemy's airfields on Formosa, yet nothing was done, and Brereton's aircraft were neatly lined up on Clark Field and satellite airfields when the Japanese arrived overhead at 12.15. Eighteen B-17s and fifty-six fighter aircraft were destroyed, as were airfield installations. The only American fighter squadron to get airborne shot down seven enemy fighters but was virtually destroyed itself.

On 10 December General Masaharu Homma's Japanese Fourteenth Army , consisting of 50,000 experienced troops, began a series of landings on the islands of Luzon and Mindanao that lasted for the remainder of the month. Faced with so many threats from different directions, MacArthur decided that he could not defend Manila without the probability that his troops would be encircled and destroyed piecemeal. He ordered his remaining seventeen B-17s to fly to Australia on 27 December and withdrew his own forces into the Bataan peninsula, although he continued to exercise command from southern Luzon. A pause ensued while Homma built up his strength until he had concentrated sufficient armour, artillery and air assets. He then launched a major assault on the Bataan defences on 9 January 1942. This was thrown back with heavy losses, as were subsequent attacks, so that it was not until 23 January that the Americans had been pushed back into their reserve positions. Despite this, a counter-attack failed to prevent the Japanese making gains, although Homma decided upon an operational pause until further reinforcements reached him. Once these arrived, he was able to push the Americans back to the tip of the peninsula on 3 April.

MacArthur only made one visit to his hard-fighting troops on the peninsula and his personal standing with them fell accordingly. By now, Washington had reached the conclusion that his abilities could be better made use of elsewhere. Accepting this, he appointed Lieutenant General Jonathan Wainwright as his successor in command. With his family and favoured staff officers, he then embarked on four PT boats, reaching Cagayan in Mindanao on 14 March. The party was evacuated from there by two B-17s on 16 March and reached Darwin at 09.00 the following day. 'I have come through and I shall return,' he told a waiting press conference.

On 9 March the remaining 78,000 American and Filipino troops on Bataan surrendered unconditionally. The Japanese behaved towards them with their usual cruel indifference to wounds and sickness, forcing them to march sixty miles under a blazing sun to their designated prison camp. Those unable to keep up were clubbed to death. Of the men who began the infamous Bataan Death March, only 54,000 reached their destination. A further 15,000 men on the tadpole-shaped fortified island of Corregidor in the centre of Manila harbour continued to resist. Under constant bombardment and air attack, most lived a mole-like underground existence in a tunnel complex. On 5 May the Japanese managed to secure a beachhead on the tadpole's tail after their leading wave sustained heavy losses. By 10.30 the following morning the last defence line had been overcome and Wainwright was forced to surrender unconditionally.

Homma had been given fifty days in which to complete his task, but it had taken him 123. For the moment, that did not matter as the road to the riches of the south was open and none remained to oppose it. To their dismay, however, it would not be long before the victors would be forced to deal with an active and well-armed force of Filipino guerrillas.

CHAPTER 8

Twilight of the Empires

The removal of the threat posed by the American Pacific and Asiatic Fleets and neutralisation of the Philippine Islands was only part of the Japanese strategy for a short, victorious war. Simultaneous attacks were also launched on the British colony of Hong Kong and the Malayan mainland and Dutch possessions throughout the East Indies.

Hong Kong was invaded from Chinese territory on 8 December 1941. Kowloon, the mainland portion of the colony, was quickly overrun and the small British garrison withdrew to Hong Kong Island two days later. A Japanese surrender demand was rejected on 13 December by Major General C. M. Maltby, the British commander, who was well aware that no possibility of relief existed, despite which he was not prepared to make a present of the city and its naval base to the enemy; rather, he intended to make his opponents pay as heavy a price as he could. In response, Japanese artillery, aircraft and naval units hammered the island continuously for the next five days

On 18 December they effected several landings. Their attacks were costly but finally succeeded in fragmenting the defence. Fighting continued until the garrison had consumed the last of its water and Maltby surrendered on 25 December. A few of his men managed to escape, evade capture and reach the nearby Portuguese island colony of Macao. The Japanese had lost about 3,000 casualties in what they believed to have been a pointless battle and revenged themselves on the hated ethnic Chinese population in an orgy of rape, murder and general savagery that far exceeded their previous record.

Suddenly, the reason for Japan's earlier invasion of French Indo-China became apparent. From Indo-China it was a short step to Siam and the Siamese were simply not equipped to take on the Japanese war machine. However, its possession was of enormous importance to Japanese plans for it provided a back door into both Malaya and Burma. Malaya's natural resources included tin, rubber and timber, while Burma possessed important oilfields. Both, therefore, were essential to the continuance of Japan's war effort.

There was a strange climate of unreality in Malaya in the months immediately prior to the Japanese invasion. The general opinion was that the Japanese were a belligerent nuisance, but not enough of a threat to interfere with a rather pleasant colonial lifestyle. Numerous airfields had been built for its defence and it was the duty of the Army to protect them. Unfortunately, only 158 aircraft were available to operate from these airfields, less than half the number considered necessary by the British chiefs of staff. Of these, the majority were Brewster Buffalo fighters, slower and less manoeuvrable than the Zeros they would have to face but, in the words of Air Chief Marshal Sir Robert Brooke-Popham, Commander-in-Chief British Forces Far East, 'Quite good enough for Malaya'. The same, apparently, was true of the Vildebeest biplane torpedo bombers. There were a few armoured cars but no tanks as someone had said that the country was unsuited. In command of the garrison was Lieutenant General Arthur Percival who had at his disposal 8th Australian Division, 9th and 11th Indian Divisions, plus two independent Indian and two independent Malay brigades. An unsatisfactory situation existed in some of the Indian formations in that a proportion of their British officers were insufficiently fluent in Urdu, the Indian Army's *lingua franca*, and were therefore unable to communicate properly with their sepoys. Training for jungle warfare was considered eccentric and rarely undertaken.

British Imperial defence strategy had envisaged sending naval reinforcements to Singapore as early as 1920 and this decision had been activated as a result of the Japanese invasion of French Indo-China. Despite the Royal Navy being stretched to the limit in the

Atlantic and the Mediterranean, it had proved possible to assemble a small squadron, known as Force Z, for this purpose. It consisted of the battleship HMS *Prince of Wales*, the battle cruiser *Repulse*, and four destroyers. It was also intended that a new aircraft carrier, HMS *Indomitable*, armed with modern fighters, should accompany the squadron, but she had run aground during working-up trials in the Caribbean and was in need of repair. It was suggested that HMS *Hermes*, the Royal Navy's purpose-built carrier, should take her place, but she was considered to be too slow.

The timing of the Japanese invasion coincided with that of others taking place. On 8 December heavy pre-dawn attacks took place on airfields in Malaya and Singapore, seriously reducing the number of combat aircraft remaining. Following these, the first waves of Lieutenant General Tomoyuki Yamashita's Twenty-Fifth Army landed at Kota Bharu in northern Malaya and at nearby Singora and Patani at the southern extremity of Siam's narrow Kra Isthmus. In total, Yamashita's army contained 100,000 men, well equipped with artillery and tanks. Having consolidated their beachheads, the invaders then began advancing down both sides of the Malayan peninsula.

That evening Force Z, under the command of Admiral Sir Thomas Phillips, left Singapore and steamed north along the east coast of Malaya with the intention of destroying the enemy's invasion fleet. Phillips asked for air cover but, following the raids on its airfields, the RAF was unable to help. Unfortunately, at 13.40 the following afternoon, his ships were spotted by Lieutenant Commander Harada of the Japanese submarine *I-65*. He immediately reported their course and speed to Vice Admiral Jisarubo Ozawa. Warships of the covering force were despatched south to intercept Force Z and seaplanes were launched to locate its position. The torpedo bomber force in Siam was also warned for action.

Early on the morning of the 10th Force Z was also sighted by another submarine, Lieutenant Commander Kitamura's *I-58*. Five torpedoes were launched at *Repulse* without result, but the position of the British ships was again reported. With the coming of dawn,

Japanese seaplanes began to make their presence felt. It was late morning when the first formations of Nell long-range bombers and Betty land-based torpedo-bombers arrived on the scene. The story of the subsequent action is narrated by Masanori Ito in his excellent book *The End of the Imperial Japanese Navy*.

> *Prince of Wales* was slow in avoiding torpedo attacks, but her anti-aircraft fire was heavy and far surpassed any that might have been produced by a Japanese battleship at the time. Eight planes of the first attack group were hit at an altitude of 3,000 metres. Enemy fire was so rapid and heavy and the bomb explosions so fierce that torpedo planes of the Ishihara Group, in the second attack wave, lost sight of their companions attacking from the opposite side of the targets. The anti-aircraft from the *Prince of Wales* was relentless to the last, and damaged five of the Takeda Group bombers which delivered the *coup de grace* to the valiant warship.

Repulse absorbed no less than ten torpedo hits or her port side, four more on her starboard side and one 250kg bomb amidships. The sheer quality of her construction astonished her attackers, for she did not sink until 14.20. *Prince of Wales* absorbed less punishment – two torpedo hits on her port side, five on her starboard side, one 500kg bomb aft and another forward. She finally sank at 14.45. The survivors were taken off by the destroyers, but Admiral Phillips refused to leave his bridge and went down with the ship.

The Japanese still retained their admiration for the Royal Navy and they were deeply impressed by the way the two doomed ships had fought it out to the bitter end. For Admiral Phillips and the way he met his end they had nothing but praise. They had employed eighty-four aircraft in the action. Of these, three had been shot down, one had crash-landed with serious damage, two sustained serious damage but managed to land and a further twenty-five had sustained damage of one sort or another.

The ensuing campaign emerged as probably the greatest triumph in the history of the imperial Japanese Army. It was also the greatest disaster ever suffered by a British army. Its commander, Lieutenant General Arthur Percival, adhered to the accepted view that it was impossible to fight in the jungle and concentrated his defences along the north-south road and railway system. Contrary to post-campaign rumours, the Japanese had not received extensive training, and their methods were based on sound common sense. As soon as they were ashore they commandeered thousands of bicycles in Siam and northern Malaya. On these, they pedalled south along both sides of the peninsula. Apart from their ammunition, all they carried was a small marching ration, but this was left intact for as long as they could live on captured food, which was most of the time. They regarded the jungle and rubber plantations as friends so that whenever they were halted by a defensive position one third of their force would mount a holding attack while the remainder executed a wide loop through jungle and plantation tracks and establish a roadblock in the defenders' rear. Next, Japanese tanks and infantry would assault the defensive position, which was now isolated by the roadblock to its rear. Never having seen a tank before, the Indian troops were terrified by their mere appearance, although the Australians resented their crews' cocky self-confidence and made them pay for it. When the defenders attempted to withdraw they were halted by the roadblock and forced to escape through the jungle, leaving behind all their heavy weapons and transport. The Japanese would then break through the abandoned defences and continue their advance. This pattern was repeated again and again, with the occasional variation of a landing on the coast behind the British lines. By the end of January 1942 Percival's troops had been forced to abandon mainland Malaya and retire onto Singapore Island, blowing up the connecting causeway behind them.

It was at this point, with the overall situation deteriorating by the hour, that the military bureaucrats began making life even more difficult for those manning the island's defences. They issued instructions to the searchlight batteries to the effect that the lights must not be used without their permission, which could be obtained by way of the military telephone network, forgetting that its cables were vulnerable to enemy fire. Likewise, just when they were needed most, it was decided to withdraw the Australians' radios for servicing. Thus, when the Japanese made a night crossing of the mile-wide straits following a protracted air bombardment, they did so in welcome darkness because the searchlight operators were unable to obtain permission to use their equipment. Likewise, when further crossings in armoured barges were made the following day, the Australians were unable to call for artillery support at the critical moment. Counter-attacks were broken up by well-controlled Japanese artillery and machine-gun fire and, to make matters even worse, Yamashita's engineers repaired the causeway and his tanks crossed to join in the fighting. When the island's water reservoirs fell into Japanese hands Percival asked for terms, little realising that his opponents only had sufficient ammunition in hand for three days' serious fighting and were considering a withdrawal to the mainland. In the long term this would not have affected the outcome of the campaign, even if Percival had been aware of it, for although his troops and the large civilian population would have recovered their water supply, they depended on the mainland for food and would have reached starvation point before too long. Percival requested concessions but Yamashita bluffed brilliantly and insisted upon unconditional surrender, although he did guarantee to protect the lives of Percival's troops and the civilian population. He is understood to have kept his word, but a number of his followers did not and, as usual, it was the Chinese community that suffered most. Again, after he had left Singapore, the *kempetai* arrived to arrest those on its list, many of whom vanished without trace.

The campaign had cost each side some 9,000 casualties, but in addition some 130,000 British, Australian and Indian troops marched into a sadistic captivity that would last over three years, cost the lives of many and break the health of others. It was particularly unfortunate for the men of the British 18th Division, who had landed in Singapore just days before Percival's surrender and underlined the folly of committing fresh troops to a battle already lost beyond recovery. Those civilian refugees who had left it too late to leave by sea were intercepted by a cordon of Admiral Ozawa's warships and spent the war in internment camps. It was brutally apparent that the British Empire could not be defended and, that being the case, its demise had simply become a matter of time.

As for Yamashita, he had won the greatest victory in the history of the Imperial Japanese Army. Perversely, he was now regarded as a threat by Tojo and the Tokyo political establishment and despatched to an obscure command posting in Manchukuo. Wishing to state his case he twice requested an interview with the Emperor and was twice refused. He will, however, appear again in this story.

Meanwhile, on 12 January 1942, Lieutenant General Shojiro Iida's Japanese Fifteenth Army of two divisions invaded Burma from Siam. Burma was another of Japan's prime objective, not simply because of her oilfields but also because of the Burma Road which, starting in northern Burma, crossed the mountains into China. It was the route by which the free Western nations kept Japan's arch enemy supplied with the means to continue making war. Thus, in addition to other considerations, Iida was to close the Burma Road and keep it closed. Not all Burmese enjoyed their status as a British colony and marching with the Japanese was a small unit of revolutionaries. Against this, while the majority of Burmese were indifferent to the British presence, they were equally indifferent to the arrival of the Japanese.

Opposing Iida were two weak, under-equipped Indian Army divisions under Lieutenant General Thomas Hutton. These were driven out of Moulmein on 31 January and withdrew north to the line of the Sittang river where the premature demolition of a bridge caused the loss of heavy weapons. While the Sittang action was in progress a significant change took place in British fortunes. The experienced 7 Armoured Brigade, consisting of two regiments equipped with Stuart light tanks, reached Rangoon from the Middle East and began unloading from its transports. It had originally been destined to reinforce Percival's army in Malaya but, in the nick of time, had been diverted to Burma.

On 3 March Lieutenant General Sir Harold Alexander arrived in Rangoon to replace Hutton and some further reinforcements arrived from India. Despite this, the Japanese still possessed air superiority and, following the fall of Singapore, were being heavily reinforced themselves. Alexander therefore reached the conclusion that, as Burma could not be held against mounting odds, he must withdraw northwards to the River Chindwin, beyond which lay the mountainous frontier with India.

The withdrawal, however, was a very different matter to the disastrous retreat in Malaya. The 7th Armoured Brigade acted as rearguard, keeping the Japanese at a respectful distance for most of the time. For their part, Iida's tank unit quickly demonstrated that it knew nothing about armoured warfare and was trounced whenever it appeared. At one stage the Japanese employed gas against the British tanks, using frangible glass grenades containing hydrocyanic acid, the fumes of which were drawn into the vehicle through its air vents. The results were disappointing and there do not appear to be any further such attacks. Iida's air force also had less of its own way when part of Colonel Claire Chennault's experienced Flying Tigers fighter unit arrived from China to reinforce the RAF, downing 100 of the enemy's aircraft for the loss of five of its own. Chiang Kai Shek also despatched two of his corps-strength armies in an attempt to protect the Burma Road. They fought hard and well but were outnumbered and eventually forced to retire. Thereafter, Allied aid to Chiang had to be flown over the Eastern Himalayas, which became known to the pilots as The Hump.

The 600-mile retreat to the Chindwin was the longest in the British Army's history. Many of its Burmese soldiers simply got rid of their weapons and went home. Likewise, many British and Indian soldiers, separated from their units, became fugitives but turned up in India after the campaign was over. It was, therefore, difficult to produce an accurate British casualty return in the immediate aftermath of the campaign, and impossible in the case of the

Chinese. The Japanese admitted to 7,000 losses among their ground troops. Iida had fulfilled his mission but Burma, now at the extreme edge of Japanese holdings, was an uncomfortable command that was difficult to supply.

On 5 January the Western Allies had gone some way towards co-ordinating their response to the Japanese series of conquests throughout east Asia by forming ABDA (American, British, Dutch, Australian) Command under the leadership of General Sir Archibald Wavell, with Dutch Vice Admiral Conrad Helfrich in overall command of the Allied naval elements. In fact, matters had already gone too far for Wavell to exercise much control over events, but he did set about concentrating the Command's assets. The last of the RAF's aircraft in Malaya, for example, were flown to Sumatra for joint use with the Dutch, and warships from the various navies were placed under the command of Rear Admiral Karel Doorman of the Royal Netherlands Navy. His small fleet included the heavy cruisers HMS *Exeter* (of River Plate fame) and USS *Houston*, the light cruisers RNN *De Ruyter* (flag) and *Java*, HMAS *Perth* and *Hobart*, USS *Marblehead* and a number of destroyers.

The essence of the Allies' dilemma was that the Japanese could strike wherever they pleased, always in superior strength and always with ample air cover provided by their omnipresent aircraft carriers. However, on 23 January four American destroyers sank a small Japanese warship and four heavily-laden troop transports at Balikpapan in the Macassar Strait, and inflicted damage on several other vessels. This setback did not delay the Japanese advance for on 13/14 February an attempt to prevent an amphibious landing on the Sumatran coast near the vitally important oilfield of Palembang was foiled by Japanese aircraft which prevented Doorman's ships coming within range of the invasion convoy. The oilfield and a nearby airfield were taken by a concurrent parachute drop.

On 19 February Nagumo led the carriers *Akagi*, *Kaga*, *Hiryu* and *Soryu*, accompanied by the battleships *Hiei* and *Kirishima*, plus three cruisers and nine destroyers in an attack on the city of Darwin in Australia's Northern Territory. No less than 180 aircraft, led again by Mitsuo Fuchida, took part in the attack. Inside the harbour an American destroyer and ten merchantmen were sunk. In addition, a freighter with 200 tons of depth charges aboard blew up; warehouses, docks, fuel tanks and government buildings were wrecked, Australian and American aircraft were destroyed in the air or on the ground, 250 civilians were killed and 150 wounded, for the loss of two aircraft. A second raid, carried out by fifty-four aircraft, caused extensive damage to an airfield four miles outside the town for the loss of a further three aircraft. Fuchida thought that the results of the two raids did not justify the effort involved. Quite possibly the attacks were mounted for the benefit of Prime Minister Tojo, who remarked more than once that the Australians must 'learn' that their population was too small and their country too large for it to be defended properly.

On the same day the Japanese seized Bali and an occupation force headed for Timor. The fact that the latter was owned partly by Holland and partly by Portugal made no difference to the Japanese way of thinking; the inhabitants were simply told that they now belonged to the new Greater East Asia Co-Prosperity Sphere, led by Japan. By now it was apparent that Sumatra could not be held with the limited forces available and the ABDA Command turned its attention to the defence of Java, the richest island of the East Indies, producing tea, coffee, rice, tobacco, gold, silver and tin. Wavell committed a number of British units to assist in the defence of the island, a decision that attracted criticism because of the approaching enemy's overwhelming strength.

Admiral Helfrich was warned by a reconnaissance aircraft that the enemy's invasion force was heading for Java in three heavily protected convoys. Most of his own strength was located at Surabaya under Admiral Doorman's direct command, but a smaller group of Allied warships was based at Batavia. This included three light cruisers, HMAS *Hobart*, HMS *Danae* and *Dragon*, and two destroyers, HMS *Scout* and *Tenedos*. Although the last four were ancient, and of very limited fighting value, Helfrich ordered all five to sea on 26 February. Two days later he thought better of the decision and instructed them to proceed to Ceylon, thereby saving them and their crews from useless destruction and loss of life.

Doorman also put to sea on the 26th but, finding nothing, decided to return to Surabaya the following morning. He was about to enter harbour when a scout plane reported the presence of the Japanese convoy some eighty miles to the north. He promptly reversed course and proceeded in that direction at his fleet's best speed, which was no greater than 22 knots. His cruisers were formed into a single column with *De Ruyter* leading, followed by *Exeter*, *Houston*, *Perth* and *Java*. The British destroyers were deployed to starboard of the cruisers while the Dutch and American destroyers were to port. At about 15.00 a Japanese seaplane spotted Doorman's ships and signalled that he was sixty miles away and heading straight for the troop convoy. The troop transports turned away to the north out of harm's way while no fewer than three rear admirals (Shoji Nishimura, Raizo Tanaka and Takagi) converged on the ABDA fleet, outnumbering it by a wide margin.

Shortly after 16.00 the two fleets sighted each other. Doorman was at an immediate disadvantage as he was steering north while his opponents were heading westwards. This meant that the two leading enemy heavy cruisers, *Nachi* and *Haguro*, could use their 8-inch broadsides while only the leading heavy cruisers in Doorman's line could reply; even then, *Houston*'s rear turret was already out of action. Doorman turned 20 degrees to port with the idea of closing the range and enabling his 6-inch light cruisers to engage, without success. Incredible as it may seem, neither side had caused the other any damage after almost an hour's fighting, all the more so as the Japanese had three seaplanes reporting their fall of shot. Even more surprising is the fact that at 16.43 the Japanese destroyers launched forty-three of the terrible Long Lance torpedoes far beyond their range. At 17.00 *Nachi*, *Haguro* and a swarm of destroyers launched a total of fifty-two Long Lances without result, at the cost of a destroyer seriously damaged. Such a prodigal waste of expensive ordnance surely deserved a court of enquiry.

However, at 17.08 an 8-inch shell exploded in *Exeter*'s boiler room, putting six out of the eight boilers out of action. To avoid being rammed from astern by the *Houston*, her captain turned to port. Unfortunately, the rest of the line followed suit, thinking the turn had been ordered to avoid torpedoes. The exception was Doorman's flagship *De Ruyter*, leading the line, which was forced to turn herself in order to remain with the fleet. It was, however, clear from the enemy's seaplane reports that the Allies were in some confusion. At about this time a Long Lance torpedo hit the Dutch destroyer *Kortenaer*, blowing her into two halves.

Meanwhile, by dint of Herculean labours, *Exeter*'s damage control parties had managed to increase her speed from 5 to 15 knots, covered the while by a smokescreen laid by *Perth*. Doorman ordered his destroyers to counter-attack while *Exeter* withdrew to Surabaya, escorted by the Dutch destroyer *Witte de With*. The destroyer melee resulted in HMS *Electra* being sunk and the Japanese *Asagumo* seriously damaged.

At 18.40, shortly after sunset, Doorman once again steered to the north-west in the hope not only of avoiding his recent opponents but also of intercepting the Japanese troop transports. Instead, he ran into *Nachi* and *Haguro* once more, halted while *Nachi*'s seaplane was hoisted aboard. The two cruisers quickly got under weigh, shielded by a smokescreen and covered by another abortive torpedo attack at 19.37. This caused Doorman to believe that somehow the troop convoy had by-passed the earlier fighting and he reversed course, heading for the coast of Java. Gradually, his ill-starred command began shredding away. The American destroyers, now critically short of fuel, returned to Surabaya. HMS *Jupiter* was fatally damaged by an explosion and sank four hours later. The source of the explosion was believed to be a rogue mine drifting free from a recently-laid Dutch minefield.

At about 23.00 Doorman again ran into *Nachi* and *Haguro*. After a brief exchange of gunfire both heavy cruisers launched Long Lance torpedoes, hitting *De Ruyter* and *Java*, both of which sank. Doorman's last signal to *Perth* and *Houston* was that they should make for Batavia and not pick up survivors. This ended what Winston Churchill called 'the forlorn battle of the Java Sea', but it was not quite the end for some of Doorman's ships. The four American destroyers that had been forced to return to Surabaya for lack of fuel made good their escape through the Bali Strait on 28 February. At dusk that same day the repaired *Exeter,* accompanied by two destroyers, HMS *Encounter* and USS *Pope,* also left Surabaya. The Bali Strait was too narrow and shallow to be used by the heavy cruiser and she was ordered to use the Sunda Strait. On 1 March Japanese aircraft reported her presence and course. Two heavy cruisers, *Ashigara* and *Myoko,* were ordered into her path. At 09.35 *Nachi* and *Haguro* were spotted closing in from the south. After a short firefight *Exeter* and her destroyers turned east. The four Japanese heavy cruisers pursued, catching *Exeter* in their crossfire. Once again, she was hit in the boiler room and quickly reduced to a blazing wreck by a rain of shells. Shortly after the order to 'abandon ship' was given she was struck by several Long Lances and rolled over to sink by the stern. *Encounter* followed her to the bottom a mere five minutes later. *Pope* escaped briefly into a squall but was discovered by Japanese aircraft, seriously damaged by their bombs and finally sunk by the enemy cruisers.

Having refuelled at Batavia, *Perth* and *Houston* were ordered by Admiral Helfrich to make for Tjilijap by way of the Sunda Strait between Java and Sumatra. Late on 28 February they reached Bantam Bay where, to their astonishment, they discovered the Japanese invasion fleet with a number of warships nearby. They both went into action immediately. In his excitement, the captain of the destroyer *Fubuki* launched nine Long Lances, forgetting that if they missed they would head straight into the troop convoy. Two exploded against the transport *Sakura Maru,* sending her to the bottom. Allied gunfire so seriously damaged three more transports that they were forced to beach themselves. The commander of the Sixteenth Army, Lieutenant General Imamura, was blown overboard, which cannot have improved his temper. It was too good to last. *Perth* and *Houston* found themselves under fire from three heavy and one light cruisers, plus destroyers and both went down fighting, *Perth* at 00.05 on 1 March after being struck by not less than two torpedoes and innumerable shells, and *Houston* at 00.50, having absorbed six torpedoes and a score of shells. Subsequent Allied air attacks on the enemy's Bantam Bay landing area caused heavy loss of life and destroyed three light tanks. Nevertheless, the Japanese landings were made in overwhelming force with complete air superiority. The Allies fought back to the best of their abilities but on 9 March the Dutch commander in Java surrendered the island.

The Battle of the Java Sea and the successful invasion of the island were the last clear cut Japanese victories. There would be Japanese successes but they would be transient and of little or no value. The long-term effects of recent months would only become apparent after the war. Neither the inhabitants of the Dutch East Indies nor French Indo-China would welcome back their former colonial masters. The British Empire would endure for longer and most of its constituents would depart in a spirit of friendship, but the catastrophic defeat in Malaya can be seen to have marked the beginning of the process.

CHAPTER 9

The Last Notes of the Victory Song

During the early days of June 1942 the most popular songs to be sung in the home islands of Japan were those of victory, of celebrating the superiority of the Japanese race and how it had triumphed over so many enemies who had proved to be contemptible opponents. After all, Japan had conquered a huge area of East Asia and in six months the Imperial Navy had become the dominant force in an area stretching from the Central Pacific to the Indian Ocean, an achievement unequalled by any other navy in history. Given that the enemy's main force had yet to be encountered this was an unhealthy attitude, described by Rear Admiral Chuichi Hara as the Victory Disease, a term taken into general use after the war by Japanese historians, including Masanori Ito, the author of *The End of the Imperial Japanese Navy*. It was, of course, quite wrong for the ruling establishment to allow such an outlook to remain unchecked when the most critical days of the war lay ahead, but throughout the war the need to preserve face remained of paramount importance in the government's dealings with its people.

Anyone who, like Yamamoto, was familiar with the United States would by now be aware of America's iron determination to punish Japan for her act of treachery, and punish her severely. They would also be aware of the American expertise in matters of mass production and be aware that along the coasts of the United States yards had begun to turn out fleet carriers, escort carriers, cruisers, destroyers, destroyer escorts, submarines and landing craft in quantities that Japan could never equal, to say nothing of the tools of land warfare being turned out by heavy industries across the country. In addition, the enormous number of recruits required for the vastly expanded Navy, including its air arm, received a thorough training in the technical aspects of their work, whereas the wartime graduates of Japanese training establishments were generally less proficient.

Since the attack on Pearl Harbor there had been a number of changes in the American command structure. Admiral Ernest J. King had become Chief of Naval Operations in Washington, and Admiral Chester W. Nimitz was the new commander of the Pacific Fleet. Of necessity, this was having to be rebuilt, but the public was anxious that some active measures be taken against the Japanese. Some of the damaged battleships were undergoing repair but any effective counter-strike would have to be delivered by the fleet's three carriers, *Lexington*, *Saratoga* and *Enterprise*. Unfortunately, *Saratoga* had sustained torpedo damage from a Japanese submarine on 11 January and while she was undergoing repair the fleet's ability to strike was reduced by one third.

Nevertheless, under Vice Admiral William F. Halsey, *Enterprise* and *Yorktown* inflicted damage on Japanese bases in the Gilbert and Marshall Islands on 1 February and returned safely to Pearl Harbor. Between 24 February and 4 March, Halsey employed a task force led by *Enterprise* to attack Wake and Marcus Islands, while on 10 March a task force led by Vice Admiral Wilson Brown, consisting of *Lexington*, the repaired *Saratoga* and their escorting cruisers and destroyers, now operating in the Coral Sea, despatched aircraft across Papua to raid Lae and Salamaua, sinking or damaging a number of small warships and transports in both places.

On 26 March Yamamoto despatched Nagumo into the Indian Ocean with the carriers *Akagi*, *Shokaku*, *Zuikaku*, *Hiryu* and *Soryu* to attack British bases on the island of Ceylon. Following the loss of the *Prince of Wales* and *Repulse*, the Royal Navy's Eastern Fleet, now commanded by Vice Admiral Sir James Somerville, had been heavily reinforced and now contained five battleships of First World War vintage, plus three aircraft carriers. Two of the latter were the modern *Indomitable* and *Formidable*, both of which were fast and armoured. However, the third, *Hermes*, dated from 1919 and was actually the Royal Navy's first purpose-built aircraft carrier and was not only too slow to keep up with the fleet but was also equipped with just a dozen Swordfish biplanes. She was, therefore, more suited to escort duties.

An RAF Catalina flying boat detected the arrival of the Nagumo's fleet on 4 April and managed to transmit a contact report before it was shot down. The following morning Commander Mitsuo Fuchida led a concentrated attack on Colombo, hoping that he would be presented with a similar array of targets to that which he had attacked in Pearl Harbor. He was disappointed, for Somerville's fleet was nowhere to be seen. However, there was plenty of maritime activity and a warship or two in the harbour. A number were hit and the port installations sustained serious damage, but overall the results of the raid were disappointing. The RAF had put up a small number of Hurricanes, most of which were out-performed and shot down by the nimble Zeros, but together the British fighters and the port's efficient anti-aircraft defences inflicted unwelcome losses on the carrier aircraft. Back aboard, Fuchida expressed his disappointment and obtained Nagumo's permission to search for the British warships. At about noon over fifty aircraft from the *Soryu* discovered the heavy cruisers *Cornwall* and *Dorsetshire* patrolling well to the south of Ceylon, without air cover. Within twenty minutes both had been sent to the bottom. Once again, Fuchida had the satisfaction of knowing that he had earned his day's pay.

Accurate British intelligence reports predicted that Trincomalee, the Royal Navy's second base in Ceylon, would be raided on 8 April. *Hermes* put to sea without her aircraft, but with the Australian destroyer *Vampire* as escort. At 07.30 Fuchida led an attack by over 100 aircraft against the base, the results being similar to those of the raid on Colombo. On his return to *Akagi*, Fuchida was informed that *Hermes* had been located. A force of dive and torpedo bombers was promptly despatched and both warships, with only their own anti-aircraft weapons to rely on, were quickly reduced to a sinking condition.

At this point both Nagumo and Fuchida felt that while their foray into the Indian Ocean had cost the Royal Navy several warships, it did not justify the loss of highly trained aircrew, especially as the training establishments were not sending out replacements of an equivalent standard. Ideally, fully-trained aircrew were an asset that should be preserved for a major action with the Americans, although Nagumo might have compromised if his carriers had been able to engage Admiral Somerville's fleet in a daylight action. Ironically, Somerville would have welcomed a night action in which the Japanese aircrew fought at a disadvantage while his big guns knocked the Japanese carriers about. As it was, both admirals played a game of cat-and-mouse but remained out of contact with each other. Nagumo had also been tasked with assessing the feasibility of supplying the army in Burma by sea. His view was that Rangoon, the only major port, was vulnerable to Allied submarine activity and unable to handle the large quantities of cargo required. Furthermore, Burma's coastal province, the Arakan, was a maze of islands and tortuous chaungs in which Akyab, the only harbour, was little more than a fishing port. A range of jungle-covered mountains up to 2,000 feet in height separated the Arakan from central Burma and in this environment movement during the torrential rains of the monsoon period was extremely difficult. The Arakan, as one British soldier put it, was simply 'not fit to fight in', although both sides fought hard for its possession. Nagumo's conclusions were, *inter alia,* a contributory factor in the decision to build the infamous Burma Railway that cost the lives of many thousands of prisoners of war and local people. Having completed his task and made his presence felt, Nagumo steamed east, out of the Indian Ocean.

If the earlier American air raids had given the Japanese an unpleasant surprise, what happened next generated such alarm and fury in the Japanese home islands that the country's naval and military high command was forced to change its basic policy. On 18 April the carrier USS *Hornet*, escorted by Halsey's *Enterprise* task force, launched no less than sixteen of the Army's twin-engined B-25 Mitchell bombers under Lieutenant Colonel James H. Doolittle. Fully laden, these flew 800 miles to release their bomb loads on Tokyo and other cities in Japan. Some damage was caused but the real results were near-panic among the Japanese civilian population and a boost to American morale. Those aircraft that were not shot down managed to crash land in unoccupied areas of China, and one reached Vladivostok, where the crew were interned by the neutral Russians. True to their *Zeitgeist*, the Japanese beheaded two crewmen who fell into their hands.

Yamamoto felt personally responsible for creating conditions in which the enemy could attack his homeland. He retired into his study where he brooded over the fact for several hours and when he emerged he ordered his staff to take the matter to heart. The feeling among the Japanese High Command was that the time had come for the extension of the Empire's outer defensive perimeter in the south and central Pacific. It would be necessary to secure Midway Island as a base for operations against the American Hawaiian Islands, while possession of southern Papua-New Guinea and the southern Solomon Islands would isolate Australia and interfere with Allied trans-Pacific shipping routes. Furthermore, this outer perimeter would make it even more difficult for the Allies to recover their lost territories.

In fact, this grandiose plan was to have consequences from which Japan would never recover. As already mentioned, the Americans had already cracked the Japanese naval code and were listening to the string of fresh orders that were being issued. At the tactical level the Allies possessed a decisive advantage because of a very remarkable organisation established by the Australian government under Commander Eric Feldt, RAN. This was the Coast Watcher Service, recruited from former planters, traders, colonial officials and officers who had volunteered to stay behind when the Japanese invaded their territories. Aided by loyal natives, they remained in hiding in the jungle, reporting Japanese naval, air and troop movements by radio as they happened, thereby giving advance warning that was often critical to the outcome of an engagement. Their survival depended upon their becoming skilled bushmen and constant movement to confuse the enemy's radio location equipment. If captured, they could expect no mercy.

To initiate the process of fresh expansion, Yamamoto ordered Admiral Shigeyoshi Inouye, commanding the recently established naval base at Rabaul, to establish bases in the southern Solomons and capture Port Moresby on the southern coast of Papua. In the Solomons, Tulagi, off the coast of the major island of Guadalcanal, was occupied without difficulty on 3 May. The Port Moresby operation, however, was rather more complicated. Nagumo had detached Vice Admiral Takeo Takagi with the carriers *Zuikaku* and *Shokaku* with two cruisers and six destroyers to provide cover for the operation while the smaller *Shoho*, a converted submarine depot ship, covered the landings themselves. Simultaneously, Admiral Nimitz ordered Rear Admiral Frank Fletcher's Task Force 17, consisting of the carriers *Yorktown* and *Lexington* with eight cruisers and eleven destroyers to penetrate the Coral Sea.

Late on 6 May a US Army reconnaissance aircraft spotted the Port Moresby invasion force and relayed its position to Fletcher. The following day American carrier aircraft located the *Shoho* and, despite her wild evasive movements, sank her for the loss of just three aircraft. The Japanese assault landing was cancelled immediately and the troop transports headed out of the area. At approximately the same time a Japanese scout plane spotted Fletcher's fleet oiler *Neosho* and her escorting destroyer *Sims*, which were identified respectively as a carrier and a cruiser. Presented with two such apparent prizes, Takagi despatched some sixty bombers that experienced no difficulty in sinking both ships. On their return they were re-armed and sent out again in a rain-laden dusk. Not surprisingly, they found nothing and ditched their ordnance. On the way home one twenty-eight-strong group flew directly over Task Force 17 and found themselves set upon by snarling Wildcat fighters; only seven survived to touch down on a friendly flight deck.

The following morning both sides waded into each other with maximum effort. Two 500lb bombs slammed into the *Shokaku*, damaging her flight deck and starting a serious fire. *Yorktown* was hit by an 800lb bomb that exploded inside her. *Lexington* was hit by two torpedoes and two bombs. Her damage control parties struggled for five hours but finally had to accept that the ship was beyond saving. A burning hulk, she was sunk by five torpedoes from the USS *Phelps*. Remarkably, over 2,700 of her crew survived, but 216 died with her. *Zuikaku* escaped damage and was able to absorb *Shokaku's* surviving aircraft.

So ended the Battle of the Coral Sea, the first naval battle in history in which the contending ships never sighted each other. American losses amounted to sixty-six aircraft, 543 men killed, a tanker, a destroyer and the fleet carrier *Lexington* and a second fleet carrier, *Yorktown*, seriously damaged. Japanese losses were put at seventy-seven aircraft, 1,074 men and the light carrier *Shoho*. On the basis of tonnage sunk the Japanese claimed a victory. Masanori Ito adds the destroyer *Kikuruki* and three auxiliary vessels to the Imperial Navy's toll of losses, but still claims a Japanese victory. However, as the Germans found in the aftermath of Jutland, physical losses are not the whole story. The most important result of the battle was that the Japanese had to cancel and re-plan their Port Moresby operation.

The new plan involved converging thrusts from Milne Bay, on the eastern tip of New Guinea, and from Buna on the north coast across the Owen Stanley Range by means of the Kokoda Trail. On 24 August a coastwatcher reported seven landing barges moving in the direction of Milne Bay along the northern coast. The following day Kittyhawks were scrambled from Milne Bay's three airstrips, driving the barges ashore on Goodenough Island and setting them ablaze, thereby leaving the 350 infantrymen aboard completely stranded. However, during the night of 25/26 August the Japanese put a regimental-sized group and several light tanks ashore at Ahioma on the bay's eastern shore. The Japanese could only advance along the narrow strip of land between the sea and mountains clad in impenetrable jungle and restricted themselves to night attacks. They made slow but steady progress until their two leading tanks were knocked out and the remainder bogged down. Reinforced by 800 naval infantry, they reached the edge of the bay's most easterly airstrip but failed to capture it with a series of desperate charges. The Australians counter-attacked and pushed them back towards their landing area. Ships entered the bay during the night of 5/6 September and daylight revealed that the enemy had gone. The Australians lost 161 men killed or missing and about the same number wounded, while over 600 Japanese had been killed. Though small in scale, the fighting provided the Allies with their first indisputable victory and exploded the myth of the Japanese superman.

The second and major thrust at Port Moresby confirmed the result. On 21 July Major General Tomitoro Horii's South Seas Detachment, containing some 13,000 veterans from China, Malaya and the Philippines, began landing at Buna. They began moving along the precipitous, switchback Kokoda Trail at once. Exhaustion and tropical diseases quickly began thinning their ranks. The lessons of Malaya had been taken to heart and this time there were no captured food dumps to feed from as they had been back-loaded out of harm's way. When, on 17 September, the Japanese reached Imita Ridge, just thirty miles from Port Moresby, they had already sustained the loss of 1,000 men killed and 1,500 wounded, more than three times that of the Australians. Their logistic system had broken down, many were suffering from tropical diseases, most were on the verge of starvation, and now they were confronted by a formidable defensive position, any attack against which was doomed to failure. As it happened, no such attack was made as Imperial General Headquarters in Tokyo, taken aback by the failure of the Milne Bay operation, disheartened by the lack of progress towards Port Moresby and worried by the prospect of an Allied landing at Buna, sent Horii a signal on the night of 24 September ordering him to leave the Owen Stanley Range and concentrate on defending his base. The Australians followed up his untidy withdrawal, fighting their way through weak rearguard positions. The way was marked by fresh corpses and gleaming skeletons from the earlier fighting, stripped clean by ants. Horii himself never reached Buna, having drowned while trying to cross the Kumasi River on a raft.

Following Horii's death the Japanese forces in New Guinea were designated the Eighteenth Army and placed under the command of Lieutenant General Hatazo Adachi, who wisely established his headquarters in distant Rabaul. Reinforcements were rushed into Buna where they demonstrated the traditional Japanese skill in constructing extensive field fortifications with interlocking arcs of fire around the perimeter. These were reinforced with earth-filled oil drums and roofed with layers of palm logs and earth so that they were only vulnerable to a direct hit from a heavy-calibre round. They were then expertly camouflaged and the fire slits covered with transplanted greenery, making them invisible save at close quarters. Several bunkers might be connected by crawl passages to form a complex. Most Japanese preferred to die in their bunkers rather than escape from them. When Buna finally fell to MacArthur's Australian-American army on 22 January 1943 some 7,000 Japanese had been killed in its defence. About 1,200 sick and wounded were evacuated by sea and 1,000 managed to escape to Lae.

The only Japanese remaining in New Guinea were located in small pockets on the north coast or on offshore islands. There was no hope for them as they could only be supplied or reinforced intermittently because the Japanese hold on the sea lanes had finally been broken. Together, the fighting at Milne Bay, along the Kokoda Trail and at Buna, removed the threat to Australia and created a virtual prison camp for over 100,000 Japanese soldiers. In the eighteen months following the capture of Buna, MacArthur remorselessly pursued his advantage with a series of landings that resulted in the piecemeal destruction of the battered, disorganised and fragmented Japanese Eighteenth Army.

CHAPTER 10

Who Will Tell the Emperor?

To achieve a war's final, crushing victory in a major decisive battle was a constant theme running throughout Japanese naval history. That was how Yamamoto had been brought up and now he intended to make the Midway extension of the new Japanese expanded strategy produce the required result. Midway Atoll was situated halfway across the Pacific and consisted of just three square miles of land above sea level. However, on this tiny space the Americans had built an air base and if it was threatened Admiral Nimitz could hardly avoid reacting to the threat. Yamamoto's plans, therefore, were intended to draw the remnants of the Pacific Fleet into an action that would result in its destruction and were made in the misplaced belief that both American carriers had been sunk during the Battle of the Coral Sea, when the truth was that the *Yorktown*, though badly damaged, had reached Pearl Harbor, where the dockyard crews were working round the clock to restore her to fighting trim. Furthermore, Nimitz had strengthened his fleet by the arrival of the carriers *Enterprise* and *Hornet* (Task Force 16) the commander of which, Vice Admiral William F. Halsey, was ill and required immediate hospitalisation, his place being taken by Rear Admiral Raymond A. Spruance. Having replenished, Spruance's carriers left Pearl Harbor on 28 May and, escorted by six cruisers and nine destroyers, headed for the operational area indicated by intercepts of the Japanese radio traffic. *Yorktown*, the surviving carrier of TF 17, had entered Pearl Harbor the previous day and after forty-eight hours of working around the clock, sailed again on 30 May under Rear Admiral Frank Fletcher's command, accompanied by two cruisers and five destroyers. Fletcher also assumed overall command when his ships joined TF 16 in an area designated Point

Luck, some 350 miles north-east of Midway. In addition, the large Japanese carriers that had fought in the Coral Sea battle would not be ready for action for some time to come, *Shokaku* because she was in need of major repair and *Zuikaku* because casualties among her air crew had been serious and the replacements needed time to settle down and reach the required standard.

Notwithstanding this increment to the American's strength, Yamamoto's fleet still possessed the greater number of carriers. Like the majority of Japanese operational plans, what he proposed was complex and contained elements of bluff and double bluff that he hoped would confuse the Americans. A Northern Force under Vice Admiral Hoshiro Hosagaya, led by Rear Admiral Kakuta's 2nd Carrier Striking Force, consisting of the small carriers *Ryujo* and *Junyo*, two cruisers and three destroyers, was to leave northern Honshu for the Aleutians on 25 May, followed two days later by escorted transports carrying the troops detailed for the invasion of Attu and Kiska Islands. If Admiral Nimitz attempted to intervene he would be intercepted by a Guard Force under Vice Admiral Shiro Takasu, consisting of four battleships, two cruisers and twelve destroyers, which had been positioned on the direct route between Pearl Harbor and the Aleutians. Meanwhile, Vice Admiral Chuichi Nagumo's 1st Carrier Striking Force, consisting of the fleet carriers *Akagi, Kaga, Hiryu* and *Soryu*, with an escort consisting of two battleships, four cruisers, a light cruiser and eight destroyers under the command of Vice Admiral Nobutake Kondo, was to neutralise Midway's defences with an air attack on 4 June. Following this, the Invasion Force would take possession of the atoll with direct gunfire support provided by four heavy cruisers and two destroyers under Vice Admiral Takeo Kurita. The Japanese Main Body, commanded personally by Yamamoto aboard his new flagship *Yamato*, one of two super-battleships armed with eight 18-inch guns, plus two 16-inch gun battleships, the light carrier *Zuiho*, a light cruiser, nine destroyers and two seaplane tenders, was positioned centrally so that it could intervene decisively, however Nimitz chose to react. To this end, two flying boats delivered by submarine to French Frigate

Shoal, some 500 miles north-west of Hawaii, were to keep Pearl
Harbor under observation from 31 May until 3 June and report on
American activity. In addition, submarine patrol lines were to be
established north, north-west and west of Hawaii by 2 June.

Yamamoto seemed to have thought of everything, little suspecting
that the enemy were in possession of the broad outline of his plans.
Nimitz identified the threat to the Aleutians but was more concerned
about the security of Alaska and directed a task force of five cruisers
and ten destroyers in that direction. At sea, Fletcher enjoyed the
definite advantage of being aware of the enemy's general intentions,
while Yamamoto was not even aware of his presence. In fact, both
carrier task forces had sailed over the Japanese patrol lines before
the scouting submarines had reached them and the flying boat
mission was cancelled when French Frigate Shoal was found to
be in American hands. Against this, although he obviously had no
idea as to the precise figures, Fletcher knew that he was seriously
outnumbered. His three carriers would be opposed by the enemy's
five, he had no battleships at all, his eight cruisers would be pitted
against sixteen, and fourteen destroyers against forty-six. In the
air, the situation was more balanced for although he could put up
230 aircraft against the Japanese 262, another fifty aircraft based on
Midway could be added to the equation.

Early on 3 June a Catalina flying boat based on Midway sighted
the Japanese some 700 miles west of the atoll. Later in the day nine
USAAF B-17 bombers delivered a high altitude bombing attack on
the enemy ships without loss to either side. During the night bright
moonlight encouraged four Catalinas to mount a torpedo strike in
which a tanker was hit but not sunk. Details of these actions were
transmitted to Fletcher who ordered TFs 16 and 17 to concentrate at
a position 200 miles north of Midway.

With the eastern sky lightening in a pre-dawn glow on 4 June, scout
aircraft left Nagumo's 1st Carrier Striking Force to fan out across an
area extending 300 miles to the east and south. Simultaneously, the
decks of his four large carriers were a scene of busy preparation
as Kate torpedo bombers and Val dive-bombers were both armed

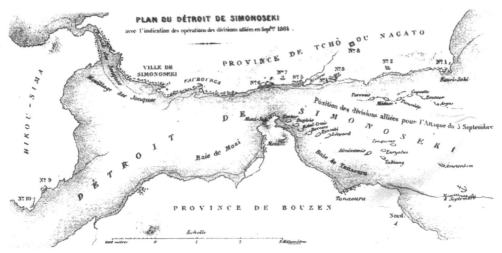

A pictorial map of British and allied warships forcing the Strait of Simonoseki in 1864, an encounter that convinced the Japanese that they must have a modern navy. *US Navy Historical Records Centre*

The Battle of the Yalu River during the Sino-Japanese War. The Chinese ships are distinguished by triangular pennants showing the Chinese Imperial dragon. The warship in the foreground is the ironclad *Chen Yuen*. *Battles of the Nineteenth Century*

The Battle of the Yalu River. The destruction of the *King Yuen*. *Battles of the Nineteenth Century*

A triptych by a Japanese artist depicting the battle. The fact that almost all the seamen are wounded and their ship has sustained extensive damage suggests that the Chinese were actually held in some respect. *Boston Museum of Fine Art*

Admiral Togo's flagship *Mikasa* has been preserved as a memorial to the admiral. Togo is regarded in Japan as the Admiral Nelson of the Far East. *US Navy Historical Records Centre*

The Russo-Japanese War. Japanese artillerymen manning one of the heavy siege guns that destroyed Port Arthur's fortifications. *US Navy Historical Records Centre*

Admiral Togo's fleet heads off the Russian Pacific Squadron as it makes a vain attempt to escape from Port Arthur to Vladivostok. *US Navy Historical Records Centre*

The remnant of the Russian Pacific Squadron returned to Port Arthur where they came under fire, not only from the besiegers' artillery but also from Togo's warships outside the harbour. Their wrecks are seen here resting on the bottom of the harbour. *US Navy Historical Records Centre*

The Battle of Tsu Shima. Admiral Rozhestvensky's flagship *Suvoroff*, having led the Russian fleet round the world from the Baltic, was quickly battered into a dis-masted, sinking wreck by accurate Japanese gunnery. *US Navy Historical Records Centre*

The Battle of Tsu Shima. Rozhestvensky had assembled every warship he could lay his hands on, including a number of unsuitable coast defence vessels that he scathingly referred to as 'flat irons'. That shown here is the *Admiral Apraxin*. *US Navy Historical Records Centre*

Despite this, the *Admiral Ushakov*, another of the 'flat irons', distinguished herself and went down fighting. There were no survivors. *US Navy Historical Records Centre*

A rare Japanese postcard showing the surrender of the surviving Russian warships by Admiral Nebogatoff on the morning after the battle. *Boston Museum of Fine Art*

In 1937 Japanese aircraft sank the river gunboat USS *Panay* on the Yangste River without the slightest provocation. *US Navy Historical Records Centre*

Pearl Harbor under attack, as seen from the cockpit of a Japanese aircraft. Ford Island is in the centre of the photograph with bombs exploding beside Battleship Row. *US Navy Historical Records Centre*

Ford Island Naval Air Station in Pearl Harbor following the Japanese attack, with Battleship Row beyond. The aircraft in the centre of the picture is a Catalina flying boat. *US Navy Historical Records Centre*

Alvin Henning's painting showing the final minutes of the defence of Wake Island. *US Marine Corps*

The Battle of Midway. The carrier USS *Yorktown* sustained damage during an air attack on the first day of the battle, although the ship remained operational thanks to the efforts of her damage control parties. *US Navy Historical Records Centre*

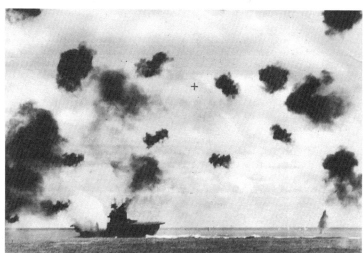

The Battle of Midway. *The Famous Four Minutes*, a painting by R.G. Smith illustrating a defining moment of the Pacific War when Dauntless dive bombers flying from the carriers *Enterprise* and *Yorktown* destroyed the Japanese carriers *Kaga*, *Akagi* and *Soryu* in just four minutes. *US Navy Historical Records Centre*

The Battle of Midway. *Hiryu*, the sole survivor of the Japanese carriers present, was destroyed on the second day of the battle. An internal explosion seems to have blown her forward lift backwards so that it resembles the lid of a sardine tin. *US Navy Historical Records Centre*

The Battle of Midway. *Yorktown* sustained further damage from air attack on the second day of the battle. Here, seamen and aircrew make their way along the heavily listing flight deck. *US Navy Historical Records Centre*

The Battle of Midway. *Yorktown* received her death wound from torpedoes fired by the Japanese submarine *I-168*, one of which also sank the destroyer *Hamman*. The carrier sank shortly after this photograph was taken. *US Navy Historical Records Centre*

The Battle of Midway. American aircraft turned the Japanese heavy cruiser *Mikuma* into a battered, sinking wreck as she withdrew from the scene of the action. *US Navy Historical Records Centre*

Alarming but nothing more. In the aftermath of the battle one of the destroyer *Phelps'* fuel oil tanks ran dry, resulting in lost suction and a huge cloud of smoke that was alarming but harmless. The cruiser *Atlanta* offered assistance but *Phelps* managed to sort out her own problems. *US Navy Historical Records Centre*

Dauntless dive bombers commence their dive towards an enemy vessel making smoke far below. *US Navy Historical Records Centre*

Japanese shipping under air attack take violent evasive action. *(US Navy Historical Records Centre)*

The Battle of the Philippine Sea virtually destroyed what remained of Japan's naval aviation strength. *(US Navy Historical Records Centre)*

A Kate torpedo bomber blown apart and set ablaze by the impact of a 5-inch shell. The torpedo can be seen falling away from its mounting clamps on the aircraft. *(US Navy Historical Records Centre)*

The Fabuki class Japanese destroyer *Amogiri* (Heavenly Mist) served off China, Malaya, the Solomon Islands, in the Indian Ocean and at the Battle of Midway. She is, however, best remembered for running down the American *PT 109*, commanded by Lieutenant John F. Kennedy, the future President of the United States. *US Navy Historical Records Centre*

During the Solomon Islands campaign Japanese transports frequently ran themselves aground, this being the only way of delivering their cargo. *US Navy Historical Records Centre*

During the naval Battle of Guadalcanal on 14-15 November 1942, the Japanese battleship *Kirishima* was sunk within seven minutes by the accurate fire of the USS *Washington*. *US Navy Historical Records Centre*

Three torpedoes from the Japanese submarine *I-19* initiated a series of fires and explosions that finally destroyed the USS *Wasp* off the Eastern Solomons on 15 September 1942. *Wasp* was unique among American carriers as she had flown reinforcement aircraft to Malta earlier that year.

Nothing could be taken for granted. Gun crews aboard an American cruiser strain to identify the nationality of a strange aircraft overhead. *US Navy Historical Records Centre*

The Invasion of the Philippines

The crew of the destroyer *Barton* claim a victim for the twin high-angle mountings of their 5-inch guns. *US Navy Historical Records Centre*

Smoke billows from sinking Japanese warships attacked by American aircraft supporting landings in Ormoc Bay, Leyte Island. *US Navy Historical Records Centre*

The Battle of Leyte Gulf. The Japanese battleship *Fuso* formed part of Admiral Nishimura's force during the battle. She was sunk during a torpedo attack carried out by American destroyers. *US Navy Historical Records Centre*

The Battle of Leyte Gulf. An early view of the Japanese battleship *Nagato* showing her original tripod command tower. *Nagato* formed part of Admiral Nishimura's force during the battle and was damaged by air attack. *US Navy Historical Records Centre*

The Battle of Leyte Gulf, action off Samar. American destroyers make smoke to conceal the withdrawal of their escort carriers. *US Navy Historical Records Centre*

The Battle of Leyte Gulf, action off Samar. The last sighting of the escort carrier *Gambier Bay*, on fire, abandoned and surrounded by shell bursts. *US Navy Historical Records Centre*

The Battle of Leyte Gulf, action off Cape Engano. The Japanese hybrid battleship/carrier *Ise* takes a hit on her forecastle. *US Navy Historical Records Centre*

A suicide bomber smashes into the forward lift of the USS *Enterprise*, blowing most of it into the air, 14 May 1945. *US Navy Historical Records Centre*

Damage control parties working on the fire caused by a suicide bomber below *Enterprise*'s forward lift. *US Navy Historical Records Centre*

The end of *Yamato*, the world's largest battleship, which had been despatched on a suicide mission to assist the defenders of Okinawa but was intercepted and sunk by American aircraft before she reached the battle zone. A bomb can be seen exploding on the ship's A Turret. *US Navy Historical Records Centre*

On 2 September 1945, senior Japanese officers and politicians boarded the battleship USS *Missouri* to sign the formal document of surrender, watched by representatives of all the Allied nations. *US Navy Historical Records Centre*

The end of it all. Photographed on 9 October 1945, the heavy cruiser *Aoba* rests on the bottom of Kure harbour, having been sunk by American air attacks the previous 18 and 24 July. All that now remained of the once-mighty Imperial Navy was a handful of miscellaneous warships and some sunken hulks like the *Aoba*. The Imperial Navy was never resurrected. In its place Japan's Self Defence Force maintains a small naval element. *US Navy Historical Records Centre*

with bombs while the pilots of the escorting Zeros went through their final pre-flight routines. By 04.45 the raiders were well on their way to Midway. Some thirty-five minutes later a Catalina was spotted shadowing the carriers. More Zeros were scrambled to intercept it, but by then the flying boat had vanished into a cloud and its radio operator was transmitting details of Nagumo's force, its composition, course and speed, together with a warning that a heavy enemy raid was heading towards Midway. By 06.03 Fletcher was aware that Nagumo was just 200 miles away to the south-west. TF-16 was ordered to proceed in that direction and attack as soon as the Japanese carriers had been located, followed by Fletcher himself as soon as *Yorktown* had recovered her scout aircraft.

As soon as the raiders had been picked up on Midway's radar the bombers and flying boats were flown south out of harm's way while the island's Marine Corps fighters, mainly obsolete Brewster Buffalos, climbed to their combat height and a counter-strike force of ten Avenger and Devastator torpedo bombers headed for the enemy carriers. In the ensuing brawl the garrison lost all but five of its fighters but shot down four of the enemy in return and damaged more, plus two Zeros and a further three shot down by anti-aircraft fire. Hangars and other installations were damaged, but the officer leading the attackers, a Lieutenant Joichi Tomonaga, signalled Nagumo at 07.00 to the effect that a second raid would be required to suppress the island's defences. At about the same time Midway's counter-strike arrived and although it proved possible to evade the slow-running American torpedoes of the time and shoot down all but three of the attackers, it was clear that the garrison was still full of fight. At that moment Kates, armed with torpedoes, were ranged on the decks of *Akagi* and *Kaga*. Nagumo gave orders that they should be struck down and re-armed with fragmentation, incendiary and high explosive bombs, a process that would take about an hour.

However, at 07.28 he received a report from one of his scout aircraft, the launch of which had been delayed by technical problems with her catapult. The transmission reported the presence of ten apparently enemy ships about 240 miles from Midway, but did not specify their type. This placed Nagumo on the horns of a terrible dilemma, for if the enemy force included carriers he must strike as soon as he was within range. At 07.45 he gave orders that the Kates should be re-armed with torpedoes and armour-piercing bombs. The admiral relaxed visibly when, at 08.10, the scout aircraft described the composition of the American group as being five cruisers and five destroyers.

Shortly after, Midway's second counter-strike came in. It was delivered by fifteen B-17s which attacked from 20,000 feet and twenty-six dive-bombers and light bombers that came in much lower. Their reception was less severe and only accounted for two Vindicators. The attack was watched through his periscope by Lieutenant William Brockman, commanding the American submarine *Nautilus*, which he had successfully brought through Nagumo's screen of escorts. Brockman noted a large number of near misses but no hits. He decided to join in the action and fired two torpedoes at a battleship. The track of one and the plume of spray was spotted. *Nautilus* was immediately treated to such protracted depth-charging that Brockman was forced to take her down to 150 feet and stay there until things had quietened down. His courage deserved a better reward, for his target had swerved out of the way of one torpedo while the second had jammed in its tube.

While the raid was in progress the scout aircraft came through again. Its' pilot confirmed that the American group *did*, after all contain a carrier. At that moment the aircraft which had raided Midway began to return, some of them shot up and all of them short of fuel. Nagumo sought advice, but it was contradictory and made it clear that the final decision was his. His deputy, Rear Admiral Tamon Yamaguchi, was for an immediate strike against the American task force. Against this, his operations officer, Commander Minoru Genda, commented that he was opposed to wasting either aircraft or trained pilots. Carriers were unable to launch and recover aircraft simultaneously, and if the strike was mounted those now returning from Midway would have to ditch.

It would take just half an hour to recover Tomonaga's force, after which the strike against the American task force could proceed. Nagumo accepted this and every aircraft on deck was struck while the raiders landed. Refuelling and rearming began at once, the aircraft being brought up and re-ranged as soon as they were ready. At 09.18 Nagumo ordered the 1st Carrier Striking Force to steer towards the reported American task force.

Admiral Spruance's aircraft had begun lifting off their flight decks at 07.02, but all had not gone well for them by any means. In four groups, they had headed for Nagumo's estimated position but because of the Japanese change of course they found nothing. *Hornet*'s dive-bombers and their fighter escort flew on until lack of fuel forced the former either to land on Midway or return to the ship, while all the fighters ditched in the sea. At about 09.30, however, the torpedo bombers from *Enterprise* and *Hornet*, under the command respectively of Lieutenant Commanders Eugene Lindsey and John Waldron, had turned south and were rewarded almost immediately by the sight of the enemy's funnel smoke. Although they were out of contact with their fighters, they decided to launch an immediate attack, knowing that it would be virtually suicidal. Waldron attacked first, his slow Devastators diving low through the wall of anti-aircraft fire coming up from the escorting cruisers and destroyers, only to be bounced by the Zeros of the carrier's combat air patrols. A few torpedoes were launched but failed to find a mark and the attack ended in virtual massacre. Five minutes later it was the turn of Lindsey's squadron. *Soryu* and *Hiryu* were near missed but only four of Waldron's ten aircraft survived.

The *Yorktown*'s air group arrived shortly after, having set off later than those of TF-16 but flown straight to the target area. Lieutenant Commander Lance Massey, commanding *Yorktown*'s torpedo bombers, decided that, as the earlier attacks had been delivered against the enemy's port side, he would attack from the opposite side at about 10.25. The results of the attack were the same. Only two Devastators survived, while one Wildcat was shot down and two driven off with serious damage. Understandably, there was wild jubilation among the Japanese carrier crews, now convinced more than ever that the 1st Carrier Striking Force was absolutely invincible. Unfortunately for those celebrating, within minutes events would take place that would alter the entire complexion of the battle.

Enterprise's dive bomber squadron, under Lieutenant Commander C. Wade McClusky, had reached the estimated point of interception only to find a deserted sea. McClusky had continued on a south-westerly direction for a while before starting a sweep to the north-west. Through a break in the clouds he spotted a Japanese destroyer travelling at high speed. She was the *Arashi*, left behind to continue depth charging the *Nautilus*, and now hurrying to catch up with the rest of the fleet. McClusky correctly deduced her intention and decided to follow. He arrived above Nagumo's carriers just as *Yorktown's* dive-bombers, under Lieutenant Commander Maxwell Leslie, were approaching from the west.

On board the carriers most eyes were watching the destruction of the Wildcats and Devastators, whose self sacrifice had not been in vain. Nagumo had just given the order to launch a counter strike against the American task forces and the attention of most senior officers was concentrated on their flight decks, where the massed aircraft were ranked tightly together. Then, at about 10.25, the rising roar of aero engines overhead made them glance up. To their horror, they saw the first of McClusky's and Leslie's thirty-five Dauntless dive-bombers, growing larger by the second as they bored down on their targets. In desperation the Zeros of the combat air patrol, their ammunition almost expended, strove to gain height, but it was too late.

In *Akagi*, Nagumo's flagship, one bomb landed among the packed aircraft. Exploding petrol tanks, bombs and torpedoes creating a giant fireball which killed everyone in the vicinity and threw wrecked aircraft about like toys. A second bomb smashed its way through the flight deck and exploded in the hangar below, where the discarded bombs from successive re-armings still lay about. Explosions followed each other in succession and raging fires rapidly became infernos as they were fed by ruptured fuel lines. The carrier's commander, Captain Taijiro Aoki, knew that the ship was doomed and managed to persuade Nagumo to transfer to the light cruiser *Nagara*.

Aboard *Kaga*, one bomb exploded just forward of the carrier's superstructure, hitting a parked fuel truck. A huge fireball swept back over the bridge, incinerating everyone on it. Three more bombs landed among the ranks of parked aircraft, triggering such fires and explosions that it was immediately apparent that the ship was beyond saving. On *Soryu* the story was much the same. One bomb smashed its way through to the hangar deck. Its explosion blasted the aircraft lift back against the bridge. Two more landed among the parked aircraft, starting more explosions and fires. Within twenty minutes the order was given to abandon ship. In the meantime, Brockman had brought *Nautilus* forward to join in the action. He fired a torpedo that struck *Kaga*, only to suffer the too common disappointment of the time in having it fail to explode.

The three blazing hulks continued to burn for the rest of the day. One observer recalled that the sound resembled huge blow torches. *Kaga* and *Soryu* went down during the evening, but *Akagi* had to be despatched with torpedoes fired from one of her own destroyers. Most of the combat air patrol's Zero pilots were now without a home but flew on until their fuel was exhausted then splashed down beside one of the escorts to await rescue.

It had taken just ten dramatic minutes to alter the balance of power in the Pacific. The carrier *Hiryu* had avoided destruction because her earlier manoeuvres to avoid the torpedo attack had taken her some distance from her sisters, and when the American dive-bombers appeared she had been concealed by cloud cover. Aboard her, Rear Admiral Yamaguchi ordered a retaliatory strike which began leaving the carrier at 11.00, following the direction taken by the American aircraft. Shortly after noon they were picked up by *Yorktown's* radar and were shot to pieces by the combat air patrol and anti-aircraft fire. Nevertheless, several Vals bored in to land three bombs on the carrier. The first started a hangar fire but this was brought under control as the fuel system had been drained down and flooded with inert carbon dioxide gas. The second penetrated deep into the ship, starting fires that threatened the forward fuel tanks and magazine until they too had been brought under control. The third exploded inside the funnel, extinguishing half-a-dozen furnaces and destroying three boiler uptakes. The carrier slowed down and twenty minutes later was lying dead in the water. Fletcher handed over tactical control of the battle to Spruance, some sixty miles distant, and transferred his flag to the cruiser *Astoria*.

The opinion was that *Yorktown* would have to be taken in tow, but her engineers managed to effect repairs and she managed to work up to 20 knots. At that moment the second wave of the Japanese strike appeared. It consisted of escorted torpedo bombers and was led with suicidal courage by Lieutenant Tomonaga, who insisted on taking part in the raid although he knew that his tanks contained only sufficient fuel for a one-way trip. Once more, many of the attackers fell victim to the American fighters and anti-aircraft fire, but two torpedoes slammed into *Yorktown*'s port side, blasting holes in her fuel tanks. Water flooded into her hull, quickly producing a list of 26 degrees. All power was lost and at 15.00 her commander, Captain Elliot Buckmaster, believing that a capsize was a real possibility, ordered his crew to prepare to abandon ship. Stubbornly, *Yorktown* remained afloat and refused to roll.

Over on *Enterprise*, Spruance was fully aware that a fourth Japanese carrier was still at large and at this juncture received a report on her whereabouts from one of *Yorktown*'s search aircraft. At 15.30 twenty-four dive-bombers, including ten that had flown across from *Yorktown*, took off from *Enterprise*, followed by sixteen more from *Hornet*. Yamaguchi's combat air patrol, by now reduced to just thirteen Zeros, failed to spot them until they commenced their dive in succession at about 17.00. In a desperate but vain attempt to avoid the rain of bombs, *Hiryu* twisted and turned this way and that. One bomb peeled back the forward lift like the lid of a sardine tin and four more initiated the same sequence of explosions and fires that had destroyed her sisters. Hardly had the dive-bombers droned away than a fresh attack was delivered by Midway's B-17 bombers. No hits were recorded but coming on top of the day's earlier events their arrival served to confirm the magnitude of the Japanese failure. *Hiryu's* crew fought the flames until 02.30, then abandoned their hopeless task. The ship was then torpedoed and sunk by her escorting destroyers.

By then, Yamamoto, some 350 miles distant with his Main Body, had already received the shattering news that not only were Midway's defences still intact, but also that Nagumo had lost all his carriers. He despatched the light carrier *Zuiho* to render such assistance as she was able, then, in towering rage, assembled his battleships and began steering east at speed in the hope of using his heavy guns to batter the American task force to destruction. This was exactly what Spruance expected him to do, so he also steered an eastward course, maintaining the same distance between the two fleets. Gradually, Yamamoto recovered his composure. By 02.55 he accepted the point that the striking range of the American carriers was thirty times that of his battleships. He ordered a general withdrawal, together with a dawn bombardment of Midway by Vice Admiral Takao Kurita's squadron of four heavy cruisers.

What followed seemed to confirm that Japan's glory days had finally come to an end. As Kurita's cruisers were approaching the atoll from the west they spotted the American submarine *Tambor*, commanded by Lieutenant Commander John W. Murphy, observing them in the moonlight. She dived almost immediately but Kurita was not inclined to take chances and ordered his ships to make an emergency turn to port. At the rear of the column the flashed signal was not seen by *Mogami* and she collided with the next ahead, *Mikuma*, sustaining very serious damage. Kurita decided to abort his mission and, leaving *Mikuma* and two destroyers to escort the crippled *Mogami*, he set off to rejoin the fleet.

Tambor transmitted a contact report at 03.00. At 06.00 Midway's B-17s took off but were unable to find the ships because of an early morning haze. However, at 06.30 a Catalina reported 'two battleships (sic) streaming oil' 125 miles west of the island. Marine dive-bombers took off and, using the oil slick as a pointer, were able to launch an attack shortly after 08.00. No direct hits were scored but Captain Richard E. Fleming's burning aircraft crashed on top of *Mikuma*'s after turret. Petrol poured down the starboard engine room intakes and exploded below, killing the crew and causing extensive damage. Both cruisers were now forced to proceed at a mere 12 knots.

During the afternoon of 5 June Spruance learned that Yamamoto could be found in the general area of the previous day's action. A strike of fifty-eight dive-bombers was launched but found only Commander Motomi Katsumi's destroyer *Tanikaze*, sent by Nagumo to confirm that the *Hiryu* had finally sunk. Somehow, Katsumi managed to avoid every bomb aimed at his twisting, turning, circling ship, including a number dropped by a later B-17 strike, and even managed to shoot down one of his attackers. The only damage sustained by the destroyer came from a near miss when a bomb fragment penetrated her No. 3 turret, causing an explosion that killed the six men inside.

For some reason, *Yorktown* refused to sink in the immediate aftermath of the battle. A salvage party boarded her at noon on 5 June and she was taken on tow. Unfortunately, other people had also noted that she was still afloat. The cruiser *Chikuma* was also visiting the area of the battle that morning and signalled the fact to Yamamoto. The admiral promptly signalled Lieutenant Commander Yahachi Tanabe, commanding the submarine *I-168*, ordering him to sink her.

During the previous night *I-168* had been bombarding Midway. On receipt of Yamamoto's order, Tanabe set a course for *Yorktown*'s reported position, 150 miles to the north. By first light on 6 June he was in a position to observe the crippled carrier from the west, with the sky still dark behind him. Slipping beneath the escorting destroyers he launched four torpedoes then made good his escape. The first struck the destroyer *Hammann*, moored alongside *Yorktown* and providing electric power for the salvage crew, sending her to the bottom. Two more exploded against the carrier's starboard side, blasting huge holes through which the sea poured into the hull. Even then, she refused to give up easily and did not slip under until 06.00 on 7 June.

Yamamoto, aware of the desperate straits in which *Mikuma* and *Mogami* found themselves, despatched *Zuiho,* six cruisers and eight destroyers to their assistance under Vice Admiral Nobutake Kondo. Unfortunately for the stricken cruisers, Admiral Spruance's dive-bombers found them first, sinking *Mikuma* and inflicting yet more damage on *Mogami.* The latter, with forty feet of her bows missing, somehow succeeded in reaching her base at Truk because of the fine seamanship of her skipper, Captain Akira Soji, and the work of her damage control officer, Lieutenant Suruwatari.

The Battle of Midway, one of the most decisive in naval history, was over. Spruance ended his pursuit and reversed course to rendezvous with his supply tankers. When an immediate reckoning was made the Americans had lost one carrier and a destroyer sunk, 147 land- and carrier-based aircraft, and 307 men killed. Japanese losses amounted to four carriers and one heavy cruiser sunk, one heavy cruiser and two destroyers seriously damaged, 332 aircraft (including those being transported to Midway for operational use after its capture), and approximately 3,500 men killed. As Commander-in-Chief of the Combined Fleet it was Yamamoto's duty to inform the Emperor that the Imperial Navy had sustained a disastrous defeat, the full consequences of which had yet to be felt. There was little the Emperor could say beyond thanking the Admiral for his courtesy, but in private he no doubt recalled Yamamoto's forecast that for the first six months of the war the Navy would have things all its own way, but that after that the future could not be predicted.

The loss of face was not to be borne. Imperial General Headquarters maintained a stranglehold on whatever was released for publication in the Japanese press. Now, it spun whatever happened into a fantasy of wishful thinking. There had been a wonderful victory near the Aleutian Islands, it said, in which one American carrier had been sunk and another damaged. Now Attu and Kiska, two western islands in the chain, formed part of the Japanese Empire and were to become ramparts in its expanded northern perimeter. The truth, of course, was that the Americans had never had any intention of defending these bleak, unwanted specks in the far north, and the Japanese didn't really want them either. Attu was recaptured without difficulty on 11 May 1943 and Kiska was abandoned by the Japanese shortly after. The Midway press release also mentioned, in passing, that there had been a naval action in the vicinity of Midway, the term 'action' being used deliberately to downgrade the event from 'battle'. The survivors of sunken ships were absolutely forbidden to discuss the terrible defeat Japan had suffered until they were re-assigned to warships operating far from the home islands. Yet, murder will out and not even the *kempetai* could control the whispered discussion of the disaster. Among the Navy's senior officers disbelief was followed by shock, followed by alarm that so many experienced aircrew had been lost, and anxiety about the quality of their replacements. There was, however, no sense of defeatism and a fierce determination that the next round of the war would be fought as hard as any in the Empire's history.

CHAPTER 11

Quarter Never Asked,
Seldom Given

In June 1942 Captain Martin Clemens, a Coast Watcher stationed on Guadalcanal in the Solomon Islands, reported that the Japanese were constructing a major airfield near Lunga Point. The implications were extremely serious as bombers stationed there could interdict the supply route between the United States and Australia while fighters could provide cover for strikes against American bases in the New Hebrides to the south. In fact, in the wake of the major Japanese defeat at Midway, the American Joint Chiefs of Staff were already planning to take the offensive in this area. Now, it was decided that the new airfield and the island of Tulagi would be captured by Major General Alexander A. Vandergrift's reinforced 1st Marine Division.

In overall command of the operation was Vice Admiral Robert L. Ghormley, whose headquarters was situated at Noumea on the island of New Caledonia. Command at sea was exercised by Rear Admiral Fletcher with a task force containing the carriers *Saratoga*, *Enterprise* and *Wasp*, while the amphibious element, consisting of four US cruisers, three Australian cruisers, nineteen US destroyers and nineteen troop transports, was commanded by Rear Admiral Richmond Kelly Turner.

The marines landed on 7 August and experienced no difficulty in chasing the construction troops off the airfield and into the jungle, although the Japanese on Tulagi Island fought to the death. The airfield itself, now named Henderson Field after a marine officer who had been killed at the Battle of Midway, was completed and open for use by what became known as the Cactus Air Force by the end of the month. A fighter airstrip, designated Fighter One, was constructed 2,000 yards east of the main airfield and completed on 9 September.

The reaction of the Japanese to the American incursion into their very back yard was rapid and violent. Those troops who should have captured Midway atoll were now loaded into transports and given the task of recapturing Henderson Field. At the Imperial Navy's base at Rabaul, Vice Admiral Gunichi Mikawa quickly assembled a strong squadron with which to attack the American beachhead and its supporting ships. The squadron included the heavy cruisers *Chokai, Aoba, Kako, Kinagusa* and *Furutaka,* the light cruisers *Tenryu* and *Yubari,* and the destroyer *Yunagi.* The Imperial Navy had always trained itself in the techniques of night fighting which Mikawa intended to put to good use against the covering force. Its lookouts were provided with powerful night glasses, its star shells and parachute illuminating flares gave a powerful and widespread light, and there was a direct linkage between its searchlight and guns.

Mikawa's opponent was Rear Admiral Victor Crutchley, VC, RN, who had under his command the heavy cruisers HMAS *Australia* (flag) and *Canberra,* the USS *Chicago, Vincennes, Quincy* and *Astoria,* and six destroyers. His task was to protect the American transports and beachhead from an attacker approaching from the north-west down The Slot, as the long, narrow area of sea separating the two Solomon Island chains was known. During daylight hours several Allied aircraft had spotted Mikawa's ships but were uncertain of their type and Crutchley was late in being informed of their approach.

Any Japanese force intending to interfere with the American landing would have to pass Savo Island, a circular pointed protrusion lying off the coast of Guadalcanal. An attacker could therefore by-pass the island to the north or south, or split his force and employ both options. He chose the third alternative and at 01.30 on 9 August was leading his Southern Group in *Canberra* at about 12 knots in line ahead. In recent times Allied ships had been fitted with a useful device known as 'Talk Between Ships' or TBS. This enabled real time conversations to take place but at this stage disciplined voice procedure was not being enforced so that anyone who thought he had something to say said it. Naturally, the unintended result was uproar as transmission of vital information was blocked by comparative trivia. Thus, destroyer *Patterson's* frantic call 'Warning! Warning! Strange ships entering harbour!' was heard by comparatively few ships.

One of them was *Canberra* in which the alarm bells were ringing and men were running to their action stations. At that precise moment Japanese seaplanes dropped a shower of brilliant parachute flares, illuminating every one of Crutchley's ships. There is some debate as to whether *Canberra* was struck by one or more torpedoes, but none about the fact that during the next minutes she was struck by no less than twenty-four shells of 8-inch calibre or less. They ripped her hull open, smashed her superstructure, flooded both boiler rooms and left her without light or power. Her commander, Captain F. Getting, was among eighty-four members of her crew to be killed and another fifty-five men were wounded.

As *Canberra* slowed to a standstill the USS *Chicago*, next in line, swerved to avoid torpedoes to starboard and then to port, too late, for at 01.47 a Long Lance exploded against her bow, blasting the bottom out of her cable locker. Simultaneously, her foremast was struck by a shell, showering the deck with splinters that killed two and wounded twenty-one of her crew. Wakened from a sound sleep, Captain Howard Bode ordered star shells to be fired, but not one of the four salvos fired ignited. All but blind, Bode spent the next two hours searching in vain for a particularly aggressive Japanese destroyer, the *Yubari*.

Mikawi had now passed through Crutchley's Southern Group and was running north, leaving Savo Island to port. This quickly brought him into contact with the Northern Group, under the command of Captain Frederick Riefkohl, which was steering north-west, led by *Vincennes*, followed by *Quincy* and *Astoria*, the destroyers *Helm* to port and *Wilson* to starboard. Although Riefkohl had seen flares and the flashes of gunfire to the south, for some reason he believed that the Southern Group was engaged with enemy aircraft. Having heard nothing to the contrary he simply ordered an increase in speed to 15 knots.

The Northern Group was simply not prepared for action when, at 01.50, *Chokai* illuminated *Astoria* with her searchlight. *Aoba* then lit up *Quincy* and *Kako*'s searchlight fastened on *Vincennes*. Almost immediately, all three ships were straddled by 8-inch shells. Riefkohl believed that the searchlights belonged to the Southern Group and used the TBS to demand that they be turned off. When nothing happened *Quincy* and *Astoria* opened fire briefly, but by then their respective captains had reached the bridge and ordered firing to cease in the belief that a terrible mistake had been made. Fierce arguments ensued but before they could be resolved the Japanese found the range and all three American heavy cruisers received a continuous rain of shells. Fires were started that ignited petrol from the shattered tanks of their scout aircraft on their catapults. The rest of the Japanese vessels arrived on the scene and added to the scenes of destruction and carnage. Long Lances arrived to explode against the sides of *Quincy* and *Vincennes*, opening up to an inrush of sea. The American response was sporadic and caused little damage. At 02.15 the Japanese ceased firing and switched off their searchlights. Two minutes later, as they ran into the destroyer *Ralph Talbot*, they were switched on again and the destroyer received a hammering to which she replied gamely. Ablaze and with a heavy list to starboard, the Japanese left her to her fate. Happily, she was saved by a tropical rainstorm that washed over her.

At about 02.40 Mikawa decided to withdraw, for although he now had Turner's transports completely at his mercy, he knew that it would take time to assemble his scattered command and that daylight would bring heavy and prolonged attacks from Fletcher's carriers. Yamamoto congratulated him on what had been achieved, but believed that he should have accepted the risk and attacked the transports. Captain S. W. Roskill, the Royal Navy's historian of the war at sea, agreed, commenting 'Mikawa undoubtedly sacrificed the chance of inflicting a defeat which would have brought disaster to the whole Allied expedition'.

Be that as it may, Mikawa had inflicted the most humiliating defeat ever suffered by the US Navy. *Quincy* capsized and sank at 02.35 and *Vincennes* followed her fifteen minutes later. *Canberra* was still afloat but listing and on fire at dawn and her crew were taken off. Turner ordered her to be sunk, a decision which her Australian crew thought unnecessary; the fact that it took two destroyers, over 300 shells and two torpedoes suggests that they might have had a point .Efforts to save *Astoria*, still ablaze, continued until 11.00 when the fire reached her magazine. Following the explosion her crew were taken off and at 12.15 she rolled over onto her port side. Allied personnel casualties amounted to 1,270 killed and 790 wounded. The area of Savo Island had begun to earn its title of Ironbottom Sound.

Nevertheless, the battle did have a postscript. By the afternoon of 9 August Mikawa's ships were well on their way home and apparently safe from air attack. Mikawa detached Rear Admiral Aritomo Goto with *Aoba*, *Kako*, *Kinugasa* and *Furutaka* with orders to proceed to Kavieng, while he proceeded to Rabaul with *Chokai*, *Tenryu*, *Yubari* and *Yunagi*. The following morning the American submarine *S-44*, under Lieutenant Commander J. Moore, sighted Goto's four heavy cruisers and noted that their only anti-submarine protection was a solitary circling aircraft. Carefully, he closed to within 700 yards of his prey without being detected. At 09.08 on 10 August he launched four torpedoes at *Kako*. They all hit and they all exploded. The heavy cruiser broke in half and sank five minutes later. Undetected, *S-44* slipped away.

During the next fortnight both sides built up their strength ashore. The Japanese sent fast destroyers down The Slot at night, their regularity earning them the nickname of the Tokyo Express among the Americans. The marines also received supplies and reinforcements by means of destroyer transport as well as aircraft using Henderson Field when it was completed. During this period intense air activity took place above the island and The Sound as

Japanese raiders from Rabaul and the northern Solomons battled with the Cactus Air Force and American aircraft flying from the New Hebrides. If the Japanese felt puzzled and not a little irritated that their opponents always seemed to be waiting for them, the answer lay with Martin Clemens and his fellow Coast Watchers, who regularly reported their approach long before they reached their target area.

On 22 August the Japanese ran a heavily escorted convoy carrying 1,500 reinforcements to the island under the command of Rear Admiral Raizo Tanaka. In order to provide support and air cover for this convoy, a squadron was formed at Truk under Admiral Nabutake Kondo. The air element of this included the *Shokaku*, recently repaired, the *Zuikaku*, in which her newly replaced aircrew were still shaking down, and the light carrier *Ryujo*. It was under Nagumo's direct command. Following the Midway disaster, the Japanese had changed their code, despite being by no means certain that it had been compromised. Nevertheless, their increased radio traffic was a clear indication that they were about to mount a major operation.

Ghormley instructed Fletcher to intercept the Japanese, but thanks to faulty intelligence that suggested the main Japanese body was still in the area of Truk when it was actually much closer, he detached *Wasp* to a refuelling point some 240 miles away. The effect of this was to reduce his strength by one carrier, eighty aircraft, two heavy cruisers, a light cruiser and seven destroyers. On the other hand, while *Ryujo's* aircraft were raiding Henderson Field, his own were sinking their home carrier. Welcome as this success was, it meant that his own carriers, *Enterprise* and *Saratoga*, which were operating as independent groups, were vulnerable. *Enterprise* was attacked on 24 August. The Japanese dive-bombers and Zeros became involved in a furious dogfight with the American fighters and were apparently getting the worst of it when, at 16.41, a number broke through. They not only ran into *Enterprise's* own anti-aircraft fire, but also the huge volume of fire put up by the brand new battleship *South Carolina*. At least three of the attackers blew up in mid-air while more plunged into the sea around the ships they were targeting. One bomb exploded on *Enterprise*'s flight deck without penetrating it, but two more hit close together near the after lift and broke through to explode on the lower decks, killing seventy-five men, wounding ninety-five more and setting fire to an ammunition stack. However, thanks to the same precautions that had saved the *Yorktown* for a while at Midway, the fires were extinguished and the burning 5-inch ammunition was thrown overboard. *South Carolina* sustained nothing worse than three near-misses. Nagumo ordered a second strike against *Enterprise* but this missed its target by fifty miles.

Elsewhere, two of *Saratoga*'s dive-bombers attacked the seaplane carrier *Chitose* and sent her home with a 30-degree list. However, 'Tenacious' Tanaka, whose destroyers were providing close escort for the troopships, did not want to go home. During the night, five of his destroyers bombarded American positions ashore. They were attacked unsuccessfully by a flight of six dive-bombers, one of which was so badly damaged that it had to ditch. At 09.35 next morning eight more dive-bombers from Henderson Field arrived overhead. Lieutenant Baldinus hit Tanaka's flagship, the light cruiser *Jintsu*, between her two forward turrets, causing damage to the bridge, destroying communications, flooding the forward magazine and starting fires. Tanaka transferred his flag to the destroyer *Kagero* and ordered *Jintsu* back to Truk, escorted by another destroyer, *Suzukaze*. Nearby, Ensign Fink slammed a bomb into the troopship *Kinryu Maru* which came to a standstill, sinking and burning furiously. The destroyer *Mutsuki* went alongside to take off those aboard, but while so engaged eight B-17s flying from Espiritu Santo arrived overhead and commenced high-level bombing. Three bombs hit *Mutsuki* which exploded and vanished in a cloud of smoke and steam; incredibly, her captain survived. Shortly after, Tanaka received specific orders to retire to the advance base at Shortland Island, which would be the starting point for night runs of the Tokyo Express.

What became known as the Battle of the Eastern Solomons was an American success if not an outright victory. The Japanese had sustained the loss of *Ryujo* and some smaller warships, *Shokaku* had sustained fresh damage and the loss of ninety aircraft confirmed that the Navy's air arm was not what it had been once. The Americans' carrier strength had been written down to two carriers – *Enterprise*, on her way to two months' repair work in Pearl Harbor, actually passed *Wasp* returning from the refuelling area.

The Japanese now began to introduce submarines into the battle. *I-9* and *I-16* were sunk by air attack on 25 August and *I-123* was sunk by the destroyer *Gamble* three days later. However, on 30 August the carrier *Hornet* joined Admiral Fletcher's task force, enabling *Wasp* to leave for Noumea where her crew could rest and catch up on their repairs. The following day *Saratoga* was steering a zig-zag course between San Christobal and the Santa Cruz Islands when the Japanese submarine *I-26* was detected at 07.48. At that moment the carrier was cruising at just 13 knots to conserve fuel. Her captain rang down for 'Full Ahead' and swung her hard to starboard, but it was too late, for *I-26* had already fired a spread of six torpedoes. Five missed but the sixth hit, causing damage to her electric propulsion units that would require six weeks to repair in Pearl Harbor. All her aircraft flew off safely, landing first on *Hornet* and then proceeding to Espiritu Sano and later to Henderson Field. There were no fatalities aboard the carrier but twelve men, including Fletcher, were wounded. The Admiral recovered but was sent to less demanding duties in the north Pacific. *I-26* was depth-charged but escaped.

At noon on 11 September a spread of torpedoes fired by *I-11* raced past *Hornet* and *South Carolina*, much to the alarm of those aboard. The Americans cleared the area, heading north of Espiritu Santo and rendezvoused with the *Wasp*, which was carrying reinforcement aircraft for the Cactus Air Force. Together the enlarged force formed a distant escort for a troop convoy heading for Guadalcanal. Three days later a Catalina flying boat operating to the north of the Santa Cruz Islands identified a major Japanese fleet that included the carriers *Shokaku, Zuikaku, Hiyo* and *Junyo* plus escorting vessels. *Wasp* and *Hornet* changed course to intercept and at 14.30 sent out scout aircraft, followed by dive- and torpedo-bombers. The Japanese had vanished and had apparently been heading for their base at Truk.

Early afternoon on 15 September found *Wasp* steaming into the wind at only 16 knots while she recovered some of her aircraft. Watching her through his periscope was Commander Shogo Narahara of the submarine *I-19*. Having reached a decision, he ordered his torpedo officer to launch six torpedoes at once. Their immensely fast tracks would only have been visible during the final stage of their run at the carrier. Three exploded against her starboard side, blasting great holes through which the sea rushed to create a heavy list. All the forward water mains were shattered so that the damage control parties were unable to bring the raging fires under control.

From a point five miles north-north-east those aboard the *Hornet*, *North Carolina* and their escorts could only watch in horror as an enormous pillar of smoke rose above the stricken carrier. At 15.00, *Wasp* all but blew herself apart. Twenty minutes later, Captain Sherman gave orders for what remained of his ship to be abandoned. Still burning but afloat at 21.00, she was finished off by three torpedoes from one of her escorting destroyers. Of her 1,800-srong crew, 193 were killed and 366 were wounded. Narahara was watching them and when the moment came he ordered *I-19*'s remaining three torpedoes to be fired. One raced past two destroyers, *Lansdowne* and *Mustin*, to strike *North Carolina* on the port side, killing five of her crew and blasting a hole thirty-two-feet long by eighteen-feet high. The battleship remained in formation until evening when she withdrew and subsequently left for repairs in Pearl Harbor. The destroyer *O'Brien* succeeded in dodging one torpedo but the last of the Long Lances exploded against her bow. She, too found it necessary to retire, first to Noumea for temporary repairs and then to the United States. Unfortunately, the extent of her damage had been under-estimated and, on 19 October, she broke in two and sank off Samoa.

Meanwhile, the fighting ashore had been going very badly for the Japanese. Unlike the campaigns in Malaya, the Philippines and

Burma, there were neither flanks nor natural features that a tactician of even moderate ability could have exploited to his advantage. The object of the campaign was to recapture Henderson Field and eliminate the American presence on the island. The problem was that the perimeter of the airfield was held in strength and with grim determination. One failed attack after another was mounted over ground that had become a stinking charnel house, notably at the aptly named Bloody Ridge. Furthermore, the Americans were reinforcing their troops at a rate the Japanese could not match, as well as enjoying the benefits of efficient logistic and medical services. In these last respects the Japanese were seriously deficient so that starvation and tropical diseases provided a constant drain on their resources. In the circumstances it was hardly surprising that they reacted violently to an amphibious raid on Taivu by the 1st Raider and 1st Parachute Battalions. These units came ashore on 8 September and, having dispersed the 300 communications personnel they found in the village, advanced westward to Tasimboko. This was taken after a fierce fight and was found to contain a main supply depot filled with weapons, ammunition, food, medical supplies, documents revealing future enemy plans and miscellaneous items of equipment. Everything save the captured documents was destroyed and the attackers re-embarked at 16.00. That night the light cruiser *Sendai* and eight destroyers bombarded Tulagi without hitting anything in particular, and on 13 September twenty-six Mitsubishi Betty twin-engine bombers, escorted by twelve Zeros, carried out a raid on Taivu believing that it was still in American hands. It had, in fact, been re-occupied by their own troops who sustained exceptionally heavy casualties.

On 18 September the Americans received a substantial reinforcement in the form of the 3,000 men of the 7th Marine Regiment, with all their tanks, artillery, ammunition, and fuel, General Vandergrift now had 19,000 men on the ground and for the remainder of the month the strength of the Cactus Air Force was steadily increased. Further reinforcements, consisting of a regiment of the Army's Americal Division, reached the island on

11 October. In addition to Admiral Turner's close escort of eight destroyer transports, Rear Admiral Norman Scott's principal escort consisted of five cruisers and five destroyers. Hardly had this reached Ironbottom Sound than Scott received warning that an enemy supply convoy consisting of two seaplane carriers and six destroyers was heading down The Slot. In addition, an enemy bombardment group consisting of three cruisers and two destroyers was also approaching along the same course. He headed north at once, surprising the enemy's bombardment group a little before midnight at a point north of Cape Esperance, the northernmost tip of Guadalcanal, which gave its name to the ensuing gun and torpedo battle. The Americans opened fire first and the Japanese, commanded by Rear Admiral Arimoto Goto aboard the cruiser *Aoba*, replied shortly after. Several salvos struck the flagship, mortally wounding Goto. A second cruiser, *Furutaka*, sustained such heavy damage that she foundered shortly after. Believing that faulty recognitions had taken place, the destroyer *Fubuki* switched on her identification lights. *San Francisco* promptly illuminated her with her searchlight. The destroyer immediately became the focus of every American ship in sight and at 23.53 she slowed to a halt, exploded and sank. The cruiser *Kinugasa* and destroyer *Hatsuyuki* made good their escape. The only American loss was the destroyer *Duncan* that found herself isolated and engaged by several of the enemy's ships. Her final act of defiance was to strike *Furutaka* with a torpedo in her forward engine room. It would, however, be wrong to assume that the Battle of Cape Esperance was a clear-cut American victory as Japanese gunnery had been of a high standard and both *Boise* and *Fahrenholt* had sustained serious punishment.

The Japanese supply convoy, commanded by Rear Admiral Takaji Joshima, had successfully completed unloading its troops, artillery and supplies under cover of darkness and then set off for home. However, during the early hours of 12 October Joshima was informed of the bombardment group's fate. He detached two of his destroyers, *Shirayuki* and *Murakomo*, to look for survivors from *Furutaka* and *Fubuki*. Some 400 men had been rescued when the first aircraft from Henderson Field appeared overhead. They inflicted only minor damage but subsequent attacks by dive- and torpedo-bombers crippled *Murakumo* and she had to be scuttled. Joshima sent back another destroyer, *Natsugomo,* to assist *Shirayuki* with the growing number of survivors, but at 16.45 that afternoon Dauntless dive-bombers scored a direct hit amidships on the new arrival, followed by two near misses. *Natsugumo* blew up, rolled over and sank.

The struggle for Guadalcanal had now reached its climax. It was a battle neither side could afford to lose, and one in which both sides recognised that the key to ultimate victory lay in the possession of Henderson Field. The Imperial General Headquarters in Tokyo had already declared that the campaign in New Guinea – which was going nowhere anyway – was now of secondary importance only and that the Army's most pressing task was the recapture of Guadalcanal. To that end Lieutenant General Harukichi Hyakutake was to leave his headquarters in Rabaul and take personal charge of the offensive. His Chief of Staff, Major General Miyazaki, would remain behind and co-ordinate the shipment of reinforcements and supplies. Yamamoto promised that the offensive would receive maximum support from the Navy and large numbers of additional aircraft arrived in the operational area.

Thus, on the night of 13 October Vice Admiral Takeo Kurita led the battleships *Kongo* and *Haruna* down The Slot, accompanied by the light cruiser *Isuzu* with Rear Admiral Tanaka aboard, and six destroyers. At 01.00 on 14 October Japanese seaplanes began dropping parachute flares over Henderson Field, floodlighting every detail below and enabling corrections to be signalled to the gunnery officers aboard ship. A continuous rain of 14-inch shells flew inland, supplemented by 5-inch shells from the destroyers. Flames soared skywards from every quarter of the airfield as high explosive shells burst among the parked aircraft, fuel dumps and ammunition stacks. At 02.30 Kurita, satisfied with his night's work, withdrew.

Morning revealed a scene of scorched desolation to the marines. Forty-eight aircraft had been wrecked, the metal matting of the runway had been holed and torn apart, craters gaped everywhere but particularly on the sites of fuel and ammunition dumps. Yet, surprisingly, only sixty casualties had been sustained and of these just forty-one were fatalities. The remaining aircraft were moved to the fighter airstrip known as the 'cow pasture' and concealed dumps were opened up for use.

For the Japanese, all seemed to be going to plan. The Americans were aware that another supply convoy had arrived but could do nothing about it for the moment and during the evening Vice Admiral Mikawa led the heavy cruisers *Chokai* and *Kinugasa*, accompanied by two destroyers, onto their bombardment line to land 752 eight-inch shells on Henderson Field. Confident that they would not be disturbed by the Cactus Air Force, the supply convoy continued to disembark troops and unload food, equipment and ammunition long past dawn on 15 October. Then, to the horror of those involved, every American aircraft on Guadalcanal, by now refuelled and re-armed, headed for the unloading area, shooting down six patrolling Zeros as they did so. While C-47 Dakota transport aircraft flew in fresh fuel from Espiritu Santo, the Americans continued their attacks without pause. Every one of Tanaka's transport vessels sustained varying degrees of damage, three of them – *Azumasan Maru, Kyushu Maru* and *Sasako Maru* – being so badly hit that they had to be run hard aground. By 15.50 Tanaka had had enough and left with his damaged survivors, some with half their cargoes still in their holds. The day's fighting cost the Cactus Air Force three dive-bombers and four fighters.

Shortly before midnight that evening two more of Mikawa's cruisers, *Myoko* and *Maya*, plus several destroyers, took up the bombardment role, landing 800 eight-inch and 500 five-inch shells on Henderson Field, causing yet more serious damage but not quite enough to put the complex out of action. Nevertheless, General Hyakutake had considerable cause for satisfaction. He had assembled some 22,000 men, many of them fresh and healthy, with which to oppose 23,000 Americans, plus another 4,500 on Tulagi. Many of the marines, however, were tired to the point of exhaustion and starting to suffer from malaria, dysentery and malnutrition. For his part Yamamoto also had cause to be pleased with his efforts for he had concentrated four battleships, five carriers, ten cruisers and twenty-nine destroyers under the overall command of Admiral Nabutake Kondo to blockade the approaches to the Solomons. The gravity of the threat and its implications had already been digested by Admiral Nimitz and his staff at Pearl Harbor. Their blunt assessment was that 'It now appears that we are unable to control the sea in the Guadalcanal area. Thus our supply of the positions will only be done at great expense to us. The situation is not hopeless but it is certainly critical.' In the light of this a number of changes were made at the higher levels of command. Vice Admiral William Halsey replaced Ghormley as commander of the South Pacific Area and Rear Admiral Thomas Kinkaid relieved Fletcher as commander of the carrier force, which now included *Hornet* and the hurriedly repaired *Enterprise*.

While these changes were being implemented, Hayakutake commenced his planned offensive, intended to crush the American perimeter and capture Henderson Field. This began on 23 October and lasted for three days. The Japanese attacks were repetitive, piecemeal, uncoordinated and simply piled up casualties in the face of an interlocked defensive fire plan in which the flexible American artillery, controlled by radio, adjusted its fire against the enemy's forming up areas from concentrations to barrages and back again as required. Over 2,000 Japanese died to no purpose and twice that number of wounded staggered back into the jungle; American casualties amounted to less than 300. Vandergrift promptly went over to the offensive and during the next six weeks extended the area under American control until Henderson Field was beyond the range of Hyakutake's artillery, notably 150mm pieces the marines named Pistol Pete after a baseball pitcher noted for the speed of his delivery. Simultaneously, the 2nd Marine Division began relieving its comrades ashore.

At sea, the Japanese had greater success. Yamamoto had hoped that Hyakutake's anticipated victory would be equalled by a similarly important success for the Imperial Navy. He had ordered Nagumo's striking force, containing the *Shokaku, Zuikaku,* the light carrier *Zuiho,* 157 aircraft, one heavy cruiser and eight destroyers, to eliminate the American carrier force operating in the area of the southern Solomons. An advance group under Rear Admiral Abe included the battleships *Hiei* and *Kirishima,* three heavy cruisers, one light cruiser and seven destroyers. Bringing up the rear was Vice Admiral Nabutake Kondo's group with the battleships *Kongo* and *Haruna,* four heavy cruisers, one light cruiser and twelve destroyers. They were opposed by Rear (later Vice) Admiral Kinkaid's Task Force 16 with the *Enterprise* and eighty-seven aircraft, and Rear Admiral George Murray's Task Force 17 with *Hornet* and eighty-seven aircraft. The rest of the American fleet consisted of the new battleship *South Dakota,* six cruisers and fourteen destroyers. Kinkaid's orders from Halsey were virtually a mirror image of those given to his opponent – he was to return to the waters off Guadalcanal and restore them to American control. It can be seen, therefore, that the odds were heavily stacked against Kincaid from the outset.

On 26 October the two fleets came into contact to the north of the Santa Cruz Islands, which gave their name to the ensuing battle. In the event, fighting was largely confined to the opposing carrier strike forces. They launched simultaneous strikes against each other and passed on opposite courses in mid-air. At this stage several of the American aircraft were shot down by Japanese fighters, but the remainder damaged the *Zuikaku* and the light carrier *Zuiho* and hit the *Shokaku* so hard that she was out of action for the next nine months. The heavy cruiser *Chikuma* also sustained damage. In return, a blazing Val deliberately dived into *Hornet*'s superstructure, wrecking the signal bridge, then smashed its way through the flight deck, detonating two of the bombs it was carrying and starting a huge fire. Shortly after, two torpedoes blew a hole in the carrier's starboard side, causing extensive damage in the engine and boiler rooms so that she had to be taken in tow by a cruiser. *Enterprise* had also sustained serious damage when the two remaining Japanese carriers launched a second strike and at 14.00 was forced to retire to Noumea for immediate repairs. Elsewhere, the submarine *I-21* slammed a Long Lance into the destroyer *Porter*'s boiler room, causing such damage that she had to be sunk by gunfire from one of her sister ships after her crew had been taken off.

Incredibly, *Hornet*'s fires had been brought under control by 10.09 and hopes for her survival began to rise. By 11.23 the heavy cruiser *Northampton* had taken the carrier in tow, only for the cable to cable to break. By 13.30 a stronger cable had been attached. Gradually, the cruiser managed to coax her 20,000-ton burden up to a speed of three knots. However, *Hornet* was located by Japanese aircraft two hours later. *Northampton* slipped the tow and orders were given for the carrier to be abandoned. Frequent air attacks inflicted yet more damage on *Hornet,* yet she simply refused to sink. Yamamoto was informed of the fact and indicated that he wanted her captured so that she could be towed into Truk as proof of the Imperial Navy's might. For their part, the Americans were not going to permit her to fall into enemy hands; after all, it had been from *Hornet* that the Doolittle raid on Tokyo had been mounted. Two destroyers, *Mustin* and *Anderson*, launched sixteen torpedoes at her, of which seven missed and the remainder failed to explode. They then fired a total of 430 five-inch shells into her, without apparent result, but were forced to retreat when the Japanese began to close in. All her opponents found at about 21.00 was a roaring inferno that was impossible to board. Vice Admiral Hiroaki Abe ordered two destroyers, the *Makigumo* and *Akigumo*, to administer the *coup de grace;* even then, it took four Long Lances to send her on her way to the bottom.

There is no point in pretending that the Battle of the Santa Cruz Islands was anything but a Japanese victory, albeit a poisoned one that cost seventy aircraft and their trained crews; there were so few trained aircrew left that they were unable to man *Zuikaku*, which was as effectively removed from the action as was her sister ship

Shokaku which had months of repair work to attend to. Kondo seemed disinclined to exploit his success and on 27 October led his fleet back to Truk, having been encouraged to do so by an overnight attack by Catalinas that narrowly failed to torpedo *Zuikaku*. Equally, while the Americans continued to dominate the skies above Henderson Field, *Enterprise*, their only carrier left in the Pacific, was being forced to operate with one lift out of action. Consequently, Admiral King took the unusual step of asking the Royal Navy to send a carrier to the Pacific. In due course HMS *Victorious* reached Pearl Harbor and began re-equipping with American aircraft and absorbing American operational methods.

The principal result of the battle was to provide a fresh incentive for Hayakutate to bring the fighting on Guadalcanal to a successful conclusion. There were plenty of Japanese troops ashore, but many were wounded and more were riddled with disease. He was critically short of ammunition, food and supplies of every kind and, thanks to American naval and air activity, very little was being landed. The Americans also had the benefit of fighting on interior lines within their perimeter, whereas moving his own troops from one side of the enemy's beachhead involved days of exhausting marches through some of the most difficult jungle in the world, often with disastrous results. For example, a battalion-sized group under a Colonel Toshinaro Shoji, while undertaking such a march, found itself trapped between several American units. At the cost of 350 men killed, all his artillery and most of his rations, Shoji managed to break out. His column was pursued by Lieutenant Colonel Evans Carlson's Raider Battalion, accompanied by native guides and porters. Carlson's tactics were simple. While his main body moved parallel to Shoji's column, snipers were detached to pick off the enemy's officers and senior NCOs. Simultaneously, a fighting patrol would harry the Japanese rearguard until reinforcements were sent back to help; these would be ambushed and destroyed by the rest of the Raiders. In this way the remnants of Shoji's command were savaged on no less than twelve separate occasions, over 500 of its men being killed in exchange for just seventeen Raiders.

Despite such reverses, Yamamoto shared Hayakataki's view that the Battle of the Santa Cruz Islands opened a window of opportunity through which it was possible to achieve final victory in Guadalcanal. During the night of 12/13 November, Abe, now a vice admiral, would carry out a bombardment of Henderson Field with the battleships *Hiei* and *Kirishima*. The following morning the airfield would be raided by aircraft from the carriers *Hiyo* and *Junyo* while no less than eleven transports with 13,500 reinforcements aboard, approached the island under the close escort of eleven destroyers under the command of Admiral Tanaka. This brought the total number of Japanese troops ashore to 30,000, sufficient it was believed, to swamp Vandergrift's defences, although those on the spot were fully aware that many of those already present were unfit for duty.

Unfortunately for Yamamoto, American code-breakers provided ample warning of his intentions. On 11 November Rear Admiral Thomas Kinkaid left Noumea with *Enterprise* (still with an unrepaired forward lift), battleships *Washington* (flag of Rear Admiral Willis Lee) and *South Dakota*, the heavy cruiser *Northampton*, light cruiser *San Diego* and eight destroyers. In the meantime, Rear Admiral Turner had decided to reinforce Vandergrift before Tanaka could reach the island. He had already embarked the 182nd Infantry Regiment aboard five transports at Noumea on 8 November and, escorted by the heavy cruiser *Portland* and the destroyers *Barton, Monssen, O'Bannon* and *Shaw*, sailed for Guadalcanal, being joined en route by Rear Admiral Daniel Callaghan's command, consisting of the heavy cruisers *San Francisco* (flag) and *Pensacola*, the light cruisers *Helena, Atlanta* and *Juneau*, and a second destroyer squadron.

During the evening of 12 November Callaghan received warning that Abe and Tanaka were approaching. A number of adjustments in the balance of the different American squadrons actually placed Callaghan at a numerical disadvantage but, with Turner's approval, he set off to intercept the Japanese, relying on surprise. Callaghan had no experience of night fighting and failed to inform his captains of his intentions. In addition, he failed to interpret his radar picture correctly, so that when the two forces ran into each other unexpectedly to the south-east of Savo Island at approximately 01.40 on 13 November, both were equally surprised. The American TBS system was immediately jammed as the opposing ships became locked in a close-quarter gun and torpedo melee. In the same instant that Scott and his staff were killed aboard *Atlanta*, Callaghan ordered 'Odd ships commence firing to starboard; even ships to port'. This simply added to the confusion as not every American ship had a target visible on the designated side. Callaghan himself was also killed in this short, vicious action, generally referred to as The First Battle of Guadalcanal. American losses included the cruiser *Atlanta* and the destroyers *Cushing, Laffey, Monssen* and *Barton* sunk, and the cruisers *Portland* and *Juneau* damaged, the latter being sunk after the battle by the Japanese submarine *I-26*. Japanese losses included the battleship *Hiei,* seriously damaged, without power and wallowing, and the destroyers *Akatsuki* and *Yudachi* sunk.

A day of intense air activity followed. *Hiei* was despatched to the sea bed by land- and carrier-based aircraft. A major strike against a convoy by aircraft flying from Henderson Field sank seven out of eleven troopships, although the survivors continued their voyage to Guadalcanal. A relatively successful bombardment of Henderson Field took place during the night of 13/14 November, resulting in the destruction of twenty aircraft. Vice Admiral Mikawa had sailed from Shortland Island early on the 13th to carry out the mission that Abe had failed to execute. The only surface opposition he encountered was provided by two PT-boats whose attack was easily beaten off. He arrived off Savo Island soon after midnight and continued to patrol the area with the heavy cruisers *Chokai* (flag) and *Kinugasa*, plus the light cruiser *Isuzu* and two destroyers, while Rear Admiral Shoji Nishimura, with the heavy cruisers *Suzuya* (flag) and *Maya*, the light cruiser *Tenryu* and six destroyers closed in to their bombardment line to open fire by the light of flares dropped by the cruisers' scout planes. The bombardment ended at 02.05, having landed almost 1,000 shells on the airfield. Nishimura withdrew, no doubt satisfied with his night's work, although he might have been less so had he known that the runways were still operational, for at 08.00 the Cactus Air Force's dive- and torpedo-bombers and Wildcat fighters came in hard and fast to exact their revenge as the Japanese made their way back along The Slot. *Maya* sustained hits from the dive-bombers and two torpedoes caused serious damage to *Kinugasa*. At 09.15 two of Kincaid's pilots each landed a 500lb bomb on *Kinugasa*. An hour later seventeen dive bombers from *Enterprise* and their fighter escorts arrived overhead. What was described as a very near miss must have blown in the cruiser's hull, for she slowed, listed and went under shortly afterwards. Despite showing signs of damage, *Chokai*, *Isuzu* and the destroyer *Michishio* all returned to Shortland Island.

Then, as hour followed hour, it was the turn of Tanaka's transports. At 11.50, *Sado Maru*, in a crippled state, was forced to return to Shortland Island, taking two destroyers with her. *Canberra Maru* and *Nagara Maru* were both hit by bombs and torpedoes and sank. At 12.45 *Brisbane Maru* fell victim to dive bombers, broke in half and sank. At 14.30 B-17s flying from Espiritu Santo, made a high-level bombing run, without effect.

The Second Battle of Guadalcanal took place during the night of 14/15 November. Once again, the Japanese, under Admiral Kondo, sought to inflict a major bombardment on Henderson Field. This time, although *Kirishima* was their only battleship, they brought along the cruisers *Takao*, *Atago*, *Nagara* and *Sendai*, plus nine destroyers. Kondo's position and course were signalled by the submarine USS *Trout*, so that when he entered Ironbottom Sound he was intercepted at close range by an American task force under the command of Rear Admiral Willis Lee. This consisted of the two battleships *Washington* (flag) and *South Dakota* plus the destroyers *Walke*, *Benham*, *Preston* and *Gwin*.

When, at 22.10, the Japanese sighted the Americans, silhouetted against the moonlight, they mistook Lee's battleships for cruisers. Kondo therefore dispersed his ships so that when the time came they could launch a converging attack from different directions. At 22.50 Lee altered course to the west, intending to pass south of Savo Island. Minutes later the enemy appeared on his radar screen. At 23.22 the Americans opened fire, with the battleships using their secondary armament only. Almost immediately, the Japanese skills in night fighting became apparent, although their destroyer *Ayonami* was crippled and left wallowing. In return, the Japanese concentrated their fire on *Preston* which was reduced to a sinking wreck and abandoned at 23.36. Two minutes later a Long Lance wrecked *Benham*'s bow, forcing her to turn out of the fight. Simultaneously, a second Long Lance blew off *Walke*'s forecastle as far back as the bridge and started serious fires. Just four minutes later the destroyer sank. Her depth-charge settings had been reported as 'Safe', yet hardly had she disappeared than a series of eruptions directly beneath her survivors suggests that they were not. *South Dakota* suffered a major electrical failure that prevented her using her guns and, having been illuminated by the enemy's searchlights, was being hit repeatedly by 14- and 8-inch shells.

By now, *Washington* had pulled clear of the melee enabling Lee, who had a reputation for keeping a cool head and was also an authority on radar-controlled gunnery, to assess the situation. He concentrated his attention on the largest enemy target on his screens and at a range of 8,400 yards opened fire with his main and secondary armament. In just seven minutes, nine 16-inch and forty 5-inch shells smashed into *Kirishima*. With her steering wrecked, two turrets out of action, superstructure ablaze and her hull riven, the battleship was reduced to a sinking condition. She was scuttled by her crew, as was the damaged destroyer *Ayanami*. Shocked at the loss of two battleships in three nights, at 00.25 Kondo withdrew from the scene of the action. Elsewhere, Tanaka had enjoyed a qualified success in that he had landed 2,000 reinforcements, plus some ammunition, although to achieve this he had been forced to run four of his transports hard ashore, where they were destroyed by the Cactus Air Force the following morning.

The Second Battle of Guadalcanal was the last major sea battle of the campaign, but not the last action at sea. Following the loss of the two battleships, Yamamoto abandoned the idea of bombarding

Henderson Field and withdrew his heavy units to Truk, thereby leaving open the option of fighting a decisive fleet action. He also rejected the idea of employing slow merchant vessels to supply the troops still fighting on Guadalcanal. Instead, supplies would be delivered by Tanaka's fast destroyers. The usual slow methods of unloading was replaced by metal drums containing food or medical supplies that would be thrown overboard and collected by small craft operating from the shore.

The first such supply drop was to be made at the end of November. Tanaka arrived at the southern end of Bougainville with eight destroyers and prepared for the first run. Unknown to him, the American code-breakers had already informed the newly promoted Admiral Halsey of the plan's details and he had responded by forming a fast cruiser-destroyer unit that was trained in the appropriate counter-measures by Vice Admiral Kinkaid prior to his departure to command the North Pacific Force. His successor was Rear Admiral Carleton Wright.

Thanks to the Coast Watchers, Tanaka's departure was promptly reported to Halsey, who ordered Wright to put to sea on the evening of 29 November with five cruisers and seven destroyers. Radar provided a warning that the Japanese were entering Ironbottom Sound and the Americans opened fire on one of Tanaka's point destroyers, the *Takanami*. This was a situation that Tanaka had allowed for, introducing a manoeuvre to be adopted in such a situation and rehearsing frequently. It involved the leaders of each division reversing course simultaneously with their remaining ships following them round and firing their torpedoes independently. Concurrently, as the ships were off the landing beach of Tassafaronga, seamen aboard the supply destroyers began frantically flinging drums overboard.

Wright had maintained a steady course and speed, thereby providing easy marks for the enemy's torpedo crews. The results were horrendous. At 12.37 two Long Lances struck Wright's flagship *Minneapolis*. One partially blew away her bow, the wreckage of which dangled some sixty feet below the waterline. The second exploded in her boiler room, starting fires. The cruiser fired her tenth, eleventh and twelfth salvos, then lost power and slid to a standstill.

New Orleans was swinging sharply to starboard to avoid a collision with Minneapolis when a Long Lance crashed through the hull and exploded in the forward magazine. Approximately 120 feet of her bow was blown off, including A (8-inch) Turret, simultaneously killing the crew of B Turret. The torn bow grated on the plating as it passed along the ship's port side, ripping out plating and causing damage to her propellers before sinking.

The American line disintegrated as ships changed course individually to avoid collision with those already damaged. Between 23.28 and 23.33 the Japanese destroyers Kuroshio, Kawakaze and Naganami launched their torpedoes. At 23.39 a Long Lance struck the Pensacola amidships. Three of the cruiser's turrets were knocked out, the after engine room was flooded, reducing her speed to 8 knots, the communications system was destroyed and serious fires broke out. Meanwhile, Northampton had been brought back on course but at 23.48 was hit by two Long Lances on the port side. On fire and listing heavily, she slowed to a halt. This ended the Battle of Tassafaronga, the last major sea battle of the campaign. The Japanese turned for home, leaving the Takanami, crippled and abandoned by her crew, to sink alone. Incredibly, thanks to efficient damage control measures and the assistance of their destroyers, all the heavily damaged American cruisers managed to reach safety. The last American naval casualty of the campaign was the cruiser Chicago, disabled and sunk by air strikes on 20 and 21 January.

It had now become clearly apparent to most Japanese senior officers that the cost of holding Guadalcanal had become prohibitive. Battle casualties, starvation and disease were decimating the troops ashore. General Hayakutake requested permission to lead a suicide attack on the American positions, commenting that this death was preferable to the other alternatives. His request was denied. General Tojo and Admiral Yamamoto were granted an interview with the Emperor to state their respective viewpoints. Tojo wished to retain the island as part of the Empire's expanded perimeter, despite the heavy casualties sustained by the Army. Yamamoto stated that although the Americans had lost the greater number of warships during the campaign (twenty-four against eighteen), these would be replaced very quickly while the Imperial Navy's would not. He was especially concerned by the Combined Fleet's heavy loss of aircraft, 600 experienced naval pilots and 300,000 tons of merchant shipping sent to the bottom, none of which could be replaced quickly. The Emperor supported the latter view and gave permission for Guadalcanal to be evacuated.

No one had done more than Tanaka to keep the island in Japanese hands. However, by December he was tired and had come to terms with the reality of the situation, commenting that it was pointless to continue fighting. He was sent to Japan for a period of rest and recuperation. His successor, who would command the Tokyo Express and carry out the evacuation, was Rear Admiral Koniji Koyanagi. Between 1 and 7 February 1943 he evacuated approximately 12,000 Japanese from Guadalcanal without attracting the Americans' suspicions. Most were informed that they were being transferred to another area of operations, but some 600 died later as a result of wounds received or sickness. It was a remarkable achievement, as Admiral Nimitz was to comment:

> Until almost the last moment it appeared that the Japanese were attempting a major reinforcement effort. Only skill in keeping their plans disguised and bold celerity in carrying them out enabled the Japanese to withdraw the remnants of the garrison. Not until after all organized forces had been evacuated did we realise the purpose of their air and naval dispositions; otherwise, with the strong forces available to us on Guadalcanal and our powerful fleet in the South Pacific, we might have converted the withdrawal into a disastrous rout.

Approximately 60,000 Americans served on Guadalcanal. Of these, only 1,592 were killed and 4,709 were wounded, although many more contacted malaria. About 36,000 Japanese fought on Guadalcanal, of whom 23,800 were killed in action or died from disease; approximately 1,000 were taken prisoner, an event remarkable in itself as to be taken alive by the enemy was the ultimate disgrace for a Japanese serviceman. Nowhere was this more apparent than in an action at sea. It is a tradition that when the fighting is done the victorious seamen save their recent enemies from drowning whenever possible. The Japanese did not want quarter. They swam away from the boats of their would-be rescuers and sang of death. It was an eerie experience, never forgotten by those who heard it.

CHAPTER 12

Pacific Jigsaw

'The conduct of war resembles the workings of an intricate machine with tremendous friction, so that the combinations which are easily planned on paper can be executed only with effort,' wrote Major General Carl von Clausewitz in his book, *The Principles of War*, published in 1812. Although Clausewitz wrote of other times and places the principles remain universal and unaltered, despite the fact that wars are now fought in three dimensions. To function efficiently, navies, armies and air forces must each consist of numerous parts which, when joined together, form the complete intricate machine. Working together, the three machines form the whole national war machine.

In this context the driving force of Japan's Pacific War was the Imperial Navy in all its constituent parts. Without it, the Army could not be transported to the various theatres of operation and supplied with the means to make war. Likewise, it was necessary for both to enjoy air superiority, without which it was difficult to achieve success. Thus far the story has been concerned with the major weapons of naval warfare and their use, yet there were also numerous smaller weapons and apparently insignificant events that helped to shape the history of the war.

There were always rich pickings for German commerce raiders in the Indian Ocean. On 11 July 1940 the raider *Atlantis*, under the command of Captain Bernhard Rogge, captured the steamer *City of Baghdad*, aboard which were found the current copies of the British Merchant Navy cipher and classified call-signs. Rogge was therefore able to plot the probable course of his victims. By employing this technique, Rogge intercepted the 7,529 ton Blue Funnel steamer *Automedon* off the Nicobar Islands on 11 November. *Automedon* continued transmitting a 'Raider Sighted' report until gunfire from the *Atlantis* turned her into a wreck, killing her captain, one other officer and a steward on the bridge.

Inside the ship's strong-room the German boarding party found top secret mail addressed to the British Far Eastern Command in Singapore. This included new Royal Navy fleet ciphers, Merchant Navy ciphers effective from 1 January 1941, Admiralty shipping intelligence summaries and six million dollars in Straits currency. Worth far more than all these items put together was a canvas bag marked SAFE HAND - BRITISH MASTER ONLY. It contained a copy of the top secret Chiefs of Staff report on the defence of Singapore and elsewhere in the Far East against possible Japanese attack and was addressed to Air Chief Marshal Sir Robert Brooke-Popham, Commander-in-Chief Far East. The report made it clear that, in the event of Japanese aggression against Hong Kong, Malaya, Singapore and the Dutch East Indies, the United Kingdom would be unable to spare forces from other theatres of war to conduct an adequate defence. Why it had been decided to send such sensitive material by means of slow merchant steamer when the rapid Imperial Airways flying-boat service was still in operation remains one of the war's unsolved mysteries.

Rogge was fully aware of the importance of his haul. By 5 December the papers were in the hands of Admiral Paul Wenneker, the German naval attaché in Tokyo. As Russia was still neutral, and Germany was not yet at war with the United States, Wenneker handed copies to Vice Admiral Kondo, the then Vice Chairman of Japan's Naval General Staff. At first Kondo could not accept that the contents of this astounding intelligence windfall were genuine, but finally accepted their authenticity when Wenneker explained the details of their capture. In due course Kondo informed Wenneker that the report had been of enormous value during the planning phase for the attacks on Pearl Harbor, Malaya, Singapore, the Philippines and the Dutch East Indies. For his part in the affair, Rogge received a samurai sword from the hands of the Japanese Emperor.

On 19 November 1941 another German commerce raider, *Kormoran*, under the command of Theodor Detmers, created what was to be a fresh mystery of the sea until the answer was discovered only recently. That day *Kormoran* was cruising south-west of Carnarvon on the coast of Western Australia. She was disguised as the Dutch freighter *Straat Malakaa* and flying the Dutch flag, which was all in keeping with her proximity to the East Indies. Her presence was detected by the cruiser HMAS *Sydney*, commanded by Captain Joseph Burnett, which closed in to investigate. *Sydney* had a fine war record, the high point of which was her disabling the Italian *Bartolomeo Colleoni*, regarded at the time as the fastest cruiser afloat, which had to be sunk by her escorts. Detmers had sent his crew to action stations and allowed the *Sydney* to come closer, noting that her guns were trained on the raider. There was nothing about *Kormoran*'s appearance to arouse suspicion and when challenged she confirmed her identity as *Staat Malakaa*. However, when Burnett began asking questions that Detmers could not answer, the game was up. The Dutch flag came down and the German ensign soared aloft as *Kormoran* opened fire with her main armament and machine guns. *Sydney* responded as soon as she was able and a murderous close-quarter gun and torpedo battle continued for the next thirty minutes. At the end of that time, both ships were burning fiercely and had sustained fatal damage. *Sydney* seems to have been without power and drifted away through the dusk to the south. The glow of her fires remained visible to the Germans until midnight, then vanished abruptly. *Kormoran* could not be saved and was scuttled by her survivors, who became prisoners of war in Australia.

There was no trace of *Sydney* or her crew. The date set for the major Japanese raid on Pearl Harbor was not too far distant and after this had taken place stories began to circulate that *Kormoran* was cooperating with a Japanese submarine that finally torpedoed the cruiser and machine gunned her survivors in the water. Careful checking of records revealed the location of every Japanese submarine on 19 November and none were present in Western Australian waters. However, on 12 March 2008 the wreck of the

Sydney was discovered 11.4 miles south of that of the *Kormoran*, lying on a sandy bottom approximately 820 feet down. The cruiser's bow had broken off – German accounts speak of it being low in the water during the closing stages of the engagement – and is separated from the rest of the ship by a 1,600-foot-long debris field. The principal portion of the wreck is lying in an upright position. This suggests that the end of the ship had come suddenly, with the bow and the remainder of the wreck reaching the bottom at different times. Photographs of the wreck show boats still aboard, although it is difficult to assess the damage they have received.

Yet another German surface raider, the *Thor*, commanded by Captain Gunther Gumprich, was responsible for Japan benefiting from one of the war's most spectacular intelligence coups of the entire war. On 5 May 1942 the Australian steamer *Nankin* left Fremantle with 180 crew, 162 passengers, eighteen naval and five military personnel aboard. During the afternoon of 10 May the ship was circled by an aircraft that then flew so low across her that it seemed to be making an attempt to tear away her wireless aerial. Shortly after, the *Thor* appeared, bearing down on the *Nankin*. Captain Stratford, commanding the steamer, immediately recognised that his ship had become the chosen victim of an enemy surface raider. He attempted to transmit the 'Raider Sighted' signal, at which the *Thor* opened fire. An hour-long engagement ensued with *Nankin* using her poop gun. It was soon apparent that the Australian ship was seriously out-gunned and unable to shake off her assailant. *Nankin*'s casualties had been light, but Stratford saw no further point in risking the lives of the women and children aboard and, having thrown overboard the ship's code books and confidential ciphers, he surrendered.

There were 120 sacks of apparently routine mail aboard the *Nankin*, yet among this the Germans discovered material with the highest security classification that someone, with criminal negligence, had allowed to travel with articles of no value. Briefly, there were documents present that proved beyond any reasonable doubt that the American cryptanalysts had broken the Japanese

JN25 fleet cipher. The evidence was transferred to the *Regensberg*, *Thor*'s supply ship, which reached Yokahama on 18 July, where it was examined by Admiral Wenneker. On 29 August Wenneker was given permission to inform the Japanese of the situation. Horrified, the latter refused to believe at first that their communications had been so heavily compromised but, in due course, they reluctantly accepted proof that this was the case and accepted German assistance in improving cipher security. Nevertheless, immediately following Wenneker's disclosures on 29 August, American code-breakers were confronted by a complete signals blackout and it was not until well into 1943 that the US Navy received any further worthwhile information. It was felt at the time that this sudden loss of signals intelligence contributed to unexpectedly serious losses during the Battles of Cape Esperance (11– 12 October), Santa Cruz (26 October) and Guadalcanal (13–15 November).

Commerce raiders were generally employed by smaller navies to prey on the merchant shipping of their enemies. It is, therefore, mildly surprising that the Imperial Japanese Navy should resort to their use at a time when it still possessed the third largest fleet in the world, although that position was to change shortly after their introduction. Quite possibly, the Imperial Navy was impressed by the achievements of the German commerce raiders in the Indian and Pacific Oceans and was keen to produce similar results. Whatever the truth, it converted two of its merchantmen, the 7,529-ton *Hokoku Maru* and the 10,437-ton *Aikoku Maru* to the commerce raiding role, the former being armed with eight 5.9-inch guns, two 7.62mm anti-aircraft guns and four 21-inch torpedo tubes, while the latter's armament consisted of eight 5-inch guns, four 25mm anti-aircraft guns and four 533mm torpedo tubes. With their maximum speed of 21 knots, both ships were quite capable of running down the average merchantman. Unfortunately for them, their commanders had little or no instinct for the mission they had been set. As their German allies demonstrated repeatedly, the ideal commerce raider acted alone, disguised herself to maintain an innocent, unremarkable appearance and only met her support ship when necessary at classified positions far removed from busy shipping lanes. However, *Hokoku Maru* and *Aikoku Maru* were sister ships that had originally belonged to the Osaka Shosen Kaisha Line and were identical cargo-passenger liners with fine, unmistakable lines. That two such ships should be sailing together in wartime was quite sufficient to raise anyone's suspicions. They had, however, enjoyed a limited degree of success, having sunk or captured five merchantmen totalling 31,303 tons within a twelve-month period. On 5 November 1942 they left Singapore to begin their fourth cruise.

Simultaneously, the 6,000-ton Dutch tanker *Ondina*, owned by the Shell organisation, was leaving Fremantle on her regular run to Abadan, Persia, where she would fill her tanks with fuel and then return to Australia. *Ondina*, under Captain Willem Horsman, was armed with a 4-inch poop gun manned by service personnel and several machine guns and escorted by the 650-ton sloop HMIS *Bengal*, commanded by Lieutenant Commander William Wilson. It was a matter of some debate just who was escorting who as, thanks to a shortage of 4-inch guns, *Bengal* was having to make do with one 3-inch gun, one 40mm and two 20mm anti-aircraft guns.

At 11.58 on 11 November radio operators in Fremantle received a transmission from *Bengal* reporting that she and the *Ondina* were being attacked by two surface raiders at a given position. The tanker and her escort turned away to the north-north-west but *Bengal* then reversed course and opened fire at 12.12 at a range of just 3,200 yards, hoping to buy sufficient time for *Ondina* to make good her escape. That was wishful thinking, as the tanker could make just 12 knots and the sloop 15.5 knots. On the other hand, *Ondina* also opened fire at 8,000 yards and it was clear that Captain Horsman intended to fight.

Both raiders, the *Aikoku Maru* under Captain Oishi Tamatsu and the *Hokoko Maru* under Captain Imazato Hiroshi, opened fire in return, straddling the tanker and slicing through her mainmast. In reply, *Ondina's* third round slammed into the *Hokoko Maru's* superstructure, after which Captain Horsman's gunners concentrated their fire on the enemy's stern. It is uncertain whether the next hit was fired by the tanker or the sloop. It exploded on the raider's starboard torpedo mount. A huge explosion engulfed the ship. As she emerged from the smoke it was clear that she was listing to starboard and down by the stern. A second explosion tore the stern away and pitched the ship's two floatplanes into the sea. The superstructure was now an inferno that was beyond control. Captain Hiroshi had no alternative but to order 'Abandon Ship'. At 13.12 the raider was blown apart by another mighty explosion as the flames reached her magazine.

Meanwile, *Aikoku Maru* was trading shots with both the sloop and the tanker. *Ondina* was hit several times but, because their hulls are subdivided into separate tanks, tankers are very difficult ships to sink. *Bengal* was also hit several times and, with her ammunition almost expended, she turned away and made smoke. Her crew could see *Ondina* surrounded by shell splashes and one hit on her bridge, but by 13.45 both she and the surviving raider had disappeared. Having made good her damage, the sloop headed for the island of Diego Garcia, which she reached on 17 November.

Ondina, too, had almost expended her ammunition when the *Aikoku Maru* closed in to within 3,500 yards. To avoid loss of life, Captain Horsman stopped his engines, ordered lifeboats to be lowered and hoisted a white flag. Sadly, he was killed by a shell splinter before he could leave the ship. The raider closed to within 400 yards of the tanker, fired two torpedoes that blew holes in her starboard side, causing a 30-degree list, then machine gunned those in the lifeboats, killing the First Engineer and three Chinese stokers. She then steamed away to pick up the survivors from the *Hokoko Maru*. There were 278 of them out of a crew of 354. Captain Hiroshi was not among them and many had sustained serious injuries or burns. *Aikoku Maru* then returned to the *Ondina*, fired a torpedo at her, which missed, then went on her way. First Officer Rehwinkel and a few hands returned to the tanker, extinguished a number of small fires, corrected the list by counter-flooding and managed to start the engines. The remainder of the crew then returned to the ship and a course was set for Fremantle, which was reached on

18 November. Gallantry awards were made to crew members of *Ondina* and the *Bengal* who had distinguished themselves during the engagement.

Together *Haikoko Maru*, *Aikoko Maru* and *Kyosumi Maru* formed the 24th Raider Squadron, but after the engagement resulting in the loss of the *Hokoko Maru* the Japanese lost interest in the idea of commerce raiding, partly because of the poor returns it was producing, but mainly because of a pressing need for more transports to support the vast area of their recent conquests. Altogether, the Imperial Navy converted fourteen merchant vessels into armed merchant cruisers. By the end of 1943, five AMCs had been sunk and seven reconverted to their original use. The remaining two were lost in 1944.

Submarines clearly provided a far more efficient means of raiding. Japan possessed a large submarine fleet, consisting in the main of boats capable of carrying out long-range patrols, the fact that they possessed little or no crew comfort being of secondary importance in Japanese eyes. Some of the submarine service's achievements have already been recounted and the reader will have noted that in every case the opposition consisted of Allied warships. Japanese submarine commanders showed little interest in attacking merchantmen or even naval transports, considering such targets to be unworthy. This ignored the probable effects on the enemy's civilian morale of troopships being sent to the bottom. In the view of the Japanese admiralty, the correct employment for submarines was either in defensive patrol lines, scouting or taking part in fleet attacks on the enemy's warships. However, work could still be found for midget submarines. On 30 May 1942 several attacked the British battleship *Ramillies* while she was moored in the harbour of Diego Suarez, Madagascar, and damaged her so badly that she was out of action for the next twelve months. The following day four midgets penetrated Sydney harbour and damaged an accommodation ship, although all were lost in the process.

Two years later, to quote Samuel Eliot Morison, the US Navy's historian,

There began a series of exploits by the destroyer escort *England* (Lieutenant Commander W. B. Pendleton) that are unparalleled in anti-submarine warfare in any ocean. Although but one of a group, *England* delivered the death blow to six submarines within a period of twelve days. Newly built, named after an ensign in the naval reserve killed in the Pearl Harbor attack, she had had about ten weeks' sea experience.

On 18 May *England*, in company with two more destroyer escorts, *Raby* (Lieutenant Commander James Scott) and *George* (Lieutenant Commander J. E. Page), left Purvis Bay with the intention of preventing fresh supplies reaching the by-passed Japanese garrison of Buin. In overall command was Commander Hamilton Hains, aboard *George*. The three ships were armed with Hedgehog projectors, which threw a pattern of high explosive bombs ahead of the ship, thereby preserving the ASDIC signal, and depth charges that could be rolled off the stern. They were proceeding on a north-easterly heading to the north of Manus Island in the Admiralty Group with *George* in the centre, *Raby* to port and *England* to starboard, about two miles apart. At 13.35 on 19 May *England* picked up an ASDIC contact approximately a mile distant. She headed straight for the target, firing five salvos with her Hedgehog. A minute after the last there was a heavy explosion that lifted the ship's stern out of the water and sent most of her crew sprawling. Some thought that the ship had been torpedoed, but when a long oil slick appeared, followed by furniture, mattresses and assorted debris, it was apparent that the submarine, later identified as the 2,100-ton *I-16*, had met her end just beneath *England*. A school of sharks quickly disposed of any human remains.

At 03.50 the following morning all three ships picked up a sonar echo estimated to be seven miles ahead. Their commanders rang down for 'Full Ahead' and began a converging run on the contact. *George* clicked on her searchlight to reveal a diving submarine, then made a run at the target, without result. *England* followed and two minutes after her first salvo the submarine exploded, leaving an oil slick and splintered rubbish heaving on a ground swell to mark the end of *RO–106*.

On 23 May the entire team caught *RO–104* moving up to her patrol line in full daylight. The submarine was evidently aware that she had been spotted as she dived and avoided several runs by *Raby* and *George*. Commander Hains called *England* forward and at the end of Pendleton's second run the usual quantities of oil and flotsam broke the surface. *George*'s radar picked up *RO–116*'s radar in the pre-dawn darkness of 24 May but, before the destroyer escort could close, the submarine disappeared beneath the surface some four miles distant. *England* established sonar contact and her fathometer indicated that the target had dived to a depth of 168 feet and was deliberately pursuing an erratic course in the hope of throwing her opponents off the scent. *England* fired a full Hedgehog salvo. After a brief interval there was a loud rumbling sound from below and then debris shot to the surface. After dawn, a quantity was recovered, including wood from a chronometer box or sextant, suggesting that at least one bomb had blasted the conning tower apart.

On 25 May, a quiet day, the group returned to Seeadler Harbor to refuel and replenish its supply of Hedgehog ammunition. Returning to the hunt, all three destroyer escorts picked up a radar contact some eight miles distant shortly before midnight. Haines, not wishing to be accused of favouritism, gave *Raby* the chance to score a kill. Unfortunately, *Raby* lost contact. *England*'s instruments quickly restored it, showing *RO-108* was lying some 250 feet below the surface. Pendleton gave her the benefit of a full salvo. Four or five explosions were followed by the rumble of a submarine tearing herself apart. Haines waited until daylight to recover evidence, then headed for Seeadler Harbor. On the way he met a fourth destroyer escort, *Spangler*, with extra *Hedgehog* ammunition. *Spangler* joined the group and at noon joined a hunter-killer group based on the escort carrier *Hoggatt Bay*.

Late on 30 May the destroyer *Hazelwood* made a sonar contact with *RO–105*. As she was acting as escort for *Hoggatt Bay*, she appointed the destroyer *McCord* to maintain contact while *Raby* and *George* hunted. The Japanese captain proved very difficult to pin down, but after several hours he surfaced between *Raby* and *George* and foolishly turned on his searchlight, hoping to locate his pursuers. The two were joined by *Spangler* but Hains prohibited any attack before first light. As soon as possible, the three attacked by turns, but all missed. *England* was called in. At 07.35 her first Hedgehog salvo hit the water. Nine seconds later a tremendous explosion signalled the end of *RO–105*.

Naturally, Pendleton and his crew received congratulations from many quarters, not least from Admiral Ernest King, the US Navy's Chief of Naval Operations, who somehow suppressed his Anglophobia sufficiently to signal from Washington, 'There'll always be an England in the United States Navy!'

A small number of Dutch submarines escaped to Australia when the Japanese invaded the East Indies and as the war progressed ran up a commendable number of kills. The Americans steadily increased the number of their submarines operating in the Far East, although they were initially hampered by faulty torpedoes. By the end of the war the US Navy had acquired a huge fleet of ocean-going submarines capable of distant deployment. The philosophy of the American submarine service was almost the reverse of the Japanese. The destruction of the enemy's sea-going traffic held almost equal importance to the elimination of his warships, for without it the Japanese Army would lose the ability to fight. Towards the end of the war, British submarines based in Ceylon and Fremantle began operating as part of the Royal Navy's Eastern Fleet. British submarines, having been designed for service comparatively close to their bases in the North and Mediterranean Sea, had a smaller operational radius than the much larger American boats and operated around the Malacca Strait, the Malayan peninsula and Sumatra. Together, Allied submarines were a major factor in what amounted to the virtual destruction of the Japanese merchant marine by the end of the war, losses from all causes amounting to 2,345 merchantmen with a total tonnage of 8,617,234.

The life of a submariner is always one in which danger is his constant companion, even in circumstances where Japanese anti-submarine warfare techniques and the ability to escort convoys efficiently had not been developed to the same degree as in western navies. Here there is insufficient space to tell more than the story of more than one distinguished submarine commander, although the career of Commander Richard O'Kane, US Navy, is in itself unique in the annals of undersea warfare. O'Kane was born in 1911 and entered the Navy in 1930. During his career, most of which was spent in submarines, he was awarded the Medal of Honor, the Navy Cross with two Gold Stars, the Silver Star Medal with two Gold Stars, the Legion of Merit with Combat 'V', the Commendation Ribbon and the Ribbon for the Presidential Unit Citation with three blue stars (USS *Wahoo* and USS *Tang*), plus campaign and service medals. He retired from the service with the rank of rear admiral on 1 July 1957.

The following is the text of the citation that accompanied the award of his Medal of Honor.

For conspicuous gallantry and intrepidity at the risk of his life above and beyond the call of duty as Commanding Officer of the USS *Tang* operating against two Japanese convoys on October 23 and 24, 1944, during her fifth and last war patrol. Boldly maneuvering on the surface into the midst of a heavily escorted convoy, Commander O'Kane stood in a fusillade of bullets and shells from all directions to launch smashing hits on three tankers, coolly swung his ship to fire at a freighter and, in a split-second decision, shot out of the path of an onrushing transport, missing it by inches. Boxed in by blazing tankers, a freighter, transport and several destroyers, he blasted two of the targets with his remaining torpedoes and, with pyrotechnics bursting on all sides, cleared the area. Twenty-four hours later, he again made contact with a heavily escorted convoy steaming to support the Leyte campaign with reinforcements and supplies and with crated planes piled high on each unit. In defiance of the enemy's relentless fire, he closed on the concentration of ships and in quick succession sent two torpedoes into each of the first and second transports and an adjacent tanker, finding his mark with each torpedo in a series of violent explosions at less than 1,000 yards range. With ships bearing down on all sides, he charged the enemy at high speed, exploding the tanker in a burst of flame, smashing the transport dead in the water and blasting the destroyer with a mighty roar which rocked the *Tang* from stem to stern. Expending his last two torpedoes into the remnants of a once-powerful convoy before his own ship went down, Commander O'Kane aided by his gallant command, achieved an illustrious record of heroism in combat, enhancing the finest traditions of the United States Naval Service.

The citation does not mention that one of the last two torpedoes fired was a rogue that circled and exploded against the submarine's stern, sinking her immediately. O'Kane was picked up by a small Japanese warship and was imprisoned, first on Formosa and then in a secret prison camp near Tokyo.

One of the most successful British submarine commanders of the war was Lieutenant Commander Stephen Maydon, who was awarded the DSO and Bar, plus the DSC. He served as a lieutenant aboard the submarine HMS *L26* between 21 February and 24 April 1941 and was then transferred to command the submarine HMS *Umbra*, in which he served with distinction in the Mediterranean between 7 July 1941 and 11 January 1943, sinking the Italian heavy cruiser *Trento* and twelve Italian or German merchant vessels as well as damaging others. He received promotion to lieutenant commander on 1 February 1943.

On 29 January 1944 he took over the submarine HMS *Tradewind* and, having concluded her trials satisfactorily, completed her first war patrol, which took her beyond the Arctic Circle and North Cape. On her return she docked in the Holy Loch before setting out for the Far East via the Mediterranean, Port Said and Aden, reaching her new base of Trincomalee, Ceylon, on 21 May 1944. From Trincomalee she carried out a reconnoitring of the west coast of Sumatra and its off-lying islands. During her second patrol, Maydon took her into the Sunda Strait where he picked up one Chinese and two Javanese from a *prau* on 19 June and took them to Trincomalee for interrogation. Eight days later *Tradewind* surfaced and pumped thirteen rounds of gunfire into the oil storage tanks at Sibolga.

The submarine's third patrol took her into the Malacca Straits, where she was depth charged without result on 7 July. Her fourth patrol involved two special operations and an inspection of the west and south coasts of Sumatra. On 15 September a sampan loaded with coconuts was captured. Her crew were made prisoners, as was a monkey trained to climb palm trees and collect coconuts; according to the boarding party, the latter objected strongly to his new job as a submariner in King George's navy. Next day a large prau, apparently loaded with nutmeg and cinnamon bark, was captured but released. Shortly after, a second *prau* was intercepted and found to be carrying 400 sacks of cement for the Japanese among her cargo. With the exception of one man who wished to join the *Tradewind*, the crew were sent ashore and the *prau* was blown up. Maydon's suspicions were now aroused. He returned to the first *prau*, where more cement and building materials were found under the nutmeg. Again, the crew were sent ashore and their craft was rammed and sunk.

On 18 September *Tradewind* unwittingly became involved in one of the war's most tragic losses at sea. The submarine's view of events is recorded in her log:

15.16 – The officer of the watch sighted a small plume of smoke through the low power periscope (the high power periscope was flooded). The smoke was sighted at a range of over 13,500 yards. This was an excellent sighting. The smoke was first sighted bearing 173 degrees. Course altered to attack.

The target was later seen to be an old-fashioned merchant vessel, 4,000 to 5,000 tons, of the three island type, two masts, single tall thin funnel and counter-stern. She was about two-thirds loaded. She was escorted by two motor launches, one on her starboard beam and the other on her port quarter.

15.51. Fired four torpedoes. The target speed was estimated at eight knots. Upon firing *Tradewind* went deep. 1 min 30 sec after firing explosions were heard. After these explosions the HE [hydrophone echo] of the target ceased. Three depth charges were dropped by the escort but these did no damage.

16.13 – Heard loud crackling noises – must have been the target breaking up.

When *Tradewind* returned to Trincomalee on 4 October Commander Maydon still knew nothing about his victim or the business on which she had been engaged. She was the *Junyo Maru*, one of thousands of tramp steamers that sailed the world's oceans with whatever cargo they could pick up. The encounter had taken place off Mukomuko on the west coast of Sumatra. The Japanese had no qualms about employing prisoners of war and conscripted local labour on projects demanding heavy physical labour throughout their newly-acquired empire. In this case the *Junyo Maru* had aboard some 2,200 Dutch, British, American and Australian prisoners of war and 4,320 romushas (conscripted Javanese labourers). Conditions aboard the ship were overcrowded and insanitary. After landing at Padang the prisoners and conscripts were to have been put to work building the Pakaburu–Muara Railway, in its way as infamous as the better known Burma Railway, if somewhat shorter. Those captives who drowned in the sinking of the *Junyo Maru* included 1,382 Dutch, fifty-eight British, eight American and three Australian prisoners of war, a number of Dutch civilians and about 4,000 of the romushas.

On 22 October *Tradewind* left Trincomalee on her fourth patrol and 30 October was spent laying a minefield off the Mergui Archipelago, Burma, after which she headed south-west to patrol the Andaman Sea. Returning to the Burmese coast, she sank four Japanese sailing vessels with gunfire on 8 November, plus a further two, also with gunfire, on the 10th, ending her fifth patrol five days later. After spending some days in dock at Trincomalee, she left on 5 December and carried out a special operation on the west coast of Sumatra before continuing her voyage to Fremantle, Western Australia, which she reached on 24 December. It was subsequently learned that, on 1 January 1945, the 593-ton Japanese freighter *Kyokko Maru* sank off the Mergui Archipelago after striking one of the mines laid by *Tradewind*. On 7 January 1945 Commander Maydon relinquished command of the submarine.

It was not until 1962 that he learned that the *Junyo Maru* was carrying prisoners of war and conscripted labourers. Like many submarine commanders he dreaded the prospect that such a situation might arise.

CHAPTER 13

This Way To The Turkey Shoot

The fact that the Japanese had been ejected from Guadalcanal did not mean that the rest of the Solomon Islands would fall into Allied hands without a struggle. It was necessary that the Allies should secure the rest of the islands if the enemy's Southern Area was to be penetrated and his important naval base at Rabaul neutralised. The first step, of which both sides were aware, would be to strike at the New Georgia group in the centre of the island chain. This included the islands of New Georgia, Kolombangara, Vella Lavella, Rendova, Vanguni and a number of other smaller islands. Naturally, the Japanese intended to forestall any attempt at occupation by establishing their own presence, which was a joint service command under General Naboru Sasaki and Rear Admiral Minoru Ota. Airfields had been established at Munda on New Georgia and Vila on Kolombangara; although the Americans bombed and shelled them regularly, they knew little or nothing about any other defensive systems that the Japanese might have established. That they intended to strengthen them was beyond doubt, for on the night of 6 March 1943 a bombardment force of three American cruisers and three destroyers, closing in on the coast to shell Vila, picked up the destroyers *Murasame* and *Minegumo* on their radar. The cruisers' radar-controlled gunfire and torpedoes sank both before they were fully aware what was happening. It was apparent that the Tokyo Express was back in business and, having noted its preferred routes, the Americans laid mines across them. The result was that on the night of 7 May these accounted for the destroyers *Oyashio*, *Kuroshio* and *Kagero*.

The following month, the Imperial Navy sustained a loss that led to universal mourning throughout Japan. During April's early days Yamamoto had been fed details of heavy American and Allied losses that were hopelessly inflated. Pleased that important successes seemed to have been achieved, the Admiral decided to make a morale-raising tour of bases on Buka and Bougainville, little suspecting that his every move was being followed by American code-breakers. Details were passed to fighter squadrons on Guadalcanal and, on 18 April 1943, his aircraft was intercepted and shot down by P-38 long-range fighters. Sincere as was the sadness at his passing, the 'Victory Disease' was as virulent as ever. Few cared to recall the Admiral's prophetic words predicting the short spell of Japan's victories. This was not the sort of thing to be communicated to the press or the people. Recent disappointments would be overcome and, anyway, the map showed virtually no change since the glory days of 1941 and early 1942. Yamamoto was succeeded by Fleet Admiral Minechi Koga, essentially conservative in outlook, who remained an advocate of the big-gun battleship as a battle winner.

American troops landed on New Georgia on 2 July and quickly consolidated their position. The Japanese reacted by despatching a reinforcement convoy for the Kolombangara garrison down The Slot on 5 July. This was led by Rear Admiral Teruo Akiyama with the destroyers *Nitzuki, Tanikaze* and *Susukaze,* followed by seven more destroyers carrying troops and supplies. It was Akiyama's intention to despatch the latter into the Kula Gulf between Kolombangara and New Georgia. They would enter separately, unload quickly and then make their exit. As usual, the Americans had received advance warning of the convoy's route and were already steaming to intercept it with a force consisting of the 6-inch gun cruisers *Helena, Honolulu* and *St Louis,* plus four destroyers, under the overall command of Rear Admiral W. Ainsworth.

Akiyama entered the gulf first with his escort, followed by the first three transport destroyers. At that moment Ainsworth's ships were sailing across the entrance to the gulf. Akiyama turned about and sent in the next four transports. At 01.47 he sent the remaining transports down the gulf and prepared to leave. However, at that moment his lookouts spotted the Americans. He recalled all his destroyers, unloaded or otherwise, and went straight into the attack. At 01.57 the Americans concentrated their fire on his flagship, *Nitzuki*, and battered it into a sinking wreck in which Akiyama lost his life. Simultaneously, *Tanikaze* and *Suzukaze* launched their Long Lance torpedoes at the American line. Three exploded against the *Helena*, blowing off her bows, and six minutes later she sank. Now under intense shellfire, all the Japanese turned away and coolly completed their unloading. There was sporadic firing at intervals during the night but by dawn they had gone, leaving the transport *Nagatsuki* hard aground and abandoned.

A week later a second attempt was made to reinforce Kolombangara. It was led by Rear Admiral Shunji Izaki aboard Tanaka's former flagship, the light cruiser *Jintsu*. In addition, there were the five destroyers *Mikazuki, Yukikaze, Hamazaze, Kiyonami* and *Yugure*, escorting four destroyer transports. This time the Americans were waiting for them in even greater strength, including the cruisers *Honolulu, St Louis,* and HMNZS *Leander*, plus nine destroyers. The approaching Japanese were first detected by a Catalina flying boat, but now they were equipped with radar detection sets that revealed the American presence. Both sides headed towards each other at speed. At 01.08 the Japanese launched their Long Lances and a minute later the Americans launched their own torpedoes. Ainsworth subsequently attracted criticism for not opening fire with his main armament while still outside the range of the Long Lances. However, at 01.12 his cruisers did open fire simultaneously, taking *Jintsu* as their mark. By 01.45 she had become a total wreck and went to the bottom. Meanwhile, Ainsworth had ordered his line to reverse course and while doing so *Leander* was hit by a Long Lance and so crippled that she required two destroyers to escort her to Tulagi. The Japanese broke contact to reload their tubes and then came in for a second strike. *St Louis* and *Honolulu* both sustained hits in their bows and the destroyer *Gwin* was blown apart, after which the Japanese faded away into the darkness, bringing the Battle of Kolombangara to an end.

If the Japanese seemed to be holding their own at sea, the reverse was true of the land fighting on New Georgia. Their final counter-attack was broken up on 17 July and the arrival of fresh American reinforcements enabled their front to be broken on 5 August. After this, their survivors were evacuated to Kolombangara. Too late, two infantry battalions were despatched from Bougainville to the latter aboard the destroyers *Shigure, Hagikaze, Arashi* and *Kawakaze*. By now, the Allies had no cruisers to spare with which to intercept them, but six destroyers under Commander F. Moosbrugger were waiting for them in the Vella Gulf between Vella Lavella and Kolombangara. At 23.23 on 6 August the Japanese appeared on Moosbrugger's radar screen. The Americans immediately prepared to make a torpedo attack in two divisions of three. They were lying inshore of the Japanese and therefore invisible to them against the dark outline of the land. The wide torpedo spread hit *Kawakaze, Arashi* and *Hagikaze*, all three of which were finished off with gunfire and sank. Aboard them had been the 1,500 reinforcements, all of whom drowned. So sudden and complete had been the disaster that *Shigure* vanished into the night at full speed.

It was the mistaken Japanese belief that Kolombangara was the next American objective. In fact, General MacArthur and Admiral Halsey had set their sights on Bougainville, possession of which would make the continued tenure of Rabaul difficult, if not impossible, for the Japanese. In a series of diversionary operations on 27 and 28 October, the islands of Mono and Sterling were occupied and a landing was effected on Choseul Island, across The Slot. The 3rd US Marine Division landed in Bougainville's Empress Augusta Bay on 1 November and had secured its beachhead by nightfall, although its transports still had to complete their unloading. Covering this was Admiral A. S. Merrill with the new 6-inch cruisers *Montpelier, Cleveland, Columbia* and *Denver*, plus two four-ship divisions of destroyers. These were deployed in a long arc across the entrance to the bay with his cruisers in the centre and the destroyers ahead and astern of them.

Heading for the bay at his best speed was Rear Admiral Sentaro Omori with the heavy cruisers *Myoko* and *Haguro*, the light cruisers *Sendai* and *Agano*, and six destroyers, his intention being to destroy the American transports while they were still at anchor. He had adopted a trident formation for his ships with the light cruiser *Sendai* and the destroyers *Shigure, Samidare* and *Shiratsuyu* in the left hand column, the heavy cruisers in the centre and the light cruiser *Agano* and the destroyers *Naganami, Hatsukaze* and *Wakatsuki* in the right hand column.

Omori's ships began to appear on American radar sets at 02.30 on 2 November. Merrill planned to delay opening fire until his destroyers had launched a long-range torpedo attack, but a flare dropped by a Japanese scout plane at 02.46 revealed the presence of the American warships. Omori immediately ordered his ships to form line on the starboard column but while this manoeuvre was being executed Merrill's cruisers opened fire, concentrating on *Sendai*, which became a blazing wreck in minutes. Two of the light cruiser's destroyers, *Samidare* and *Shiratsuyu*, collided heavily while trying to avoid her, while the third, *Shigure*, swung out of line to join Omori's column. The Japanese right column was faring no better. *Hatsukaze* turned out of line in a dangerous attempt to avoid the concentration of American shellfire but was run down by *Myoko* and sustained crippling damage. Omori, recognising that he stood little or no chance of damaging the American transports, cut his losses at 03.37 and withdrew to the north-west, abandoning *Sendai* and *Hatsukaze*. Despite months of heavy fighting on the island, the Imperial Navy made no further attempts to interfere with the course of the Bougainville campaign, which ended in an American victory in January 1944.

The campaign in the Solomon Islands was ending on a satisfactory note and that in New Guinea seemed likely to follow suit. This came about as a result of MacArthur's successful landings on the island's north coast early in 1944, followed by the subsequent advances westward by Australian and American troops, all of which convinced the Japanese General Staff that their troops on the island must be reinforced quickly and in some strength. A convoy consisting of eight troopships and the same number of destroyers was detected on 2 March heading for the island. The subsequent engagement became known as the Battle of the Bismarck Sea.

Together, the Royal Australian Air Force and the United States Army Air Forces assembled a formidable force of thirty-seven heavy bombers, forty-nine medium and light bombers and ninety-five fighters, plus reconnaissance aircraft. They opened the battle on 3 March with an attack on Lae airfield by Douglas A-20 Boston intruders which kept the Zeros fully occupied while the convoy was attacked by B-17 Fortresses that sank a transport, although a number of the troops aboard were taken off by a destroyer and put ashore at Lae. The next day a swarm of B-25 Mitchell bombers closed in on the convoy, employing the recently developed 'skip bombing' technique. This followed the lines of the children's game Ducks and Drakes in which a flat stone was skimmed across the surface of a pond or lake, bouncing each time it touched the water; the player who could make his stone bounce most often was declared the winner. In this context bombs were skipped off the surface of the sea and, having inherited considerable velocity from their aircraft, broke through the sides of their targets and exploded within, doing enormous damage. At the same time Beaufighters strafed bridges and upperworks with their four nose cannon and six wing-mounted machine guns. Every transport was sunk, as were four of the destroyers. The destroyer crews and 2,700 men from the transports were picked up, but at least 3,000 more were killed or drowned. Thus, in addition to their material losses, the better part of an infantry division had been destroyed. Allied losses amounted to one fortress, three Lockheed P-38 Lightnings and a Beaufighter forced to crash-land. During the next few days the Japanese made retaliatory strikes against Allied airfields but usually came off worse in such encounters. The consequences of the battle were such that the Japanese, under-strength, barely supported by a wretched supply system and heartily disliked by the native population, were driven out of one of their coastal enclaves after another until, on 30

July 1944, the Allies had reached the westernmost tip of the island. Even so, although the surviving groups of Japanese were contained, New Guinea had been completely cleared of their presence by May 1945.

Experienced Allied airmen had noticed a decline in the performance of their opponents. There were two reasons for this. First, while the Japanese continued to use the aircraft with which they had started the war, namely the Val dive-bomber, the Kate torpedo bomber and the now outclassed Zero fighter, the Allies had introduced a new generation of aircraft. The Americans were now employing Hellcats, Avengers, Lightnings and Corsairs that were faster, better armed and capable of absorbing more punishment. In Burma the arrival of the legendary Spitfire had quickly cleared the sky of Oscars. The consequence for the British and Indian troops was that they no longer feared being surrounded and cut off as they were confident of being supplied by air. For the Japanese, no longer able to feed on captured rations, it meant near starvation and the constant failure of their operations.

The Japanese view of the changed situation in the air war was succinctly expressed by Saburai Sakai, a former Zero ace who received serious head wounds over Guadalcanal and was subsequently employed at a pilot training school. The following extract is taken from his book *Samurai!*

> Everything was urgent! We were told to rush the men through, to forget the fine points, just teach them to fly and shoot. One after the other, singly, in twos and threes, the training planes smashed into the ground, skidded wildly through the air. For long and tedious months I tried to build fighter pilots from the men they thrust on us at Omara. It was a hopeless task. Our facilities were too meagre, the demand too great, the students too many.

This alone was sufficient to generate serious concern, had not attrition reduced the naval air arm to a ghost of its once mighty self.

It was true that thirteen carriers, albeit of different sizes, still existed and also that, in theory, they could put up 525 aircraft. The reality was that they carried nothing like that number, the reason being that in 1943 Japanese aircraft factories only managed to produce something over 19,000 combat aircraft while the United States production facilities turned out 90,000. Furthermore, acquisition of oilfields in the East Indies and Burma had not provided the expected supplies, partly because it had taken longer than expected to repair the damage inflicted on them by the real owners before the Japanese arrived and partly because only small tankers were available to transport the oil to Japan when supplies came back on stream; naturally, the tankers became prime targets for American prowling submarines. In 1941 Japan's oil stocks amounted to 48,900,000 barrels, but by 1943 this had shrunk to 25,300,000 barrels, whereas American production amounted to 700 times that quantity.

Japanese Navy and Army Headquarters in the South West Pacific were located at Rabaul, a town located at the north-eastern end of the island of New Britain, having the advantage of a large harbour and three airfields. Before the Allies could carry their advance further into the Central Pacific it was decided that that island, plus the neighbouring island of New Ireland, which contained the naval sub-base of Kavieng, would have to be contained. This meant driving the Japanese garrison into confined areas that effectively became self-feeding prisoner of war camps. The Japanese, correctly suspecting such a strategy, had reinforced their naval presence in Rabaul with warships brought down from their major base at Truk in the Caroline Islands, hoping that the recent arrivals would also be able to play a part in the New Guinea fighting.

The Americans mounted their first attack on Rabaul on 5 November 1943. Rear Admiral Sherman's carrier group, consisting of the carriers *Saratoga* (2) and *Princeton*, launched ninety-seven aircraft in a raid on the harbour. Complete surprise was achieved and the results included serious damage inflicted on the cruisers *Agano, Atago, Maya, Mogami, Noshiro* and *Takao* for the loss of six aircraft. On 11 November Rear Admiral Alfred Montgomery's carrier group, consisting of the carriers *Essex, Bunker Hill* and *Independence*, despatched 185 aircraft, inflicted more damage on *Agano* and sank a destroyer. Rabaul harbour also contained the sunken hulks of supply ships and the scale of air attacks convinced the Japanese that it was no longer safe to use.

Elements of the 1st and 7th US Marine Divisions landed at Cape Gloucester, at the western end of the island, on 26 December. Thanks in part to atrocious weather, their progress eastwards along the island was slow, although they were reinforced by the 5th US Marine Division in March 1944 and the Japanese were finally compressed into an enclave at the eastern end of the island. Meanwhile, during February and March 1944, the nearby Admiralty and St Matthias islands were taken by the Americans, isolating Rabaul and Kavieng. With advanced US air bases established in the Admiralties and St Mathias and ground troops in firm control of both, New Britain and New Ireland had been successfully neutralised and remained so for the remainder of the war.

The American advance into the Central Pacific would present those involved with a number of problems not yet encountered. In the main, these revolved around the great distances that existed between objectives and the coral reefs that surrounded the atolls that would have to be taken, save for one or two gaps through which the sea entered. Often insignificant in themselves, the islands forming the atolls were sometimes large enough for an airstrip to be constructed on them, and this gave them a strategic importance that was impossible to overstate. The process would become known as 'Island Hopping' and American planning for it was every bit as thorough as it was in providing the hardware necessary to fight the war and training those who would use it. The coral reefs would rip the bottom out of a conventional boat and the gaps in them were obvious aiming marks for the Japanese defenders. It was, therefore, necessary to produce and manufacture a specialist vehicle capable of clawing its way over the reef and providing a degree of protection for those within as it swam across the lagoon to the island's internal shore, on which it would discharge its infantry on top of the enemy's defences. These vehicles were known as amtracs (amphibious tractors) or LVTs (Landing Vehicles, Tracked) and in due course a whole family of them was developed, including some mounting heavy weapons. As far as the logistic aspects of the campaign were concerned, a fleet train organisation was formed, consisting not only of tankers and supply ships, but also hospital and repair ships. The fighting element of this included purpose-built headquarters ships, LSIs (Landing Ships, Infantry) that mounted the LCIs (Landing Craft, Infantry) that would be slung out and in which the infantry would be delivered to the shore itself, LSTs (Landing Ships, Tank) that would deliver tanks through their bow doors onto the beach, and LCMs (Landing Craft, Mechanised) that brought wheeled vehicles ashore. An operation would begin with heavy air attacks followed by a bombardment carried out by battleships (the US Navy having decided that this was the correct role for them), cruisers and destroyers. The assault landing would take place shortly after and after this the troops ashore would have the close support of naval gunfire, controlled by a naval gunfire support officer working with them, or ground support aircraft directed by a forward air controller.

On 19 November 1943 some 700 aircraft flying from eight carriers attacked targets in the Gilbert Islands. Their principal objective was Tarawa Atoll, the capture of which was the first step in the American drive across the Central Pacific towards Japan. The most important feature in the atoll was the airfield on Betio Island, which would provide air cover for the next phase of the advance. The various islands in the atoll were known to be heavily and expertly fortified. The garrison consisted of the 7th Special Naval Landing Force and the 3rd Special Base Force, plus attached naval personnel and a technically non-combatant labour force, a total of 4,836 men, of whom 2,619 were fighting troops. In command was Rear Admiral Keichi Shibasaki. In overall command of the American assault was Rear Admiral Turner. The assault itself would be delivered by Major General Smith's 2nd Marine Division under the tactical command of Major General Holland M. Smith's V Amphibious

Corps, giving a total, with attachments, of approximately 20,000 men. Admiral Turner's fleet contained eight escort carriers with 216 aircraft available to provide ground support once the troops were ashore, while the pre-landing bombardment would be delivered by the battleships *Colorado, Idaho, Maryland, Mississippi, New Mexico, Pennsylvania* and *Tennessee*, plus six heavy and two light cruisers, and thirty-eight destroyers.

Incredible as it might seem, the heavy bombardment left the Japanese fortifications largely untouched. Many landing craft became 'hung up' on the reefs, forcing their occupants to wade across the lagoon in the teeth of the enemy's fire. On the other hand, the LVTs, in combat for the first time, undoubtedly saved many American lives. Even they were unable to cross the palm-log sea wall behind which Marines were pinned down until individual acts of heroism eliminated the source of the enemy's fire beyond. In total, the 2nd Marine Division lost 997 killed, eighty-eight missing presumed killed and 2,233 wounded, while the US Navy's casualties amounted to thirty killed and fifty-nine wounded. With the exception of 146 prisoners, all but seventeen of whom were Korean labourers, the entire Japanese garrison was wiped out. American public opinion was shocked by the heavy price that had been paid for an apparently insignificant objective, but the lessons of Tarawa were quickly absorbed and put to good use in subsequent amphibious operations.

Again, no two battles are quite alike. Nimitz wished to secure Kwajalein Atoll in the Japanese Marshall Islands as quickly as possible and use them as air bases for the continued American drive across the Central Pacific. The atoll was held by approximately 8,000 Naval Infantry under the command of Rear Admiral Akiyama. Given that the American force deployed against him consisted of 190 aircraft, plus the gunfire support of the battleships *Colorado, Idaho, Maryland, Mississippi, New Mexico, Pennsylvania* and *Tennessee*, nine cruisers and forty-five destroyers, Akiyama stood not the slightest chance of being able to conduct a protracted defence. From 31 January, when the Americans began coming ashore, until

4 February 1944 they fought to the death, save for a handful of mainly Korean labourers. American personnel casualties incurred during the atoll's capture included 486 killed and 1,295 wounded. The battleships also bombarded landing sites at Roi and Namur on the northern rim of the atoll where the 4th Marine Division would effect its landing.

Next, between 17 and 18 February, the former Japanese fleet base and anchorage at Truk was attacked by aircraft from the carriers *Yorktown (2), Intrepid, Essex, Enterprise, Bunker Hill, Monterey, Cowpens, Cabot* and *Belleau Wood*, with gunfire support provided by the battleships *Alabama, Iowa, New Jersey, North Carolina, Massachusetts* and *South Dakota*, plus ten cruisers and twenty-nine destroyers. There was ample evidence that the base had been all but abandoned by the Imperial Navy's heavy warships. The cruiser *Naha* was sunk by aircraft while naval gunfire sank the training cruiser *Katori* and two destroyers. Twenty-six merchant vessels with a tonnage of 200,000 were also sent to the bottom. No less than 365 Japanese aircraft swarmed to the attack, of which 300 were shot down in exchange for only twenty-five American aircraft. A counter-attack by seven Japanese torpedo bombers scored a single hit on *Intrepid* without putting her out of action.

Truk had been to the Japanese Combined Fleet what Scapa Flow was to the Royal Navy's Home Fleet. Prior to the main American attack, Admiral Koga had decided to establish Palau as his main base, a decision that could only be regarded as an unfortunate setback that inevitably involved loss of prestige. For the Americans, however, Truk was simply the next stop on the road to Eniwetok Atoll, and the Marianas. Eniwetok was held by Major General Nishida's 1 Amphibious Brigade, an experienced force some 2,000 strong which had been expected to offer even tougher resistance than usual. On 17 February Admiral Turner's command put the 22nd Marines and some Army troops ashore on Engebi Island, situated on the northern rim of the atoll, which was taken without difficulty. Moreover, Eniwetok Island, inside the atoll, and Parry Island, on its southern rim, were all captured in turn by three American battalions.

The Japanese caused 339 fatal casualties, and many more wounded, by the use of land mines. Determined to reduce their casualties, the Americans made extensive use of flamethrowers, which inflicted a heavy toll. By 21 February the garrison had been annihilated.

Fate now took a hand. On 1 April Admiral Koga was killed in an air accident. His place as Commander of the Combined Fleet was taken by Admiral Soemu Toyoda, regarded as possessing a more aggressive character. He immediately made it clear that the primary mission of the Imperial Japanese Navy remained the destruction of the US Navy and its allies. Vice Admiral Jisaburo Ozawa, commanding the carrier striking force, now repaired, rested and in receipt of recently trained pilots, as well as the First Mobile Fleet, was ordered to entice sizeable elements of US naval strength into the locality Palau–Yap–Woleai, in which land-based aircraft could assist in their destruction. Ozawa's fleet assembled off the southern end of the Sulu Peninsula during April and May. Its presence was quickly detected by American submarines, which harassed it and, later, warned Admiral Spruance that it had moved into the Philippine Sea.

During June and August Admiral Turner's V Amphibious Force, numbering over 530 warships and auxiliaries, with the 127,000 troops of Lieutenant General H. M. Smith aboard, headed north into the Marianas. Between 11 and 17 June the carrier aircraft of Vice Admiral Marc Mitscher's Task Force 58 destroyed the enemy's air defences throughout the islands. During this period two carrier groups also attacked the Bonin Islands, halfway between Japan and the Marianas, to inhibit their use as a refuelling base. This air activity also resulted in the loss of 300 Japanese aircraft as opposed just twenty-two American.

On 15 June landings took place on the island of Saipan, covered by eight escort carriers, 170 aircraft and the battleships *California, Colorado, Idaho, Maryland, New Mexico, Pennsylvania* and *Tennessee*, plus eleven cruisers and fifty destroyers. Also present were four escort carriers with spare aircraft. The landings were made by the 2nd and 4th Marine Divisions, the approaches to the landing beaches having already been cleared by underwater demolition teams. Confronting them were Lieutenant General Yoshitsugo Saito's garrison, reinforced by 6,000 sailors. A beachhead had been established by nightfall but so determined had been the resistance that the US 27th Division had to be committed as reinforcements. The difficulties of the ground troops increased when, on 17 June, Mitscher's carriers and – later – all warships departed for the Battle of the Philippine Sea (see below). Deprived of naval gunfire and air support, the infantry advanced slowly and at heavy cost over difficult terrain that had been expertly prepared for defence. The airfield fell on 18 June but not until 9 July, following the defeat of a final suicidal counter-attack by the surviving 3,000 Japanese, did organised resistance end. The capture of Saipan cost the Americans 3,126 killed, 326 missing and 13,160 wounded. Some 27,000 Japanese died, including hundreds who leapt to their death from the cliffs. Only 2,000 prisoners were taken. General Saito and Admiral Nagumo, the doyen of Japanese carrier warfare, took their own lives.

Two days before the landings on Saipan, Admiral Ozawa's 1st Mobile Carrier Fleet had put to sea from its anchorage at Tawi Tawi on the north coast of Borneo, chosen in preference to Palau because of its proximity to fuel oil supplies, and steamed north-eastwards, passing through the Guimeras Straits between the Philippine islands of Panay and Negros at about 09.00 on 15 June. Its intended destination was Saipan, but on the morning of the 16th Ozawa read the following message from Admiral Toyoda to the men under his command:

I humbly relay the message which has been received from the Emperor through the Navy's Commander-in-Chief. The enemy has invaded the Mariana Islands and we must annihilate them. This operation has immense bearing on the fate of the Empire. It is hoped that all the sailors and airmen of this command will exert their utmost to achieve as magnificent results as the Battle of Tsu Shima.

Ozawa had a total of nine carriers under his command. He personally commanded CarDiv 1, consisting of the carriers *Taiho*, *Shokaku* and *Zuikaku*. CarDiv 2, under Vice Admiral Tajaji Joshima, consisted of *Junyo*, *Hiyo* and *Ryuho*. CarDiv 3, under the command of Vice Admiral Sueo Obayashi, contained *Chitose*, *Chiyoda* and *Zuiho*. This looked very well on paper, although the nine carriers only had 473 aircraft aboard. Despite this, Ozawa believed that the forthcoming battle would take place within range of 100 more aircraft flying from the islands of Guam, Rota and Yap. Even then, he would still be fighting against odds, as the Americans would be flying off no less than 956 aircraft.

The Japanese battleship fleet, known as the Batjan Force, had left its base at Halmahera in the Dutch East Indies at about the same time that Ozawa left Tawi Tawi. It was under the command of Vice Admiral Matome Ugaki and consisted of the four battleships *Haruna*, *Kongo*, *Musashi* and *Yamato* (flag). The last two were the largest battleships in the world with a main armament of 18-inch guns, the muzzle blast of which made life intolerable for anyone nearby. The Batjan Force also included eight heavy cruisers and eight destroyers. By 09.00 on 15 June it had also entered the Philippine Sea and was steaming north-west, intending to rendezvous with Ozawa on the 17th. The Emperor's message was read to the crews.

Some commanders are lucky, some are not. Ozawa was not. On 15 June the brand new American submarine *Cavalla*, commanded by Lieutenant Commander Hermann J. Kossler, sighted a small convoy consisting of two tankers and two destroyers. He surfaced at 05.45 next morning and transmitted a contact report. The answer instructed him to follow the tankers, which were prime targets. However, at 20.15 on 17 June the Batjan Force ran directly over his position. At 22.25 he transmitted a further contact report containing details of the enemy's course and speed. In response to this, all American submarines in the area were informed that both Japanese groups had now been reported and that they were to shoot first and send reports later.

At 10.12 on the morning of 19 June *Cavalla*'s radar scope revealed a number of aircraft. At 10.39 the aircraft seemed to be circling and the masts of ships appeared. By 11.00 Kossler could see four ships distinctly; the carrier *Shokaku*, two cruisers ahead and to port of her and a solitary destroyer on her port beam. The situation could not have been better as the carrier was landing her aircraft and could not change course. The range shortened and at 11.18 Kossler fired a spread of six torpedoes. His periscope revealed the destroyer heading straight for him, some 1,500 yards distant and he took the submarine down to a safe depth. Three huge explosions confirmed that he had hit his target, although he was forced to remain where he was for the next three hours, during which no less than 105 depth charges exploded around the boat, causing damage to the sonar and air induction pipelines. Only after the war did a prisoner confirm that *Cavalla* had sunk *Shokaku*, one of only two carriers surviving from the attack on Pearl Harbor.

Early that morning the submarine *Albacore*, under Commander J. W. Blanchard, was stationed on a patrol line north of Yap. Blanchard took her down to avoid being spotted by the numerous Japanese aircraft overhead. At 07.50 he sighted an aircraft carrier, a cruiser and several more ships along the horizon. The range to the carrier was 13,000 yards but the angle of attack was poor. He ordered full ahead and swung towards his target. As he did so, a second group, consisting of a carrier, a cruiser and several destroyers suddenly entered his lens at a range of only 10,000 yards, placing him just ten degrees on the carrier's starboard bow. She was travelling at 27 knots and the firing range was shrinking to 1,500 yards. At 08.08 he went through the final preliminaries before giving the order to fire, only to discover to his horror that there were problems with his Torpedo Data Computer. With the target bearing down on him at speed he took the only possible course and fired all six tubes. There was just one heavy explosion followed by the thudding of depth charges as Blanchard took *Albacore* deep. His report suggested that he had only damaged the enemy carrier and he never knew that he had witnessed the beginning of the Battle of the Philippine Sea, for his boat was lost on her next patrol. Nearly a year later a prisoner confirmed that Taiho, Japan's newest carrier, had been struck by a single torpedo that had caused the petrol fires and ammunition explosions that had finally sunk her.

Ozawa's search aircraft were launched in the pre-dawn darkness of 19 June. As the streaks of first light began to appear in the eastern sky they sighted the leading elements of Mitscher's Fifth Fleet, which they estimated to be some 300 miles from their own carriers and Ozawa himself calculated to be 500 miles from the Batjan Force. The opposing fleets were running south on approximately parallel courses. The American carriers were deployed in four groups, half about ninety miles north-west of Guam and the remainder approximately 110 miles south-west of Saipan with Vice Admiral Raymond Spruance's battle fleet.

Prior to this, Ozawa had re-organised his various formations into three elements. Of these the strongest was the van under Vice Admiral Kurita Takeo, consisting of the three light carriers Chitose, Chiyoda and Zuiho, the four battleships Yamato, Musashi, Kongo and Haruna, and the four cruisers Atago, Takao, Maya and Chokai, screened by nine destroyers. Some way to the rear were Forces A and B. Force A, commanded personally by Ozawa, had contained the fleet carriers (Taiho and Shokaku both already lost), and Zuikaku, the cruisers Myoko, Haguro and Yahagi and a screen of nine destroyers. Force B, under Rear Admiral Takaji Joshina, consisted of the carriers Junyo, Hiyo and Ryuho, the battleship Nagato, the heavy cruiser Mogami and a ten-strong destroyer screen. Ozawa hoped to trap the American carriers between his own and land-based bombers flying from airfields in the Marianas, partially eliminating his opponents' superiority in numbers.

Starting at 08.30 Ozawa commenced launching a series of four strikes from his carriers at thirty-minute intervals. While these were on their way, land-based aircraft flying from Guam closed in to attack the American carriers. Mitscher responded by sending up his fighters to intercept and instructed his bombers to keep the flight decks clear so that they could remain in constant use. Those

Japanese aircraft that did manage to break through fell victim to the American ships' combined anti-aircraft fire. By 10.00 the survivors were heading back to their airfields, followed by the American bombers which began rendering their bases inoperable.

The first of Ozawa's strikes was picked up by the American radar just as the raiders from Guam were leaving. There followed a series of air battles that lasted from 10.00 to 12.00. It speaks volumes for the efficiency of American flight deck administration that there were never less than 300 Wildcats in the air at any one time. Hardly any of the half-trained Japanese pilots managed to break through, inflicting negligible damage on the battleship *Indiana* and the carriers *Bunker Hill* and *Wasp (2)*. Of the 373 strike aircraft launched by the Japanese fleet, only 130 returned home. The Americans lost twenty-nine aircraft and the onset of dusk put an end to the fighting.

Some confusion had been caused when Ozawa was forced to move his flag from the stricken *Taiho* to the cruiser *Haguro*. The Japanese managed to break contact during the night but much of the following day was spent in confused wrangling about the refuelling programme. This had to be suspended when *Atago* picked up an American sighting report indicating that Mitscher had launched a pursuit and that by 13.30 had closed the gap between the two fleets to 300 miles. At 16.24 his carriers launched a strike force of 131 planes, escorted by eighty-five Hellcats. By 18.40 they had the Japanese in sight, although the sun was now dropping towards the western horizon.

The only hope for Ozawa and his ships was that they might just be able to escape into the darkness, but it was not to be. Their remaining fighters fought hard but in vain to keep the enemy at a distance. They were almost wiped out and only fourteen American aircraft were shot down. By 18.35 the Americans had broken through and were launching a determined attack on the carrier *Chiyoda*, scoring two hits aft, wrecking her flight deck and destroying the aircraft on it and starting fires. Nearby, the battleship *Haruna* was hit badly and forced to flood a magazine and the cruiser *Mayo's* damage control parties were dealing with fires and flooding. Next, it was the turn of the carrier *Hiyo*. She sustained a torpedo hit aft and a second that hit squarely, setting off raging fires and explosions that blew a hole in the hull and flooded her engine rooms. Now powerless, she became a burning hulk with a 20-degree list, surrounded by vessels hoping to rescue her crew. Next, two holes were punched through the carrier *Junyo*'s flight deck and further damage was caused by the explosion of three more bombs.

Some miles to the west of the sinking *Hiyo* was the carrier *Ryuho*, making good progress. She became the target of a squadron of dive-bombers, but took expert evasive action and put up a dense curtain of anti-aircraft fire. Lieutenant Commander Alvin Priel bored straight down through it, releasing his entire bomb load. His 1,000-pounder exploded on the stern, which began belching smoke and flames. *Ryuho* swung wildly to port but more Dauntlesses took her for their target, landing eight more bombs on the carrier's bow. Flames roared up to 300 feet high from a shattered magazine, but some ships refuse to die and *Ryuho* was one of them. A bomb smashed its way into one of *Zuikaku*'s hangars but her damage control crew quickly brought the situation under control. Elsewhere, two tankers, *Seiyo Maru* and *Hayashi Maru*, were sunk and a third, *Genyo Maru*, was seriously damaged.

It was time for the American airmen to leave. Most of their fuel gauges were showing half or less full, too little to ensure reaching their home carriers, especially if their aircraft had been damaged. They could only continue back along the route out for as long as their fuel supply would let them, then they would have to splash down and await rescue. Senior officers aboard the carriers, aware of the knife-edge situation, risked the presence of Japanese submarines and illuminated their ships, each showing its own coded light colour. A surprising number of aircraft did manage to touch down on their decks, but eighty ditched and their crews spent hours in their inflatable dinghies. Destroyers in line abreast moved steadily towards them, their boats ready to be slung out at the first flash from an airman's torch or dinghy light. Some fifty airmen were picked up in this way and a small number were spotted and rescued by Catalina flying boats next day.

Meanwhile, Ozawa's shattered fleet was heading back whence it had come, aware now that Japan's naval air arm barely existed; whether any of it could be put back together remained to be seen. Ozawa tendered his resignation to Admiral Toyoda, blaming the defeat on his own incompetence. Toyoda generously refused to accept it, blaming the disaster on ill luck. Official documents and volumes of naval history would refer to the event as The Battle of the Philippine Sea, but the Americans who fought in it referred to it by a different name – The Great Marianas Turkey Shoot.

CHAPTER 14

Have A Care What You Ask For

The Battle of the Philippine Sea was the war's last carrier battle and the last that the Imperial Navy would ever fight. For Japan, the combined effect of partially trained pilots, dreadful losses and efficient American radar had destroyed the offensive potential of the fleet. The fate of the Marianas was sealed irrevocably. Tinian fell on 1 August and Guam, a pre-war American territory, followed on the 10th. The Allies now possessed a number of alternative routes by which they could reach the Japanese home islands and for Imperial General Headquarters the difficulty lay in assessing which they would choose. The most direct route led through the Bonin and the Ryukyu Islands. Alternatively, a strike at Formosa would separate the whole of the prized Southern Area from Japan. Again, the liberation of the Philippines, considered probable, would create serious problems across a wide area. Likewise, the loss of Malaya and the Dutch East Indies, the very heart of the Southern Area, would deprive Japan of the very materials for which she had gone to war.

After much thought, the Naval High Command produced a plan for defending the areas most at risk. It was optimistically named Operation SHO–Victory. SHO–1 covered the Philippines; SHO–2 covered Formosa and the Ryukyus; SHO–3 covered the islands of Honshu, Kyushu and Shikoku in the home islands; and SHO–4 covered Hokkaido and the Kuriles. In the meantime, whatever the Allies chose, it was a matter of urgency that the Combined Fleet should be returned to fighting trim. After the recent battle the surviving carriers returned to Japanese bases and repair yards. Eight new carriers were being built on any hull that would accommodate a flight deck. The largest was the *Shinano*, based on the hull of what would have been a sister ship to the *Yamato* and *Musashi* and given an armoured flight deck strengthened with concrete. Next came a number of tanker hulls. Finally, and strangest of all, was the conversion of the battleships *Hiyuga* and *Ise* into seaplane carriers by removing the after 14-inch gun turrets and raising the quarterdeck so that twenty-two seaplanes could be accommodated below. As there was no possibility of the seaplanes being able to land on the tiny flight deck they would have to land alongside and be hoisted inboard by crane. These odd-looking conversions were neither fish nor really fowl and, in any event, there were never enough trained seaplane pilots for them to be manned adequately.

Correctly, the High Command considered SHO–1 to have priority, but their reasons differed from those of the Americans. There had been long and strenuous discussions between General MacArthur and Admirals King and Nimitz as to what should follow the Battle of the Philippine Sea. MacArthur, weighed down by his memory of being ordered to leave the Philippines and his promise to return and liberate them, was at odds with the two admirals who wanted an advance westwards from the Marianas to Formosa and China. However, in September, Admiral Halsey reported that air strikes against the Philippines had met with minimal response and that the invasion should begin with a landing on Leyte Island. This was accepted and the date for the invasion was set for 20 October.

The huge concentration of shipping accumulated by the Americans alerted Kurita to the fact that the invasion was imminent. His defence plan contained four phases, as follows:

Phase 1. Aircraft flying from land bases in the Philippines were to hit the American invasion fleet at ranges up to 700 miles. Heavy damage was to be inflicted with torpedoes and bombs.

Phase 2. The Mobile Fleet was to concentrate at Brunei and sail to intercept the American fleet.

Phase 3. The Mobile Fleet's battle squadrons would engage the invasion fleet off the beaches, while,

Phase 4. Admiral Ozawa would make sorties from Japan with
the last carriers to lure the American carrier task forces
away from their invasion fleet.

When, on 17 October, the invasion actually began with a landing
on Suluan Island at the entrance to Leyte Gulf, the warning order
'Prepare for SHO–1' was flashed to the entire fleet, followed by the
command 'Execute!' the following day. Kurita took the opportunity
to make a rousing speech to his staff and senior officers. In this
he declared that the Imperial Navy had been granted a 'glorious
opportunity', adding, 'You must all remember that there are such
things as miracles. What man can say that there is no chance of our
fleet to turn the tide of war in a decisive battle.'

This was greeted with wild cheering and shouts of 'Banzai!'
Yet the moment was one of emotion rather than cool professional
assessment. There was not an officer present who believed that
victory was a realistic outcome. Instead, there was a profound
hope that the enemy would be hurt so badly that he would
consider a negotiated peace, yet even that view was the child of
wildly misplaced optimism. To start with, SHO–1 was, like every
Japanese naval plan throughout the war, incredibly and needlessly
complicated. It is often referred to as The Battle of Leyte Gulf,
yet even that is misleading as no less than four separate naval
engagements took place during its course and perhaps the easiest
way to grasp what took place is describe each in turn.

The first stage of the Japanese reaction involved Kurita's Centre
Force leaving Lingga Roads near Singapore and concentrating at
Brunei in British North Borneo, this being achieved by 22 October.
Kurita then steamed north-east with his fleet in two columns. The
leading division of the starboard column was led by the cruisers
Myoko, *Haguro* and *Maya*, followed by the battleships *Yamato* and
Musahi. The column's second division contained the cruisers
Kumano and *Suzuya*, followed by the battleship *Kongo*. The port
column's leading division contained the cruisers *Atago*, *Takao* and
Chokai, followed by the battleship *Nagato*. The column's second

division consisted of the light cruiser *Yajagi*, the cruisers *Tone* and *Chikuma* and the battleship *Haruna*. Destroyer screens were out to port and starboard, led by the light cruiser *Noshiro*. The plan then required Vice Admiral Shoji Nishimura to bear away east-north-east with one light cruiser and ten destroyers. Known as Force C, this would pass through the Balabac Strait, cross the Sulu Sea and proceed parallel with the northern coast of Mindanao. A third element of the plan was now activated. A small group of warships designated the 2nd Striking Force was already steaming south from the Pescadores Islands under the command of Vice Admiral Kihoyide Shima. It consisted of three heavy cruisers, two light cruisers and eight destroyers and would actually cross Kurita's northerly course before swinging south-east to cross the Sulu Sea, then east to reinforce Nishimura at the Surigao Strait, thereby blocking any attempt by the American invasion fleet to escape to the west. Simultaneously, Kurita would continue steaming north through the Palawan Passage, leaving Palawan Island to starboard. To the north of the Calamian group of islands he would turn east, passing south of Mindoro, and thread his way across the Sibuyan Sea and the San Barnardino Strait. At this point he would turn south and head for the Surigao Strait, trapping the American invasion fleet against the combined forces of Nishimura and Shima. Air cover would be provided by land-based aircraft. It was at this point that the fourth element of the plan began to take effect. Ozawa, with every serviceable carrier he could muster, was already heading south from Japan's Inland Sea. His orders were that, once his entry into the battle area had been detected by the Americans, he was to trail his coat and draw off the American carriers in a protracted pursuit.

There was a curious sense of *déjà vu* about the opening engagement of the battle. Two American submarines, *Darter* (Commander D. H. McClintock) and *Dace* (Commander B. D. Claggett) were patrolling west of Palawan on the day of the landings. At midnight on 22 October the two boats rendezvoused on the surface while their captains discussed patrol plans by megaphone. Whatever plans had been made had to be set aside when *Darter*'s radar operator picked up a major contact at 30,000 yards range. It was moving in a north-easterly direction and both boats increased their speed to get ahead of the western column of Japanese warships. At 05.32 on the 23rd McClintock found himself in an ideal position to attack with the range down to 980 yards. He fired all six bow tubes at one enemy cruiser and then, putting his helm hard over, fired his four stern tubes at a second. A snatched look through the periscope revealed the target enveloped in smoke and flames from 'A' Turret aft. Simultaneously, four hits were made on the second target. Meanwhile, Claggett was stalking what he believed to be a Kongo-class battleship. Aboard *Dace* Claggett heard the series of thunderous explosions caused by *Darter*'s torpedoes, followed by the drumfire of depth-charge salvos. Time was not really on his side. At 05.54 he commenced firing his bow tubes at a range of 1,800 yards and was rewarded with four hits. These were followed by two major explosions, suggesting that fires had spread to the target's magazines. These were followed by breaking-up noises that were too close for comfort.

Darter had sunk the heavy cruiser *Atago*. This had been Kurita's flagship and the admiral, shaken by the experience, had transferred to *Yamato*. *Darter*'s second victim was another heavy cruiser, *Takao*. She was badly damaged and McClintock wanted to finish her off, but by now she was too closely guarded. At 22.00 that night the cripple began to move at five knots under her own power and was clearly heading back to Singapore. Because of the vigilance of her escort, McClintock decided to work round and attack her from ahead, but at this point disaster struck and *Darter* ran aground on the coral heads of the notorious Bombay Shoal and had to be abandoned. *Dace*'s victim was finally identified as the heavy cruiser *Maya*.

Kurita hardly welcomed the losses he had sustained, but the fact was that his main body was still making good time and by the evening of 23 October was swinging east towards the Mindoro Strait. In addition, neither Nishimura's Force C nor Shima's 2nd Striking Force had been discovered. The outlook for the morrow, therefore, still remained optimistic.

There had, however, been various adjustments to the Americans' position during the night, based on *Darter*'s contact reports. During the day Admiral Halsey's detached carrier groups had been operating over the Philippine Sea, but during the night they were moved to positions close to the islands' eastern coastline so that TG 38.2[1] was covering the exit from the San Bernardino Strait, TG 38.3 was off the Polillo Islands and TG 38.4 was off Leyte Gulf. From 06.00 onwards reconnaissance patrols fanned out to the west. At 07.46 Halsey received a signal to the effect that Kurita's Centre Force had been sighted south of Mindoro and was steering eastwards into the Tablas Strait. Halsey's prompt reaction was to order all three groups to the exit from the San Bernardino Strait and launch strikes while TG 38.1, on its way to Ulithi, was told to refuel at sea and return.

Nishimura's Force C was spotted heading east through the Sulu Sea and promptly attacked by aircraft from the carriers *Enterprise* and *Franklin*. A bomb striking *Fuso* aft caused a major fire that destroyed the battleship's catapult aircraft, but in other respects the ship remained fully operational. Shima had also been spotted by noon. Both he and Nishimura were expecting heavy air attacks and were delighted when none materialised. There were several reasons for this. First, Halsey's carriers were now concentrating on the area of the Sibuyan Sea, through which the principal enemy thrust was expected. Secondly, the air element of Admiral Thomas C. Kincaid's Seventh Fleet, both land-based and aboard his escort carriers, was heavily committed to supporting the landing operations. Thirdly, Kincaid was not only confident that Nishimura and Shima were heading for the Surigao Strait, but also happy that the battleships, cruisers and destroyers that he had deployed there could bring them up short.

---

1 An American Task Group was a very large organisation capable of carrying out several tasks simultaneously. The detached elements were identified by adding a numeral to their parent number, for example, detached portions of Task Group 38 would become TG 38.1, TG 38.2, etc.

At this point Admiral Fukatome Shigeru committed his land-based air squadrons, sending in wave after wave of escorted bombers against the American carriers in a vain attempt to protect Kurita's Centre Force. The result was a massacre. *Princeton*'s Hellcats accounted for thirty-four, *Lexington*'s (2) another thirteen and *Langley*'s at least five more. Then, at 09.38, disaster struck. *Princeton* had turned into the wind and was recovering her fighters when a Yokasuka D4Y-2 Susei (Judy) dive-bomber broke out of low cloud cover and commenced its dive towards the carrier, passing through an intense storm of flak put up by every other ship in the group. At 1,000 feet the pilot pulled out and released his 550lb bomb. It smashed its way through three decks before exploding. A petrol fire rapidly engulfed six armed torpedo planes. The warheads exploded, blowing out the lifts. Fires spread throughout the ship and some of her crew were taken off while the cruiser *Birmingham* closed in on her weather bow to assist in the firefighting, assisted by the anti-aircraft cruiser *Reno*.

Two hours later it began to look as though the fires were being brought under control. However, the screening destroyers reported a submarine contact, forcing *Birmingham* to cast off. She returned to take the carrier in tow once the threat had disappeared but, unknown to anyone on deck, in the interval the flames had reached a supply of bombs in the carrier's torpedo stowage compartment. They seemed to detonate simultaneously, blowing the carrier's stern apart and lashing those aboard the cruiser's deck with a blizzard of jagged steel splinters. Two hundred and twenty-nine men lay dead or dying while another 420 had lost one or more limbs, or been ripped open. Saving *Princeton* was no longer an option. At 16.00 *Birmingham* backed away to bury her dead and *Reno* sank the carrier with her torpedoes.

What became known as the Battle of the Sibuyan Sea had begun at 10.26 when Rear Admiral Bogan's TG 38. 1, consisting of the carriers *Intrepid* and *Cabot*, discovered Kurita's Centre Force steaming north-east through the Tablas Strait. Although the Japanese were known to have increased the anti-aircraft armament of their warships, the amount of flak that rose to meet the Americans was more spectacular than effective. Two torpedoes struck the heavy cruiser *Myoko,* reducing her speed to fifteen knots. As this was not sufficient for her to stay with Centre Force, Kurita ordered her to return to base. A second torpedo struck *Musahi's* starboard armour without apparently affecting the battleship's performance. *Musahi* was also the target for a second strike and was hit by two bombs and two torpedoes. This time, her speed fell away to 22 knots and although Kurita reduced the speed of his fleet *Musahi* continued to fall further behind.

It was now the turn of Rear Admiral Sherman's Task Group 38. 3 from which no fewer than sixty-eight planes homed in through overcast weather from the carriers *Lexington* and *Essex.* This was followed during the afternoon by three further attack waves, one from each of the carrier groups. Their 500lb general purpose bombs made little or no impact on *Musahi's* armour, but estimates suggest that she had sustained between ten and nineteen torpedo hits and was now over twenty miles astern of Centre Force and in company with the cruiser *Tone.* A fresh attack exploded a further three torpedoes in succession against her starboard bow. This slid under water and became a huge funnel through which the sea rushed into her hull. She was now beyond control and crawling along. Kurita ordered her to run herself aground, but it was too late. Her engines died as she sank lower. The order to 'Abandon Ship' was also given too late for the 1,000 men left aboard. At 19.35 she gave a sudden lurch, rolled onto her port side and sank without ever having fired her enormous main armament.

There now occurred a sequence of events that came very close to costing the Americans the battle. Obviously, Kurita was depressed by the events of the last twenty-four hours. In particular, he had been very disappointed by the performance of Fukadome's airmen, and none too pleased that the effects of Ozawa's coat-trailing had yet to make their presence felt. He despatched a signal to Toyoda informing him that he was about to reverse course in the Sibuyan Sea and 'to resume the advance when the battle results of friendly units permit'. The last was intended for Ozawa's benefit, for by now his almost empty carriers should have drawn off Halsey's carrier groups, thereby permitting Kurita to leave the San Bernardino Strait and head south for the climactic battle that he would fight in conjunction with Nishimura and Shima in the area of Leyte Gulf.

In fact the hiatus in the north was not matched in the south. Nishimura's state of mind seems to have been one of fatalism and, come what may, his small force was heading for the entrance to Leyte Gulf without bothering to wait for Shima, who was actually not too far behind. It has been suggested that the reason for this was that Shima was the senior of the two and Nishimura disliked the idea of taking orders from him. If he had known what lay directly across his path then perhaps he might have considered the matter anew, yet the Japanese death wish was an extremely potent force when allied with the concept of the warrior dying in the service of his Emperor.

The task of halting the Nishimura-Shima strike into Leyte Gulf was given to Rear Admiral Jesse B. Oldendorf's Bombardment and Fire Support Group. Deployed across the northern exit from Surigao Strait were his six battleships *Maryland, West Virginia, Mississippi, Tennessee, California* and *Pennsylvania*. His cruisers were divided into right and left flank squadrons, patrolling five miles further down the enemy's anticipated line of approach. The right flank squadron consisted of *Phoenix, Boise* and HMAS *Shropshire*; the left flank squadron included *Louisville* (Oldendorf's flagship), *Portland, Minneapolis, Denver* and *Columbia*. Closer still to the enemy were destroyer and PT boat squadrons

Before action was joined Nishimura received a signal from Kurita informing him of the latter's reversal of course and indicating that he would not reach Leyte Gulf until 11.00 next morning. However, Nishimura was ordered to break into the Gulf through the Surigao Strait and join Kurita off Saluan Island at 09.00. This would involve a night action, which Nishimura was quite prepared to fight, although he had no idea of the odds he would be facing and Shima was still forty miles astern.

The PT boat squadron launched a series of attacks during which numerous torpedoes were launched without success. It was then the turn of Captain J. G. Coward's destroyer squadron. Coward, aboard *Remey*, personally led *McGowan* and *Melvin* down the eastern side of the Strait while Commander Richard H. Phillips, in *McDermut,* led *Monsen* along the western shore. At 02.45 a single line of advancing dots revealed Nishimura's group at approximately fifteen miles range. First came the destroyers *Michishio, Asagumo, Yamagumo* and *Shigure*, then the battleships *Yamashiro* and *Fuso,* with the heavy cruiser *Mogami* bringing up the rear.

By 03.00 Coward's three ships were positioned 8,000 to 9,000 yards on Nishimura's starboard bow. Torpedoes were made ready and the destroyers had turned to launch when a searchlight snapped on, illuminating *Remey*. Shells began hurling their waterspouts around the American ships as they released a total of twenty-seven torpedoes. Then they turned away to vanish into darkness at 35 knots. Too late, starshells cracked into brilliant light overhead but by then the Americans had gone. The torpedoes had an eight-minute run to make and during that time Nishimura perversely declined to take evasive action and maintained a steady course. At the end of it straining eyes saw one flash – and possibly two – illuminate the side of the battleship *Fuso.* She broke away to starboard and began circling, out of control with fires raging, then stopped. Finally, she blew up and broke into two separate portions that continued to burn until they sank at 04.30.

Phillips' destroyers had reached a suitable firing position ten minutes after Coward's and launched twenty torpedoes before escaping unscathed. One exploded against *Yamashiro* without causing critical damage; another hit the *Yamagumo,* which blew up and sank immediately; the third left *Michishio* wallowing and without power; a fourth blew the bows off *Asagumo,* which limped out of action. Yet still Nishimura pressed on, now with only the damaged *Yamashiro* plus the as-yet undamaged *Mogami* and *Shigure*.

Two more destroyer divisions were committed to the battle. Near the Leyte shore Captain J. M. McManes, aboard *Hutchins*, brought

Daly and *Bache* into action, firing fifteen torpedoes between 03.29 and 03.36 without result and then engaging *Michishio* and *Asagumo* with gunfire until ordered to clear the range for the big ships. As *Hutchins* turned north she released her last five torpedoes, at least one of which hit *Michishio*, which blew up and sank at 03.58. In the centre of the Strait HMAS *Arunta* under Commander A. E. Buchanan, RAN, led *Killen* and *Beale* into torpedo range, firing fourteen torpedoes between 03.23 and 03.25 then reversing course.

Screening the cruisers of the American left flank were the three divisions of Captain Roland N. Smoot's destroyer squadron. Smoot's own Division 1 – *Albert W. Grant, Richard P. Leary* and *Newcomb* – were heading straight for the enemy line, while Captain Conley's Division 2 – *Bryant, Halford* and *Robinson* – were on his port bow and Commander Boulware's Division 3 – *Bennion, Leutze* and *Heywood L. Edwards* – were on his starboard bow. Smoot led his destroyers to a point closer to the enemy than any other destroyer commander that night and although his Divisions 2 and 3 failed to score a hit with their torpedoes, he personally scored two hits on the *Yamashiro*, which was already ablaze from the numerous hits she had received.

Shortly after, there followed what today would be called a 'friendly fire' incident. The American cruisers had opened fire at 03.51, followed by the battleships at 03.53. The Japanese ships had changed their position to the extent that on the radar screen of one light cruiser the destroyer *Albert W. Grant* appeared to be one of them, an opinion reinforced by the fact that she was taking hits from the 4.7-inch guns of *Yamashiro*'s secondary battery, although their source was not apparent. Now, she was hit and set ablaze by eleven American 6-inch shells, killing thirty-four of her men and wounding ninety-four. As soon as he was aware of the disaster Oldendorf ordered 'Cease Fire' and *Grant* was towed out of action by *Newcomb*. The two torpedo hits scored by *Grant* had, however, ripped open *Yamashiro*'s hull. By 04.09, she was being hit repeatedly by a rain of 16- and 14-inch shells and was clearly sinking. By 04.19 the latter had gone, taking Nishimura to the warrior's death he was seeking.

Admiral Shima had actually entered the Strait at 03.25 and had immediately been forced to detach the light cruiser *Abukama* when she sustained serious torpedo damage at the hands of *PT 137*. At 04.10 the admiral came across the two halves of *Fuso*, still burning. At 04.30 he came across the damaged *Mogami* and the *Shigure*, the latter still more or less intact, trying to escape to the south. *Mogami*'s damage control parties were still hard at work when Shima's flagship, the cruiser *Nachi*, steered across her bows and was rammed, sustaining damage to her stern that reduced her speed to 18 knots. Recognising that there was no point in proceeding further, Shima ordered his cruisers to launch their torpedoes at targets that had appeared on his radar screen – now believed to be a group of small islands – and reversed course to the south.

Oldendorf followed and there was a brief exchange of fire with *Mogami* at first light. Shortly after, the Americans came across *Asagumo*, which had lost her bows three hours earlier and lain stopped in the middle of the Strait ever since. She was duelling with the destroyers *Cony* and *Sigourney* when the cruisers *Denver* and *Columbia* arrived to end the matter with the crushing weight of their firepower. She impressed them not a little, for when she finally slid under, her after turret was still firing. At 09.10 seventeen Avenger torpedo-bombers located *Mogami* limping slowly across the Mindanao Sea. She, too, earned her pay and when the Avengers left she could no longer move and the destroyer *Akebono* was left to take off her crew and despatch her with a last torpedo.

Oldendorf and his staff had every right to feel pleased with their night's work. The Japanese had always talked of wanting a decisive battle and now their wish had been granted. Suddenly, and without the slightest warning, the Americans received news that struck them like a blow between the eyes. Somehow, Kurita had broken out of the San Bernadino Strait and his battleships had been encountered to the east of the island of Samar. Oldendorf's Bombardment Force was all that stood between them and MacArthur's virtually defenceless invasion fleet, and its magazines were already sorely depleted. With disaster in the offing, the question being asked throughout the fleet was, how had such a thing been allowed to happen?

CHAPTER 15

... And Then There Were None

Despite having two flagships shot out from under him in two days, Kurita was every bit as delighted by developments on the northern edge of the battle zone as Kinkaid was horrified. Somehow, Halsey's normally sound judgement had let him down and he had accepted Ozawa's coat-trailing as an invitation that simply could not be refused. Now, he was leading his force of fast battleships far to the north in pursuit of Ozawa and the remnant of Japan's carrier fleet. Kurita, finding that the exit from the San Bernardino Strait had been left unguarded, emerged with Centre Force's battleships and heavy cruisers to wreak destruction among Kincaid's escort carriers and their escorts. Thus, when the tall pagoda-like control towers of the Japanese battleships broke the western horizon at about 06.45 on 25 October, Kinkaid's only options lay in flight and a forlorn hope that Oldendorf would emerge from his overnight battle in the Surigao Strait with sufficient ammunition to meet this new and very dangerous challenge.

Some airfields ashore were already in American hands but, as yet, they were unready for general use. In the circumstances air cover and ground attack missions were being flown by the sixteen escort carriers of Rear Admiral Thomas L. Sprague's Task Group 77.4. This was divided into three sub-groups, viz: 77.4.1, 77.4.2 and 77.4.3, better known as Taffy 1, 2 and 3 because of their radio call-signs. Taffy 1, commanded personally by Sprague, consisted of four escort carriers and was the most southerly of the sub-groups, located off the coast of Mindanao. Taffy 2, under Rear Admiral F. B. Stump in *Natona Bay*, contained six escort carriers and was stationed off the entrance to Leyte Gulf, and Taffy 3, under Rear Admiral Clifton Sprague, was located off the east coast of Samar Island and consisted of the six escort carriers *Fanshaw Bay* (Flag), *St Lo, White Plains, Kalinin Bay, Kitkun Bay* (Flag, Rear Admiral R. A. Ofstie) and *Gambier Bay*. Each sub-unit was screened by three destroyers and four destroyer escorts, the former armed with five 5-inch guns and ten torpedoes, and the latter with two 5-inch guns and three torpedoes. In other respects, the individual defence of each escort carrier lay with twelve to eighteen Wildcats (sometimes Hellcats) and a dozen Avenger torpedo-bombers, plus a solitary 5-inch gun.

Following their normal routine, the sub-groups launched their reconnaissance flights at first light. At 06.47 Clifton Sprague received an alarmed transmission from Ensign Hans Jensen, the pilot of an Avenger engaged in anti-submarine patrol. Jensen's contact report indicated the battleships, eight cruisers and a number of destroyers. At first Sprague thought that Jensen was mistakenly reporting some of Halsey's ships. Then, things started to happen very quickly. The pagoda superstructures of Japanese battleships were breaking the north-western horizon. Hardly had this been digested than several huge water spouts, thrown up by exploding shells to heights beyond that of the carriers' flight decks, appeared between *Fanshaw Bay* and *White Plains*.

It was apparent that the enemy already had the range and Thomas Sprague reacted accordingly. The six escort carriers turned east together, away from the enemy yet permitting their aircraft to take advantage of a cross wind and become airborne Then, at Sprague's order, the carriers began making smoke, hanging low, black and greasy in their wakes. Before it could solidify into a screen, however, *Yamato*'s 18.1-inch guns opened fire at the astounding range of 35,000 yards, followed a little later by the 14-inch guns of the *Kongo* and *Haruna*. There were no direct hits but plenty of near misses that left coloured stains on the water indicating their respective origins. Clifton Sprague doubted whether any of his ships could survive another five minutes.

Salvation appeared in the form of a heavy rain squall into which the carriers vanished one after another between 07.06 and 07.15. The Japanese radar was insufficiently developed to penetrate this and firing ceased as soon as the targets were lost to view. Once the last of his aircraft was airborne, Sprague brought his carriers round onto a southerly course without the Japanese being aware of it. The result was that for a while the range continued to open as Kurita continued to pursue an eastwards course. Shaken by his recent experiences and lacking two nights' sleep, his judgement was less than acute and he seems to have been firmly convinced that he was dealing with some of Halsey's fast fleet carriers. The escort carriers' low maximum speed of 19 knots should have convinced him otherwise, but once he had turned south and was running parallel to the Americans he seemed happy that he now possessed the weather gauge, believing that the carriers' aircraft would be unable to take off. That they were already aloft and strafing his bridges seems to have escaped him, as did the arrival of Taffy 2's aircraft.

The fact was that Clifton Sprague was far from being out of the wood. At 07.16 he ordered three destroyers from his screen, *Hoel*, *Heermann* and *Johnston*, to counter-attack. *Johnston*, under Commander Ernest E. Evans, was already making smoke and heading directly for a group of four enemy heavy cruisers. Leading the latter was *Kumano*, the flagship of Vice Admiral Shiraishi. Opening fire at 18,000 yards, she scored several hits on the *Johnston*. However, at this point aircraft from Taffy 3 and Taffy 2 homed in on *Suzuya*, *Kumano*'s next astern, landing a bomb on her. With her speed falling away to 20 knots she wheeled out of line. The same air attack permitted *Johnston* to close to within 10,000 yards of *Kumano* and launch all ten of her torpedoes. The bows of Shiraishi's flagship were blown off and fires swept through her. The admiral transferred to the damaged *Suzuya*. This absorbed so much time that both cruisers were left far behind the running fight and played no further part in the action.

Two groups of Japanese cruisers were now attempting to isolate the carriers from the east while the battleships pursued them from astern. *Johnston* found herself between the two and the recipient of three 14-inch and three 6-inch shells. The 14-inch shells were armour-piercing and were intended to explode inside their target after their primers had been activated by striking thick armour.

Johnston's hull, however, did not consist of thick armour, with the result that the shells, fired at high velocity, were not primed until they had first entered and then left the hull; had it been otherwise the ship would have been blown to pieces. As it was, she was lucky to survive the 6-inch shells which wrecked her bridge, after engine room and boiler. Fortunately, the squall provided cover for them to be returned to working order. Emerging from the rain, she encountered *Hoel* and *Heermann* heading straight for the enemy, followed by the little destroyer escort *Samuel B. Roberts*. Evans immediately conformed to their movements.

Hoel, under Commander L. S. Kintberger, with Commander W. D. Thomas, the squadron's senior officer aboard, launched a decidedly impertinent attack on the massive *Kongo*, receiving a battering on the way in but launching half her torpedoes at 9,000 yards. Seriously alarmed, *Kongo* turned away to the north and was absent from the battle for some vital time. With her bridge and upperworks a smashed tangle of wreckage, *Hoel* went off to find work for her two remaining guns. She joined *Heermann*, *Roberts* and *Johnston* in a torpedo attack on the heavy cruiser *Haguro*. The torpedoes missed but caused such serious alarm aboard the battleships *Yamato* and *Nagato* that they turned away to the north and were absent for a critical phase of the battle. Next, the destroyers expended some ammunition on the superstructures of the *Kongo* and *Haruna*. Two more destroyer escorts, the *Dennis* (Lieutenant Commander Samuel Hansen) and the *Raymond* (Lieutenant Commander A. F. Beyer) joined the little ships in making life difficult for the Japanese and gaining precious time for the escort carriers fleeing to the south. *Hoel*, hit by more than forty shells, was finally abandoned and sank at 08.55.

About this time Halsey was informed of what was taking place. The problem was that although he sent back Task Group 38.1 he was now 300 miles to the north and it would be 13.00 before his strike aircraft could enter the action against Kurita. Likewise, Oldendorf's battleships and cruisers could not be expected to arrive for three hours. Kincaid was still on his own, and the enemy's cruisers were closing in on his escort carriers.

Four Japanese cruisers, *Haguro, Chokai, Chikuma* and *Tone,* were rapidly closing in on the two most vulnerable escort carriers, *Gambier Bay* and *Kalinin Bay,* with the first pair on their port quarter and the others closing in from astern. Fortunately, the carriers were thin-skinned and most of the enemy's shells passed straight through without exploding. *Kalinin Bay* was hit first and then at regular intervals by 8-inch shells. She was seriously damaged but, thanks to the efforts of her crew, she managed to stay afloat and keep station. *Gambier Bay* was not so lucky. She avoided the enemy's fire for some twenty-five minutes but was then hit repeatedly and set on fire. With the range down to 10,000 yards she was struck by salvo after salvo. By 08.48 her power had gone and she had taken on a sharp list. The order to abandon ship was given five minutes later. At 09.07 *Gambier Bay* rolled over and sank. The chase continued. The carriers *St Lo* and *Fanshaw Bay* had both come under fire at 08.15. *St Lo* was steaming through shell splashes that exceeded her flight deck in height but emerged unscathed. *Fanshaw Bay* also seemed to have a charmed life until four 8-inch shells caused damage and casualties, although they failed to stop her.

At this point Sprague ordered all his destroyer escorts to draw the fire of the cruisers away from the escort carriers. They included the *Butler, Dennis, Raymond* and *Roberts,* as well as the *Heermann* and the seriously damaged *Johnston.* There was not a lot they could do but their cumulative fire distracted the enemy and added to his damage. *Chikuma* seemed to have lost her steering at one point and began turning in a wild circle. The little ships were also assisted by increasingly heavy air attacks, although they could not hope to escape altogether. *Dennis* was forced to seek refuge in her own smokescreen, while *Heerman* was hit so often that she was flooding forward with her forecastle almost awash. *Roberts* avoided trouble until 08.50 when she was hit by several 8-inch shells in succession and then, at about 09.00, by a full salvo of 14-inch shells fired by the *Kongo* that turned her into a wreck. Despite this, half the crew, including her captain, managed to get off in rafts.

The American aircraft, including a contingent sent by the Seventh Fleet, were now receiving expert control and guidance onto their targets. *Chokai* was hit by several bombs and *Chikuma* was crippled by a torpedo strike. Then, quite suddenly, *Johnston* emerged from a smokescreen into the path of a division of four Japanese destroyers led by the light cruiser *Yahagi*, the flagship of Rear Admiral Kimura. *Johnston* immediately opened fire on the light cruiser, which was simultaneously strafed by a fighter aircraft. Kimura seems to have been seriously unsettled for, although the American carriers were so far ahead of him that they were hardly within range of his Long Lance torpedoes, he ordered his entire division to mount an attack. The result was that by the time the torpedoes approached the two nearest American carriers, *St Lo* and *Kalinin Bay*, they were nearing the end of their run and slowing down. One was dived on and exploded by the machine guns of a Avenger, another was thrown off course by the near misses of a 5-inch gun, and the remainder sank after being easily avoided by their intended targets. Kimura, badly infected by the Victory Disease, triumphantly signalled Kurita to the effect that he had sunk one Enterprise-class carrier, probably sunk another, and probably three destroyers. He failed to mention the one real success his destroyers had achieved, namely the sinking of the gallant *Johnston*. Under fire from all directions, including contributions from the enemy's cruisers, she was fought to a standstill and finally abandoned at 09.45, having lost 186 members of her crew, including her captain.

The crisis of the action was fast approaching. The heavy cruisers *Haguro* and *Tone* were now just 10,000 yards astern of the carriers and the battleships *Kongo* and *Haruna* were coming up fast. Then, at 0925, all four Japanese warships turned away and disappeared to the north and the shelling ceased. 'At best, I expected to be swimming by this time,' wrote Clifton Sprague later. A universal sigh of relief went up from the American ships. Inexplicably, the Japanese had gone. They had been recalled by Kurita, trailing the rest of Centre Force aboard *Yamato* some distance below the horizon, for a variety of reasons that loomed large in the fog of war despite his apparently being on the verge of an important success. He believed that he was about to be attacked by Vice Admiral John McCain's Task Group 38.1, which had been detached by Halsey to go to Kincaid's assistance and was even now pounding south towards him at a good 30 knots. By now, he was also aware of the catastrophe that had overtaken Nishimura in the Surigao Strait and saw no further point in continuing to pursue a southerly course. Furthermore, the damage inflicted on the heavy cruisers *Chokai* and *Chikuma* had crippled them to the extent that once their survivors had been taken off they were sunk. *Suzuya*, bombed a second time, was blazing beyond control, forcing Admiral Shiraishi to transfer his flag to the *Tone*. For a brief moment Kurita considered reinforcing Ozawa to the north, but with Halsey already in hot pursuit of the carrier fleet dismissed the idea as impractical. Instead, he decided to withdraw through the San Bernardino Strait and began assembling his ships for that purpose.

Meanwhile, a new and terrible kind of warfare was about to be launched against Kincaid. It was the brainchild of Vice Admiral Ohnishi Takijiro who had arrived in Manila on 17 October to take over command of the 1st Air Fleet from Vice Admiral Teraoka. He was aware that Japan was losing the war and believed that only by marshalling the forces of honourable self-sacrifice in the Bushido tradition could the enemy be shocked into a negotiated peace. Volunteers were not slow in coming forward to join the first Kamikaze Attack Unit, a name meaning 'Divine Wind' in commemoration of the mighty storm that had scattered the invading fleet of the Mongol Emperor Kublai Khan in 1281. Volunteer pilots flying aircraft armed with a bomb would deliberately crash them onto their target ship, often causing extensive damage and loss of life. The first unit, six strong, had as its target the southern group of escort carriers which were attacked at 07.40 on 25 October. Two were shot down without reaching their targets, one smashed through the *Santee*'s flight and hangar decks, starting a fire near a bomb stack that was quickly extinguished, then surviving a torpedo launched by the Japanese submarine *I-56*. However, the carrier was of stout construction and within a few hours had repaired her decks, worked up to a speed of 16.5 knots and was able to operate aircraft. Another dived vertically down on *Suwannee*, exploding as it blasted holes in the flight and hangar decks, putting a lift out of action, starting a blaze that was quickly extinguished and causing heavy casualties. Yet, within three hours, *Suwannee* was also back in business. Two more Kamikaze aircraft attacked respectively the *Sangamon* and the *Petrof Bay*, but were driven off by anti-aircraft fire and returned home to report that the raid had been a success. Subsequent raids were not only larger but also possessing in greater ferocity.

As already mentioned, Halsey had detached Vice Admiral John McCain's Task Group 38.1 from his Third Fleet to go to the assistance of Kinkaid. This consisted of the fleet carriers *Wasp (2)*, *Hornet (2)* and *Hancock*, the light carriers *Monterey* and *Cowpens*, the cruisers *Chester*, *Salt Lake City* and *Pensacola*, the anti-aircraft cruisers *Oakland* and *San Diego*, and thirteen destroyers, and was already well on its way south. The rest of Halsey's command was made up as follows:

Vice Admiral M. A. Mitscher, Commander First Carrier Task Force, Pacific Fleet, fleet carrier *Lexington*, (Flag)

Task Group 38.2
Rear Admiral G. F. Bogan
Fleet Carrier *Intrepid* (Flag), light carriers *Cabot* and *Independence*

Task Group 38.3
Rear Admiral F. C. Sherman
Fleet carrier *Essex* (Flag), light carriers *Langley* and *Princeton*, light cruiser *Birmingham*, anti-aircraft cruiser *Reno*, and fifteen destroyers

Task Group 38.4
Rear Admiral R. E. Davison
Fleet carriers *Franklin* (flag) and *Enterprise*, light carriers *San Jacinto* and *Belleau Wood*, and nine destroyers

Task Force 34, Heavy Striking Force, formed 04.30, 25 October
Commander, Vice Admiral W. A. Lee, Jr

Task Group 34.1 Battle Line
Task Unit 34.1.1 (Bat.Div. 7) battleships *Iowa* and *New Jersey*
Task Unit 34.1.2 (Bat.Div. 8) battleships *Massachusetts* and *Washington* (flag)
Task Unit 34.1.3 (Bat.Div. 9) battleships *South Dakota* and *Alabama*

Task Group 34.2 Right Flank
Rear Admiral F. E. M. Whiting
Task Unit 34.2.2 (Cru.Div. 14) *Vincennes* (flag), *Miami* and *Biloxi*
Task Units 34.2.3, 34.2.4 eight destroyers

Task Group 34.3 Centre
Rear Admiral C. T. Joy
Task Unit 34.3.1 (Cru.Div. 6) *Wichita* (flag), *New Orleans*
Task Unit 34.3.3, four destroyers

Task Group 34.4 Left Flank
Rear Admiral L. T. Du Bose
Task Unit 34.4.2 (Cru.Div. 13) *Santa Fe* (flag), *Mobile*
Task Unit 34.4.3, six destroyers

Compared to this huge and very powerful assembly, Ozawa's diversionary fleet was a rather sad little gathering. It consisted of the following:

Fleet Carrier *Zuikaku* (eighty aircraft)
Light Carriers *Chitose*, *Chiyods* and *Zuiho* (total aircraft forty)
Hybrid battleship/carriers *Hyuga*, *Ise*
Light cruisers *Tama*, *Oyoda*, *Isuzu*
Eight destroyers.

The subsequent action became known as the Battle of Cape Engano, this being the peninsula at the north-eastern tip of Luzon and the nearest land. It was a very one-sided affair and did not really merit the description of battle. Mitscher's search planes pinpointed Ozawa'a position and course at 02.20 on 25 October and four major air strikes were launched against it during the day, the first between 08.45 and 09.30, the second between 10.00 and 10.30, the third and longest between 13.10 and 15.00, and the last between 17.10 and 17.40. Ozawa, fully aware of the battle's probable outcome, had flown off most off his aircraft to land bases, but a few brave souls still rose in vain attempts to hold off the attackers and earned a warrior's death. During the first strike the light carrier *Chitose* received critical damage and sank at 09.37. The destroyer *Akitsuki* was struck by a torpedo and blew up. *Zuikaku,* the last survivor of the attack on Pearl Harbor and Ozawa's flagship, was hit near her stern by another torpedo that put her steering engines out of commission. Her radio communications were also wrecked and after two-and-a-half hours Ozawa transferred his flag to the light cruiser *Oyoda.* Next to be hit was another light carrier, *Chiyoda,* which was set ablaze and was flooding through ruptures in her hull. Further damage disabled her engines. The hybrid battleship/carrier *Hyuga* and the light cruiser *Tama* stood by her, trying to provide anti-aircraft protection. While so engaged *Tama* was struck by a torpedo that reduced her speed to just ten knots.

At 11.15 Halsey ordered Lee's battleships, followed by the carriers of Rear Admiral Bogan's Task Force 38.2, to reverse course and head south at speed, unfortunately too late either to assist Kinkaid or intercept Kurita. By midday *Zuikaku's* steering gear had been repaired and, in company with *Zuiho, Oyoda, Ise,*and three destroyers, she was able to make a steady 20 knots. Lagging twenty miles behind was *Tama,* trailing a long oil slick as her fuel drained out of her. *Hyuga* and a destroyer were preparing to take the crippled *Chiyoda* in tow. Still further behind were the light cruiser *Isuzu* and another destroyer.

Between 11.45 and 12.00 the third air strike of the day, involving over 200 planes, began leaving its flight decks with the object of crippling Ozawa's main body. Arriving over the target at 13.10 the

Lexington and *Langley* groups battered *Zuikaku* with bombs that turned her into an inferno, then administered the *coup de grace* with three torpedoes. By 14.14 she had vanished beneath the waves. The *Essex* group, joined by some of *Langley's* aircraft, caused fires aboard the *Zuiho*, although these were quickly extinguished. A second attack on the carrier, made by aircraft from the *Franklin, Enterprise* and *San Jacinto*, set her ablaze once more, although it was not until 15.26 that she was finally sent to the bottom. The hybrid *Ise* also came under attack but was saved from serious damage by her high-speed evasions. At about this time attempts to pick up survivors from the two carriers meant that Ozawa's Main Body was overtaken by the damaged *Tama* and the *Hyuga*. The latter had been standing by the crippled carrier *Chiyoda* with the object of taking her in tow, but had been ordered to desist when it became apparent that she was beyond saving. Instead, the light cruiser *Isuzu* and a destroyer were instructed to take off her crew, but were driven off by a squadron consisting of the light cruisers *Santa Fe* and *Mobile* and the heavy cruisers *Wichita* and *New Orleans*, plus twelve destroyers, specially formed under Rear Admiral Lawrence Du Bose to sink Ozawa's cripples. *Chiyoda* was hit by a rain of 8- and 6-inch shells and finished off by the destroyers' torpedoes. She finally sank at 16.55. Du Bose resumed the chase and came across three destroyers picking up survivors from the *Zuikaku* and *Zuiho*. Two made off northwards immediately but the third, *Hatsukuki*, led her pursuers a merry dance in which she remained under constant fire, initially directed by radar and finally by starshell at point-blank range; she slid beneath the surface at 20.56, burning fiercely.

No explanation has ever been offered for what happened next. The American submarine *Halibut*, under Commander I. J. Galantin, formed part of a small 'wolf pack' operating on Ozawa's line of retreat. Galantin fired six electrical torpedoes at an Ise-class battleship heading north, screened by a light cruiser and a destroyer. The range was 4,000 yards. After the correct number of seconds was counted off, five explosions were heard, followed by breaking-up noises. After an hour Galantin took *Halibut* to the surface and what seemed to be the upturned hull of a ship was clearly visible in the moonlight. Yet, no records exist of a Japanese warship being sunk in this position. Some distance to the east of *Halibut* another American submarine, *Jallao* under Commander J. B. Icenhower launched an attack at 23.01 on the light cruiser *Tama*, firing three torpedoes from his bow tubes. All missed. Icenhower turned away until his stern tubes would bear and then, at a range of 700 yards, fired four more torpedoes, three of which struck, ending the new cruiser's career.

Of Ozawa's Main Body, only *Ise*, *Hyuga*, *Oyada*, *Isuzu* and five destroyers survived. Kurita's force lost the light cruiser *Noshiro* to air attack on the way back to Brunei Bay, where running repairs were carried out to his ships prior to their departure for Japan, but the toll of Japanese shipping lost around the Philippine Islands continued to rise. On 26 October the light cruiser *Abukuma*, formerly of Shima's force, having been crippled by a torpedo in the Surigao Strait, was sunk by Army Liberator bombers. The same day the light cruiser *Kinu* and the destroyer *Uranami* were both sunk, together with two transports, returning from the delivery of reinforcements to Leyte when they were attacked by aircraft from the Seventh Fleet's escort carriers in the Visayan Sea. On the following day the destroyers *Shiranuhi* and *Fujinami*, with survivors aboard from the carrier *Chokai*, were sunk by carrier aircraft off Mindoro. The same aircraft also bombed the seaplane tender *Akitsushima* to destruction. Later, the destroyer *Hayashimo* had to be beached on Semirara Island, south of Mindoro, after being struck by a bomb. On 5 November the heavy cruiser *Nachi*, formerly Shima's flagship, was bombed and sunk in Manila harbour. Finally, on 6 November, another heavy cruiser, the *Kumano*, was set upon by four American submarines but managed to find shelter in Dasol Bay near Lingayen Gulf. There, on 25 November, she was bombed to destruction by aircraft from the new carrier *Ticonderoga*.

Together, these four engagements – the Battle of the Sibuyan Sea, the Battle of the Surigao Strait, the Battle off Samar and the Battle off Cape Engano, are generally referred to as the Battle of Leyte Gulf. It was the greatest naval battle in history involving 143,668

American and Australian naval personnel and 42,800 Japanese and a total of 282 vessels: 216 United States Navy, two Royal Australian Navy and sixty-four Imperial Japanese Navy. The battle destroyed the offensive capability of the Imperial Japanese Navy which lost four carriers, three battleships, six heavy and four light cruisers, eleven destroyers and one submarine; almost every other Japanese ship engaged sustained some degree of damage. About 500 aircraft were destroyed. Approximately 10,500 Japanese sailors and airmen lost their lives. American losses included one light carrier, two escort carriers, one destroyer escort and in excess of 200 aircraft. An estimated 2,800 Americans were killed and approximately 1,000 were wounded.

Halsey attracted criticism for abandoning the exit from the San Bernardino Strait at a critical moment to pursue Ozawa's force. He subsequently admitted that this had been a mistake, but against this his orders contained a paragraph authorising him to engage and destroy any sizeable enemy force that he encountered and he had no way of knowing that Ozawa was commanding a relatively small decoy force. Kurita attracted criticism for abandoning the action off Samar. It has been suggested that, like many senior Japanese admirals, he knew that Japan had lost the war and wished to preserve as much of her fleet as possible, rather than sacrifice it to no purpose. It has also been suggested that his recent experiences had eroded his will to fight.

The kamikaze target of destroying an enemy warship by sacrificing one aircraft and its pilot was seldom achieved. Nevertheless, the concept was developed into other areas until it included suicide motor boats, suicide torpedoes and even suicide tank destruction squads. None of this halted the Allied drive on the Japanese home islands; indeed, if those who conceived the idea had looked back into history, however briefly, they would have been hard-pressed to find a single instance in which self-destruction restored the fortunes of a lost cause.

Envoi

If October 1944 had been a disastrous month for the Imperial Navy, that which followed offered only the smallest degree of improvement. During the early hours of 21 November the American submarine *Sealion*, under Commander Eli Reich, was patrolling the East China Sea, to the north-west of Formosa, when a column of Japanese warships was spotted. In the lead was a cruiser, followed by a battleship, then another battleship and a second cruiser. A destroyer was positioned on either bow and a third destroyer on the starboard beam. At 02.56 Reich fired his six bow tubes, circled, stopped engines and fired his three stern tubes. Three explosions signalled hits with the forward spread. These were followed by a single hit. A destroyer left her position in the column to drop a string of depth charges far from *Sealion* and the rest of the Japanese ships increased speed to 18 knots. Reich, uncertain whether he had caused critical damage to any of his targets, tried to keep up but fell steadily further and further behind. Then, at 04.50, he received his reward. Three of the bigger ships maintained their course and speed, but one dropped astern, accompanied by two destroyers; of the third destroyer there was no sign. Reich recognised the bigger ship as his first target and decided to finish her off. Reaching a position ahead of the large ship, he slowed then turned and fired his torpedoes. His tracking team reported the target was now stationary. At 05.24 a tremendous explosion lit up the night sky and the target slowly disappeared from the radar screen. It was subsequently proved that *Sealion* had sunk the battleship *Kongo* and a destroyer.

Early on 28 November the USS *Archerfish*, under Commander J. F. Enright, was patrolling off the island of Inamba Shima, about ninety miles south of the entrance to Tokyo Bay. His usual task was acting as lifeguard for any B-29 Superfortress crew brought down in the sea after raiding the Japanese mainland, but air activity had been cancelled for the day and she was, for the moment, acting on her captain's discretion. At 20.48 radar indicated a large contact coming out of Tokyo Bay at a range of 24,700 yards. She was identified as a carrier, zig-zagging at 20 knots on a mean south-westerly course and accompanied by four escorts. Unfortunately, the target's greater speed was steadily taking her out of danger. Enright had almost given up hope of scoring a kill when, at 03.00, the enemy carrier reversed course and the range began to close rapidly. Luck was definitely on the side of *Archerfish* for the nearest–escort steamed past the submarine's periscope at a distance of 400 yards without reacting. *Archerfish* was now 1,400 yards on the carrier's starboard beam and commenced firing six torpedoes set for a depth of ten feet. After the first two hits Enright took the boat deep, counting four more explosions on the way down, followed by breaking up noises. Later he learned that he had sunk the 59,000-ton super-carrier *Shinano*, originally laid down as a sister ship to the two giant battleships *Yamato* and *Musahi*. Although she carried a modest number of aircraft, the intention was that she should serve as a sort of floating warehouse that would supply the needs of other carriers. Her commander, Captain Toshio Abe, was under the impression that *Shinano* was unsinkable and refused to reduce her speed after the torpedo strikes. In fact, the ship was not in a state of watertight integrity and openings existed in her bulkheads. When she began to list no attempt was made to correct this by counter-flooding and Toshio refused to ground the ship. Consequently she capsized and sank, just seventeen hours into her trials.

Another carrier, the brand-new *Unryu*, was lost to the Imperial Navy on 15 December. She fell victim to the American submarine *Redfish*, under Commander L. D. McGregor, which was not a notably lucky boat and so far had only the 2,345-ton transport *Hozan Maru* to her credit. Some said that there was a gremlin in her attack computer, but McGregor was not a man to let this discourage him. During the afternoon of 15 December *Redfish* was running submerged in the East China Sea when a group of four warships came into view. Three were destroyers steaming in an inverted V ahead of a carrier. Unexpectedly, the carrier zig-zagged, bringing her within range. At 16.35 McGregor began firing the last four torpedoes left in his forward tubes. The gremlin carried three of them off, but the fourth hit the carrier in the stern, wrecking her propellers and causing extensive damage. As the carrier slowed to a standstill, a destroyer spotted *Redfish*'s periscope at 1,700 yards and charged it. McGregor fired four torpedoes from his stern tubes. They all missed but alarmed the destroyer sufficiently for her to turn away.

On hearing a series of explosions McGregor observed the carrier through his periscope. She was on fire aft and had developed a 20-degree list which, to his delight, was causing the aircraft ranked on her flight deck to tumble over her side. Her guns were firing wildly at nothing in particular and the destroyers were dropping their depth charges indiscriminately. McGregor had one torpedo loaded, which he fired at the carrier, aiming just aft of the midships structure. The torpedo ran true, its strike being followed by heavy explosions and the ship starting to roll into a final capsize. McGregor was taking a photograph of the scene when he observed a destroyer charging at him, looking as though 'she was all bow wave'. He took *Redfish* down until she touched bottom at 232 feet and endured a well-placed barrage of depth charges for the next two hours. She sustained a crack in the forward torpedo room plating; twelve broken battery cells; bow and stern plane gear out of commission; gyro compass 50 degrees off its proper heading; and one man's ear severed by a watertight door that escaped its clamps. Once things had quietened down, McGregor surfaced and took her home to Midway. *Redfish* would no longer be regarded as an unlucky boat, and now she had a fine kill to her credit.

By the New Year of 1945 the end of the Imperial Japanese Navy was clearly visible. Its remaining battleships and carriers were more or less confined to harbour where their anti-aircraft armament was used to defend the homeland against the devastating attacks of the American B-29 Superfortresses. In this context it was found that using high explosive bombs from an altitude of 30,000 feet was less effective than unloading great quantities of incendiary bombs at 10,000 feet. Huge areas of Japan's major cities were turned into charred wastelands as wood-and-paper houses were consumed in gigantic firestorms that actually killed more people than the atomic bombs dropped on Hiroshima on 6 August and Nagasaki on 9 August 1945. Now homeless and living on the verge of starvation, the resolve of the civilian population began to crack, and still the odds against Japan continued to grow.

With the end of hostilities in the Mediterranean and increasing success in the Atlantic, the Royal Navy was able to form a Pacific Fleet and commit it to the war in the Far East. At its greatest strength this, commanded by Vice Admiral Sir Henry Rawlings, consisted of the carriers *Formidable, Illustrious, Indefatigable, Indomitable* and *Victorious* with 220 aircraft, supported by the battleships *King George V* and *Howe* (flag), plus five cruisers and destroyers. It is some measure of the United States' Navy commitment to the Pacific War that the Pacific Fleet was approximately the same size as an American task group. Its first missions involved the neutralisation of the Sumatran oil refineries, after which it supported the American landings on Okinawa. Although several British carriers were damaged by Kamikaze aircraft, their armoured flight decks provided them with a high degree of protection. Altogether, in this prolonged Kamikaze offensive, lasting six weeks, twenty-six American ships were sunk and 164 damaged. The battleship *Yamato*, escorted by the light cruiser *Yahagi* and the destroyers *Fuyutsuki, Suzutsuki, Kukikaze, Isokaze, Hamakaze, Kazumi, Hatsushimo* and *Asashimo*, put to sea on 6 April in the hope that they might bring some relief to the defenders of the island. In command was Vice Admiral Seiichi Ito, who was ordered to get in among the Allied invasion fleet off Okinawa and inflict as much damage as possible before meeting an inevitable end. The admiral's serious fuel shortage was of no account as he would not be returning. Lacking air cover of any kind, his force stood little chance of survival. *Yahagi* was the first to go, followed by *Yamato*, crippled and finally sunk by six bombs and ten torpedoes, then four destroyers. The Japanese force was still 200 miles short of its objective.

In addition to working with the Americans, the British Pacific Fleet carried out a number of interesting independent operations. During the night of 15/16 May 1945 the 26th Destroyer Flotilla (*Saumarez, Venus, Virago, Verulam* and *Vigilant*), commanded by Captain Manley L. Power, detected the Japanese heavy cruiser *Haguro* by radar in the Straits of Molucca, some fifty-five miles west-south-west of Penang. She was commanded by Captain Kajuh Sugiara and accompanied by the destroyer *Kamikaze*. After a pursuit lasting several hours, Power launched a synchronised torpedo attack by the whole flotilla, the result being that *Haguro* was hit many times and began to settle, being sent to the bottom by *Venus*. *Kamikaze* had fled into the darkness but returned after the action and picked up 400 survivors.

Between 24 and 30 July American carriers and battleships mounted attacks on Japan with the object of softening up invasion landing sites. No major unit of the Imperial Japanese Navy survived these attacks, the aircraft carrier *Amagi* and the battleships *Haruna, Hyuga* and *Ise* all being destroyed.

British midget submarines were also active during this period. *XE4* cut the Singapore-Saigon telegraph cable near Cap St Jacques in French Indo-China and *XE5* cut the Hong Kong-Saigon cable near Lamma Island, Hong Kong. *XE1* and *XE3* attacked the heavy cruiser *Takao* in Singapore Harbour. The cruiser's stern had unrepaired damage inflicted by an American submarine, and the crews of the two midgets placed explosives beneath her that blew a large hole in her bottom. She took no further part in the war. All three actions took place on the night of 31 July.

Elsewhere, the Japanese Burma Area Army had been defeated and dispersed and the Philippine Islands were once more in American hands. Japan concluded the formalities relating to her surrender aboard the battleship USS *Missouri*, anchored in Tokyo Bay. The Emperor spoke to his people, denying his divinity and telling them to accept what was once considered unacceptable.

Bibliography

Brown, David, *Carrier Fighters*, Macdonald, London, 1975

Cortesi, Lawrence, *Bloody Friday off Guadalcanal*, Kensington, New York, 1981, *Pacific Breakthrough*, Kensington, 1981

Costello, John, *The Pacific War*, Pan, London, 1985

Evans, David C. and Peattie, Mark R., *Kaigun – Strategy, Tactics and Technology in the Imperial Japanese Navy 1887–1941*, Naval Institute Press, Annapolis, 2012

Hargreaves, Reginald, *The Siege of Port Arthur*, Weidenfeld & Nicolson, London, 1962

Horton, D. C., *New Georgia*, Pan, London, 1972

Hoyt, Edwin P., *The Battle of Leyte Gulf*, Jove, New York, 1983, *The Kamikazes – Japan's Most Desperate Wartime Gamble*, Panther, 1985

Humble, Richard, *Japanese High Seas Fleet*, Pan, London, 1974

Kent, Graeme, *Guadalcanal*, Pan, London, 1972

Lockwood, Vice Admiral Charles A., USN, Rtd, *Sink 'em All – Submarine Warfare in the Pacific*, Bantam, New York, 1987

Macintyre, Captain Donald, *Aircraft Carrier*, Macdonald, London, 1968, *Leyte Gulf*, Macdonald, London, 1970

Masanori Ito, *The End of the Imperial Japanese Navy*, Jove, New York, 1986

Millot, Bernard, *The Battle of the Coral Sea*, Ian Allan, Shepperton, 1974

Padfield, Peter, *Maritime Dominion – Naval Campaigns That Shaped the Modern World* 1852–2001, John Murray, London, 2009

Schultz, Duane, *Wake Island*, Magnum, London, 1979

Stewart, Adrian, *Guadalcanal – World War II's Fiercest Naval Campaign*, William Kimber, London, 1985

Stewart, Adrian, *The Underrated Enemy – Britain's War With Japan December 1941–May 1942*, William Kimber, London, 1987

Vader, John, *New Guinea*, Pan, London, 1972

Walder, David, *The Short Victorious War – The Russo-Japanese Conflict 1904–5*, Hutchinson, 1973

Winton, John, *Sink the Haguro!*, Pan, London, 1983

Wragg, David, *Fighting Admirals of World War II*, Pen-and-Sword, Barnsley, 2009, *The Pacific War 1941–1945*, Pen & Sword, Barnsley, 2011

Index